AN END
TO
POLITICAL
SCIENCE

AN END TO POLITICAL SCIENCE

THE CAUCUS PAPERS

EDITED BY

MARVIN SURKIN
& ALAN WOLFE

BASIC BOOKS, INC., PUBLISHERS

NEW YORK

THE AUTHORS

MATTHEW A. CRENSON, a graduate of the University of Chicago and a former research fellow at the Brookings Institution, is currently an assistant professor in the Department of Social Relations at the Johns Hopkins University. His essay is adapted from a larger study, *The Unpolitics of Air Pollution: A Study of Non-decision-making in American Cities,* soon to be published by the Johns Hopkins University Press.

EDWARD FRIEDMAN teaches political science at the University of Wisconsin. A graduate of Harvard University, he has published numerous articles on Asia "in both scholarly journals and interesting ones," and is the author or editor of two forthcoming books, *The Chinese Revolutionary Party* and *America's Asia.*

DAVID KETTLER, the present chairman of the Caucus for a New Political Science, taught political theory at Ohio State University from 1955 until his move to Purdue University in the fall of 1970. His work has revolved around the political vocation of intellectuals, including studies of Adam Ferguson and Karl Mannheim.

LEWIS LIPSITZ teaches political science at the University of North Carolina and also writes poetry. A collection of his poetry, *Cold Water,* appeared in 1967, and he is the editor of *American Government: Behavior and Controversy.* He is currently working on a book on political economy in the United States.

MICHAEL PARENTI teaches political science at the University of Vermont. He is the author of *The Anti-Communist Impulse* and *Power and the Powerless* (forthcoming). He has also published numerous articles in both scholarly journals and general magazines. A slightly different and condensed version of this article will appear in the fall 1970 issue of the *Journal of Politics.*

JAMES PETRAS is associate professor of political science and research associate at the Institute of Public Administration,
Pennsylvania State University. He is the author or editor of,
among other works, *Politics and Social Forces in Chilean
Development* and *Class and Politics in Latin America,* and is
currently working on the problem of agrarian reform and
development.

MARCUS RASKIN is co-founder and co-director of the Institute
of Policy Studies in Washington, D.C. He was tried (and
acquitted) in the "Boston Five" Conspiracy Trial and has
been active as founder of the New Party. He is the author of,
among other works, *Deterrents and Reality,* with Arthur
Waskow and *After Twenty Years: Alternatives to World War
in Europe,* with Richard J. Barnet. His chapter is part of
Being and Doing: From Deliberation to Liberation (Random
House, 1970).

MARVIN SURKIN is assistant professor of political science at Adelphi
University. He is the editor of *Violence and Protest: The
Crisis in American Political Life* (forthcoming) and is a frequent contributor to both general magazines and academic
journals.

DAVID UNDERHILL is a "drifting twenty-eight-year-old participant-
observer from Idaho who has accumulated a B.A. from
Harvard, some experience in journalism, and an extended
view of various things in Alabama and Mississippi." His
article is based on inside acquaintance with the rebellion in
Columbia University where he is currently enrolled as a
Ph.D. candidate in Political Science.

JAMES L. WEEKS is currently working with the National Security
Research Project in Washington, D.C. and is a research fellow
at the Institute of Policy Studies. He wrote this paper while
he was a graduate student in science and public policy at
Case Western Reserve University, Cleveland, Ohio.

ALAN WOLFE is assistant professor of political science at Old
Westbury College, State University of New York. A frequent
contributor to popular magazines and academic journals, he
is the author of *Foundations of Political Science* (forthcoming).

CONTENTS

I

POLITICAL THEORY AND THE
CRITIQUE OF AMERICAN POLITICS

II

POWER IN AMERICA:
CRISIS IN THE STATE

III

POWER "HERE" AND POWER "THERE"

IV

POLITICAL SCIENCE AND THE
PROFESSIONAL MYSTIQUE

AN END
TO
POLITICAL
SCIENCE

Why I Became a Social Scientist

Lewis Lipsitz

                    because I saw Hitler
floating in the steady Mediterranean
of his mother's womb
                    because I loved the morning
—dawn hours
                    when surprise attacks
are made when
cavalries charge
                    a few mortar rounds
slam into the barracks
the bomb explodes 2,000 feet
over Hiroshima
                    because the priest said ·
something
to the man in the electric chair
                    because nothing
became simple because my skin changed color
because even in me cities burned up—
I starved and my bones gleamed like searchlights
                    because I couldn't help it
because
I needed quietness
                    because I saw this jar
where nations lay still
                    like malformed embryos
        And I looked at it from the
outside
            and from the inside
and I began to tremble like a child scalded
on the back of his neck by snow that
                                someone
                                had dropped from high up
                                and designed to burn

INTRODUCTION:

AN END

TO POLITICAL

SCIENCE • *Marvin Surkin and Alan Wolfe*

This book is a critique of American politics and American political science by a group of young university teachers, graduate
students, and political activists. It represents a collective effort of
the Caucus for a New Political Science (CNPS),[1] under whose
auspices most of these essays were presented at political science
conferences over the last few years. It is thus a part of a new
movement in American professional associations and universities,
seeking to create a critical or radical force among academics and
intellectuals. Many radical caucuses have been formed recently to
challenge the social and political purposes and direction of their
academic associations, disciplines, and universities.

The CNPS, a caucus within the American Political Science
Association (APSA), was formed in 1967 to challenge the complacency of American political science, its conservatism, its government links and, above all, what the dissidents called the "irrelevance" of the discipline. Political science, its critics argued, was
by and large devoted to perpetuating the dominant institutional
and ideological interests of American society. Many political scientists were doing research for and advising the CIA and the Department of Defense. Officers of the APSA, it was found, were
linked to Operations and Policy Research, a CIA-funded research
organization, and the association had also received funds from the
CIA through such conduits as the Asia Foundation.

Dissident political scientists, with a knowledge of the current
realities of the discipline, and in the light of their discontent over
the war in Vietnam and the unmet social demands at home, denounced the insidious direction so much of the profession was

taking. They did not reject the role of political scientists in policy-making, only the particular uses of knowledge to which much of the profession was now committed and the complacent—even positive—attitude adopted by many political scientists toward these developments. What the reformers attacked, therefore, was the willing use of *their* discipline to sustain and reinforce corporate liberalism in America. In a word, political science was indicted as handmaiden to the counterrevolutionary reflex of America in its policies at home and abroad. When the CNPS declared political science irrelevant, this implied that research was being used not to serve the interests of the poor and oppressed around the world, but rather to serve the interests of the U.S. government and the corporate establishment, for whom political science research was a most valuable strategic tool. (The same case is being put forward in most of the other professional disciplines as well.)

Besides this manifestation of the ideology of American political science, there were also criticisms of a different kind—those relating to the methods of research and teaching in the field. Since the behavioral explosion in political science in the 1940's, empirical research and quantification methods had come to dominate the discipline. Along with this new approach, political scientists claimed that their research was neutral or nonideological because, insofar as the researcher abided by the rules of scientific method, his results were "value-free" as in any other science. The data themselves are neutral. But, even though many members of the CNPS employed behavioral techniques and considered themselves "behavioralists," they concluded that the claim to value neutrality, in political science at least, was illusory. For, while some political scientists remained in the lofty realm of operationalism, quantification techniques, and game theory in which a superrationalistic scientism prevails, much of the discipline was now closely welded to the kind of policy-making noted above that bore only a thin veil of scientificity. This critique was underscored by John Seeley, who recently noted that "sciencizing" is politics by other means.

Furthermore, the growth of political science in America went hand in hand with the teaching of civics or citizenship in the schools. Teaching and text books extolled the virtues of democracy in order to prepare students for their responsibilities to the system. The task of political scientists and other "educators" was to supply future citizens with the appropriate "facts": democracy and free enterprise were taken for granted while other political and economic systems were denounced. The teaching of good citizenship and "law and order" reached its culmination during the 1950's when political scientists pronounced the "end of ideology" and praised the American political system for having so fully attained the democratic ideal. At the same time, however, these ideologists of American pluralism counseled against any serious extension of voter participation for fear that such a trend would threaten the delicate balance in American social relations.

The CNPS emerged as a natural response to these realities. Dissatisfied with the "old" political science, its members called for a "new" political science. To bring this about, the CNPS demanded both intellectual and organizational reform. The dissidents wanted political science to be more of a social service discipline than an instrument for America's elites. And they wanted democracy to extend to the APSA where contested elections were unknown.

Underlying this dissatisfaction with the "old" political science is a dissenting view of the pluralist theory of American politics. According to the pluralist theory, organized groups in American society function within a political process whereby each is accorded a piece of power. Groups influence the decision-making process to the extent that they express their interests or make them felt by those in power. That this theory accurately describes how power is meted out among the powerful in America is not to be denied. Powerful groups—big business, big bureaucracy, big unions—*do* have influence over the decision-making process. But the critique of pluralism is concerned with the fact that this model, while being defended by political scientists, serves to reinforce a system experienced as dysfunctional and intransigent by other segments of society (including many organized groups) in regard to their demands and interests.

Thus, from at least 1950 to the present, pluralism reinforced a false sense of social reality among political scientists. This enabled political scientists to conclude that presidential nominating conventions were models of democratic procedure, that the electoral college needed no reform, and that machine politics in Chicago under Mayor Daley gave the mass of the people the kind of government they seemed to want.[2] In other words, the existing order was praised, little change was deemed necessary; in some cases it was even thought deleterious to the established system.

However, in the light of recent turmoil and unrest these conclusions are no longer sufficient. As American society is increasingly being torn apart by racial strife, by imperialist adventures abroad, by a crisis of authority in its major institutions, by repressive tactics of the state, by poverty and pollution, it is increasingly important for the critique of pluralism to be extended and expanded. But what the editors have come to believe, in the process of preparing this volume for publication, is that a "new" political science which would be merely a revision of the "old" political science will certainly fall short of expectations of reform and social change. What we must now begin to dwell upon is not only the value of the critique of pluralism but also the limitations of that critique; not only the desire for relevance but the meaning of relevance; not only the need for reform but the possibility of reform; and finally, not only the virtues of science but its uses as well. In short, while the critique of pluralism is necessary, we must move beyond this critique insofar as it is limited by the pluralist paradigm itself. If dissident political scientists set out to revise the paradigm and its definitions of relevance or science instead of shattering it, then the result would undoubtedly be the tacit acceptance of that which is rejected. What cannot be forgotten is Thomas S. Kuhn's poignant description of "normal science" in *The Structure of Scientific Revolutions:*

Because he [the student for membership in the particular scientific community] there joins men who learned the bases of their field from the same concrete models, his subsequent practice will seldom evoke overt disagreement over fundamentals. Men whose research is based on shared paradigms are committed to the same rules and standards for scientific practice. That commitment and the apparent consensus it produces are prerequisites for normal science, i.e., for the genesis and continuation of a particular research tradition.[3]

Therefore, in our view, this book more accurately represents an end to political science than the emergence of the "new" political science. We now see the results of those attempts to bring *more* relevance and *more* science and *more* democratic procedure into American political science and its professional organizations, and can conclude that "normal science" and its attendant ideology and standards of professionalism cannot simply be transformed by good intentions and hard work. To change political science will require a critique of the current paradigm and the development of alternative modes of research, theory, and social practice. The only way this is possible is by ending the hegemony of political science over its students. Martin Nicolaus, a member of the Sociology Liberation Movement, made the same point in reference to sociology:

The "liberation of sociology," which the most militant caucus in the social sciences inscribed on its banner, is a noble cause; but even the devil knows it is a contradiction in terms. Sociology is not an oppressed people or a subjugated class. It is a branch of the tree of political power, an extension of sovereignty by other means. It has survived many a borer-from-within, a pecker-from-without, and carver-of-initials-in-the-bark. To "liberate" the branch means not to sit on it whistling the "Marseillaise," or the "Internationale," but to saw it off. . . . In the last analysis, the only moves toward liberation within sociology are those which contribute to the process of liberation *from* sociology. The point is not to reinterpret oppression but to end it.[4]

In short, because the only political science permitted in America today is that defined and determined within the existing paradigm, and because only those "responsible" critics who are content to remain within the established pluralistic mold are tolerated, we conclude that the only option now available to critics and reformers is an end to political science. This will entail a negative act but also a positive commitment. It will require, at the same time, denouncing the current paradigm and moving toward the creation, along with other radical caucuses, of what Andre Gunder Frank has called a social science that is *political*. This means the continuation of criticism and the analysis of where power exists in America, how it functions, and the elaboration of concrete ways to change the existing power relations. The essays in this volume share this concern and therefore point the way to a *political* social science.

N O T E S

1. The views expressed in this introduction are those of the editors alone.

2. For references see Marvin Surkin and Alan Wolfe, "The Political Dimension of American Political Science," *Acta Politica* (Amsterdam), 5 (October 1969): 43–61.

3. Thomas S. Kuhn, *The Structure of Scientific Revolutions* (Chicago: University of Chicago Press, 1962), p. 11.

4. Martin Nicolaus, "The Professional Organization of Sociology: A View From Below," *The Antioch Review,* 29, no. 3 (Fall 1969): 387.

I

POLITICAL THEORY AND THE CRITIQUE OF AMERICAN POLITICS

ESSENTIAL *to any effort to criticize and change the ideology of American society and to restructure its institutions and social relations is the development of new modes of radical political thought and action. While these essays share this conception, they recognize that any new theories will inevitably be judged by the incisiveness of their criticism of existing dogma as well as the ways their own thought reflects or influences the course of social action. With this in mind, the first essay by Marvin Surkin examines the claims to value neutrality in behavioral political science. He demonstrates that this methodology plays a supportive role for ideology in American society and offers an alternative methodology founded in existential phenomenology and Marxism. David Kettler then examines the limits of pluralism and sets forth a socialist analysis for New Left politics. Finally, Marcus Raskin asserts that "the violence colony" in America is the result of the extensive militarization and bureaucratization of society. He elaborates the foundations for a new social contract theory based on community.*

1

SENSE AND
NON-SENSE IN
POLITICS • *Marvin Surkin*

I take my cue for the title of this chapter from Merleau-Ponty, the
French phenomenologist, who wrote in 1948 that "the political
experiences of the past thirty years obliges us to evoke the background of non-sense against which every universal undertaking is
silhouetted and by which it is threatened with failure."[1] Merleau-
Ponty refers to the experience of that generation of intellectuals for
whom Marxism was a "mistaken hope" because it lost "confidence
in its own daring when it was successful in only one country."[2]
But this criticism is equally relevant for a new generation of intellectuals in America who have witnessed the ideals of liberalism
become little more than a superrational mystique for the Cold
War, a counterrevolutionary reflex in the third world, and a narrow-
range policy of social welfare at home. Merleau-Ponty argues that
Marxism "abandoned its own proletarian methods and resumed
the classical ones of history: hierarchy, obedience, myth, inequality, diplomacy, and police."[3] Today intellectuals in America
are making the same critique with equal fervor about their own
lost illusions.

As we search for new ways to comprehend the social realities
of American life and new modes of social thought and political
action to reconstruct "the American dream," Merleau-Ponty's
notion of sense and non-sense is useful in determining the historical
relationship between ideologies and practice, between thought and
action, between man and the world he creates. The dialectic of

sense and non-sense dramatizes that recurrent fact in history whereby reason parades as unreason, where even "the highest form of reason borders on unreason."[4] We must learn from recent history that "the experience of unreason cannot simply be forgotten";[5] that the most noble claims to universal truth, the most rational modes of philosophical or social inquiry, the most convincing declarations of political leaders are all contingent, and should be subject to revision and open to criticism and change. Marx and Kierkegaard, it should be recalled, shared in their revolt against Hegel's "Reason" insofar as the latter claimed to have attained through reason that universal truth in which history realizes itself, the real becomes rational, and the rational becomes real. The significance of this revolt against Hegelian rationalism is not its renunciation of reason itself, but rather the extent to which in Hegel's philosophical system reason is exalted and sanctified over and against the historical, human, and irrational in history.

Our primary task is therefore twofold: to recognize the historical linkage between the present social forces of reason and unreason, sense and nonsense; and unmask the guise by which the most prevalent modes of thought, their institutional expression, and their ideologies keep us from grasping their real social meaning.

My purpose in this essay is to show that the rigorous adherence to social science methodology adopted from the natural sciences and its claim to objectivity and value neutrality function as a guise for what is in fact becoming an increasingly ideological, nonobjective role for social science knowledge in the service of the dominant institutions in American society. And further, I will attempt to support the claim that the prevailing modes of inquiry in the social sciences in no way counter these recent developments in the uses of knowledge, but rather tend to reinforce them, that is, reinforce their "irrational" or, in this context, ideological uses. Moreover, I will examine what Noam Chomsky has called the double myth of the social sciences: the myth of political benevolence and the myth of scientific omniscience;[6] the view, in other words, that since we have arrived at the end of ideology, knowledge and technology are free—neutral or nonideological—to serve the interests and powers of the "benevolent" American state and corporate elite both at home and abroad.

Finally, I will outline an alternative methodology for the social sciences based on existential phenomenology the theoretical foundations of which are consistent with the position that for a social scientist to be empirical is not to assume that he must be value-free or nonideological. In fact, existential phenomenology is well suited to the view that an empirical analysis of reality is not only a way of understanding the social world, but that it is also a way of criticizing society and of changing it as well. For when one ruminates in the realm of ideas, questions of ideology or social goals need not arise, even though they may be applicable; but in the world of social reality in which ideas are always related to institutions and social practice, questions of the social use of knowledge and ideology cannot be avoided. In short, while this chapter deals with methodology in the social sciences, its primary concern is with ideology.

The New Role of the Social Sciences

In recent years, the burgeoning critique of behavioralism has put forward the claims that its proponents are guilty of "implicit and unrecognized conservative values," "fearful of popular democracy," and tend to "avoid political issues" in their research.[7] It is argued, therefore, that the study of power as the observable exercise of power is conservative because it fails to consider the nonobservable, non-decision-making process;[8] that to assume that elites are the guardians of liberal democratic values and succeed in satisfying most demands made on the American polity is to demonstrate a fear of popular democracy, especially when this view is coupled with the presumption that the masses tend to be undemocratic;[9] and that the increasing trend to build mathematical models based on the criteria of the physical sciences abstracts political science from political reality and renders such research pseudo-political or apolitical by reducing it to a sophisticated numerology.[10]

To the contrary, however, in a recent countercritique, Bert Rockman has developed the view that these troubles of social science methodology are due to the shortcomings of the researcher, his failure to understand the role his ideology plays in his research, and the limitations of the present level of knowledge, but not to the methodology itself.[11] Although this view is in many ways persuasive, it does not fully contend with the critique since it is obvious that one must judge social science on the basis of what it *knows* and what it *does,* not on the basis of what it *ought* to know or what it *ought* to do. For, to the extent that knowledge, including methods of inquiry and techniques of data collection, is socially determined, the social scientist's assertion of the purity of his methodology, "the quality of (his) operationalizations," his "resourceful utilization of technique," or the high moral virtue of his ideological biases are in themselves insufficient grounds for judging the results of empirical research. Bert Rockman's view, for example, is that "the only real issue is how well we are able to operationalize," which "is dependent upon what we define as reality."[12] But the point is that what we define as reality is also dependent on preconceived knowledge, and that the validity or relevance of methods of inquiry and the utilizatilon of technique are also implicated in the social determination of knowledge. Therefore, the limitations of behavioral methodology are to be found even in Rockman's convincing paper because while on the one hand he puts forward a view, with which I fully agree,[13] that "our 'science' will consist of developing interpretations of the political universe, based partly on data and partly on ideology";[14] on the other, he concludes that "the data should enable us to test for the invalidity of clearly defined propositions on their own terms."[15] The latter point is questioned by even some positivists, who, like Moritz Schlick, assert that there is an important distinction between verified knowledge and verifiable knowledge.[16] The former is subject to tests for validity or invalidity; but the latter, according to Schlick, cannot be verified here and now. For example in order to prove the proposition that God exists one must wait and see. This suggests that at least there are classes of knowledge for which the data will not enable us to test for validity or invalidity merely on the basis of clearly defined propositions taken on their own terms. Does social knowledge not fall into this class of knowledge? Moreover, there is no reason to conclude that because we have clearly defined propositions, they will necessarily be consistent with socially defined knowledge or socially acquired street knowledge. The point was well made by Murray Kempton, who recently noted:

I think there is a change now in our view of life; we know more than we ever knew before, but we know it instinctively, and not from the sources of public information we get. What do we know, exactly? We know now that Walt Whitman Rostow is a fool. We know that Dean Rusk is a clerk. We know that Mr. Nixon is not really very much worse than the people who preceded him (which is a sufficient judgement on them), and so on. We know all these things not because anyone told us but because events have explained them to us. And it is this explanation that people are looking for.[17]

To criticize social science methodology and its criteria of verification, operationalization, or objectivity is not to denigrate the relevance of scientific inquiry. It is rather to analyze the social and political nature of this methodology, and to see the extent to which knowledge is socially determined, the extent to which social forces decide *what* knowledge is relevant and *how* (and for what purposes) it is to be used. I will attempt to delineate three methodological approaches to social science with a view toward analyzing the linkage between scientific method and ideology or the ideological implications of research. These are (1) The New Mandarin; (2) The Public Advocate; (3) The Persuasive Neutralist.

The New Mandarin is best characterized by Ithiel de Sola Pool whose view it is that the social sciences should be devoted to the service of the mandarins of the future because psychology, sociology, systems analysis, and political science provide the knowledge by which "men of power are humanized and civilized."[18] In order to keep the actions of the men of power from being "brutal, stupid, bureaucratic, they need a way of perceiving the consequences of what they do."[19] To perceive the consequences of public policy, that is, to describe the facts, is the primary contribution of the empirical social sciences to the uses of American power. As an example of this approach, Pool informs us of what we have learned in the past thirty years of intensive empirical study of contemporary societies by formulating the central issues of order and reform in this way:

In the Congo, in Vietnam, in the Dominican Republic, it is clear that order depends on somehow compelling newly mobilized strata to return to a measure of passivity and defeatism from which they have recently been aroused by the process of modernization. At least temporarily, the maintenance of order requires a lowering of newly acquired aspirations and levels of political activity.[20]

The meaning of this analysis for American policy is clearly in accord with counterrevolutionary American policies such as recent pacification programs, counterinsurgency and the like. But the social scientist denies that this sort of analysis is ideological, claiming instead that these studies conform to the scholarly, objective rigor of his discipline.

This is sheer non-sense. Take for example the following proposition by Professor Pool on "restructuring" government as an "empirical" formulation: "I rule out of consideration here a large range of viable political settlements" for restructuring government in South Vietnam, namely, those that involve "the inclusion of the Viet Cong in a coalition government or even the persistence of the Viet Cong as a legal organization in South Vietnam." Such arrangements "are not acceptable" since the only acceptable settlement is one "imposed by the GVN despite the persisting great political power of the Viet Cong."[21] While it may argued, as Pool puts it, that "the only hope for humane government in the future is through the extensive use of the social sciences by government,"[22] the precise ideological nature of this new role, all claims of objectivity to the contrary, is not to be denied. In effect, intellectual detachment and the disinterested quest for truth—the professed essence of the value-free, neutral social scientist—are replaced by the new elite role of the masters of knowledge[23] whose knowledge is placed at the disposal of the "benevolent" political interests of the masters of power. Accordingly, social scientists become, in essence, "house-ideologues for those in power."[24]

The Public Advocate appears to be a more selfless servant of the people who is concerned primarily with reforming public policy to better the lot of the poor, disfranchised, or underdeveloped. His professed mission is to serve the public good rather than the government or the corporation. In response to the plight of the poor and black in America, Daniel P. Moynihan adopts the stance of the Public Advocate. He decries the failures of the War on Poverty to contend with the "problem."[25] His view is that the problem of poverty cannot be solved either by discouraging the rigorous inquiry into the social process that keeps men in poverty (or leads them out of it), or by falling back on the guilt complex of the white society which concludes that "white racism is essentially responsible for the explosive mixture which has been accumulating in our cities since the end of World War II."[26] Rather, for Moynihan, "American social science can do better, and so it ought."[27] This requires commitment on the part of the social scientist—the War on Poverty was such a commitment—and an honorable desire to be helpful. Therefore, even though there were many failures in the War on Poverty program, the commitment by social scientists and the government for which they worked was made, and "that commitment stands, and intellectuals, having played a major role in its establishment, now have a special responsibility both for keeping it alive and for keeping it on the proper track."[28]

The Public Advocate uses his social science knowledge to influence public policy, but he is not, so it is claimed, the servant of government since his primary objective is "to get public policy to react to unmet social demands...."[29] However, the research design, the questions posed, and the general framework of the analysis are all circumscribed by the Public Advocate's desire to do something *for* the poor and black people insofar as that "something" is possible within the known or assumed limits of the existing institutions. For the Public Advocate, "simply to blame the system is ... obscurantism"[30] and best left out of consideration. He prefers to limit his research to influencing policy within the system—to make the system work better. The Public Advocate assumes, therefore, the values of the system and its operationality as given; he does not question it. Whatever the case may be, he has obviously not arrived at this analysis by empirical, objective, or neutral investigation.

In the Moynihan Report on the Negro family, "doing something for these people" was described in a special research report for the internal use of the government. The report revealed a pattern of instability in the Negro family structure which represented a "tangle of pathology ... capable of perpetuating itself without assistance from the white world."[31] In addition, Moynihan adduced evidence to show that illegitimacy, crime and juvenile delinquency, drop-out rates and unemployment were "causally" connected to family structure.[32] The social scientist has here uncovered a case of deviant social pathology, the cure for which is to change the deviants, not the system. Christopher Jencks criticizes Moynihan's conservative analysis because "the guiding assumption is that social pathology is caused less by basic defects in the social system than by defects in particular individuals and groups which prevent their adjusting to the system."[33]

The major concern of the Public Advocate is not knowledge in itself but the policy relevance of his research findings. When he writes "a polemic which makes use of social science techniques and findings to convince others," it should be clear that he expects that "the social science data he could bring to bear would have a persuasive effect."[34] Therefore, the scholarly or "scientific" quality of his research or its political relevance for those whom he wants to help would seem to be of only secondary importance. The Public Advocate is committed primarily to advocating ways by which the existing social institutions can be made to function better. However broad a range of research or policy this may include, it is nonetheless limited to the established parameters of the system, and thus it appears that the Public Advocate always tends to tell the government what it wants to hear, i.e., to constantly reinforce existing myths and ideologies or create "a new set of myths to justify the *status quo*."[35] In no way does this qualify the Public Advocate as an objective or value-free social scientist.

The only remaining question is whether and to what extent this sort of policy science is defined by and serves the interests of governmental agencies at the expense of the public. Herein lies the background of nonsense characterized by the Public Advocate's desire to do something *for* those poor, black people while knowing that in a very real sense his commitments are elsewhere. Julius Lester has correctly perceived the social and political function of the Public Advocate when he says, "Bang! Bang! Mr. Moynihan," because

somehow . . . nothing is true for a white man until a white man says it. Let the black say the same thing, and it will not be heard, or, if heard, ignored. Let a white man say it, and it becomes truth. It should be obvious why it will be the Moynihans we go after first rather than the southern sheriff.[36]

On the surface, the case of the *Persuasive Neutralist* seems to be altogether different from the first two types, for while the New Mandarin and the Public Advocate are ideologues for the existing social system, the Persuasive Neutralist appears as a professional methodologist who is concerned "strictly" with the techniques and knowledge brought forth by the scientific or "behavioral" revolution in the social sciences. His studies are generally not policy-oriented, though he claims that policy studies may also be "objective,"[37] and he carefully eschews any sign of ideological intent in his research. The Persuasive Neutralist, not unlike the other types, may have a calling, but it is to science, not polemics, dogma, or ideology. His main function is to cumulate knowledge about the social world, *to describe, understand and interpret reality, not change it.*[38]

In my view, however, the Persuasive Neutralist is equally subject to the claim of nonobjectivity, of ideology and non-sense stated above. The view, for instance, that one's research objective is to describe reality but *not* to change or criticize it is, I would argue, fundamentally conservative and will generally tend to reinforce existing institutions and social patterns. But I think the critique can be extended further than I have thus far suggested.

First, behavioral social scientists make the basic claim that the world of thought and knowledge is objective and rational. The social scientist so oriented adapts the intellectual posture of the physical scientist whose main function is to observe the phenomena of his chosen sphere of social reality and organize his data in such a way that he will be able to understand, interpret and, hopefully, explain that segment of the world under observation. His work is piecemeal; he theorizes and hypothesizes and later, by employing the techniques of modern technology and science, cumulates data, replicates experiments, and amasses evidence for his propositions. In all events, his research is the work of the rational thinker, the "scientist," but one who is constrained by the self-imposed rules of the physical sciences to see the world from the outside, as a neutral observer. Naturally, he is also constrained in his view of social reality because for him the world is what "I think," not what "I live through." This world of science is the natural or physical world which reason alone (scientific or conceptual knowledge) can harness; but it is not the world of man and society which is always composed of reason and unreason, preconceptual knowledge and conceptual knowledge, thought and action, objective and external phenomena as well as subjective and internal phenomena. In short, for the behavioral scientist, "scientific" knowledge can overcome irrationality, contingency, and subjectivity. However, by its very nature, this knowledge has definite limitations, which William James clearly perceived when he distinguished "knowledge-about" or thought knowledge from "knowledge by acquaintance" or felt knowledge. To be empirical, according to James and contemporary phenomenologists, requires the distinction and elucidation of these different levels of knowing and meaning construction if the object of inquiry in social science is the social and human world itself. For James, "feelings are the germ and starting point of cognition, thoughts the developed tree,"[39] and therefore, a genuine empiricism "cannot simply construct experience as a logical patterning tailored to the convenience of this or that analysis of what valid propositions require."[40] Rather, "we must inquire into the ways in which logical order can relate to the concretely felt experience."[41]

Moreover, the claim of objectivity in behavioral social science is not warranted by the facts. Since objectivity refers to only external, observable, physical phenomena—the things of the world—it fails to recognize precisely those human and social experiences which also include internal, subjective, and psychical phenomena. What is essential for social science is the recognition that:

Human behavior is neither a series of blind reactions to external "stimuli," nor the project of acts which are motivated by the pure ideas of disembodied, wordless mind. It is neither exclusively subjective nor exclusively objective, but a dialectical interchange between man and the world, which cannot be adequately expressed in traditional causal terms.[42]

To put it in other words, human behavior and human knowledge are neither exclusively rational nor exclusively irrational. The quest for exclusivity from either side simply has no scientific foundation when applied to men and society. To the contrary, behavioral science is primarily concerned with theory construction and scientific *testability* rather than social *tenability*. Models tend to be viewed as theories (provable or disprovable cause-effect propositions) which purport to forecast practical results, i.e., game theory or the domino theory.[43] The replicability of experiments or the uniformity of data are given the status of causal explanation. In contrast, Max Weber asserted that

. . . If adequacy in respect to meaning is lacking, then no matter how high the degree of uniformity and how precisely its probability can be numerically determined, it is still an incomprehensible statistical probability whether dealing with overt or subjective processes.[44]

In order to avoid the objectivism and intellectualism of science, one must recognize this dependence of conceptualization on the preconceptual life-world, which Husserl called the *Lebenswelt,* because:

The whole universe of science is built upon the world as directly experienced, and if we want to subject science itself to rigorous scrutiny and arrive at a precise awareness of its meaning and scope, we must begin by reawakening the basic experience of the world of which science is the second-order expression. . . . To return to things themselves is to return to that world which precedes knowledge, of which knowledge *speaks,* and in relation to which every scientific schematization is an abstract and derivative sign-language, as is geography in relation to the countryside in which we have learnt beforehand what a forest, a prairie or a river is.[45]

Insofar as behavioral scientists ignore this social "reality," insofar as they fail to distinguish scientific facts or natural reality from world facts or social reality, their research tends to objectify or reify human and social meanings. There can be no doubt that behavioral social science has amassed "knowledge-about," but the capacity for this knowledge to reconcile its theoretical understanding of social problems with the experienced reality of, say, the black power advocates, and employ it in the quest for free, creative social activity and responsive social institutions is today indeed questionable.

Second, it is becoming more evident with recent trends in the uses of technical and social science knowledge by large-scale institutions that science and technology are not necessarily progressive, as it was once thought. As John McDermott has recently noted:

Segments of knowledge still belong to technical specialists and pieces of knowledge to the well educated, but only the very largest organizations are able to integrate these proliferating segments and pieces into systems of productive, effective, or more likely, profitable information. That is the meaning of technological progress: the systematic application of new knowledge to practical purposes. And it dictates a continual increase in the size, wealth and managerial capacity of the organizations which seek thus to apply knowledge. Corporations, government agencies, universities, and foundations have been quick to respond.[46]

In the face of this technological explosion and increasing institutionalization and professionalization of knowledge, to claim a neutral or "objective" role for social science is clearly to fall under the onus of what Merleau-Ponty called "non-sense." Briefly put, the full thrust of reason and knowledge is being turned against itself—against truth and humanity, in favor of the dominant institutions and power-centers which are now tending to the *manipulation,* rather than the *liberation* of mankind, especially its underclasses. In short, the Persuasive Neutralist who inveighs against the ideologies and utopias that want to change the world in favor of a scientific or "objective" description or interpretation of social reality turns objective knowledge upside down: a fundamentally apolitical posture becomes highly political or ideological insofar as that knowledge serves entrenched institutions and power interests, whether these be pacification programs in South Vietnam or funneling of the energies of black youth into the established channels of American society.[47] To put it another way, the meaning and social significance of rational inquiry is inverted —sense is turned into nonsense. (From this perspective it could be argued that the Wallaceites and the New Left and other so-called social deviants have correctly perceived the insane world of reason against which they rebel.)

The serious limitations of even the most sophisticated methods and techniques of social science were underscored in a recent report by the Center for the Study of Conflict Resolution at the University of Michigan which noted that, after eleven years of research using the most proficient methods and techniques they had gotten no closer to resolving conflict in the world or explaining the causes of violence. In fact, the report suggested, the situation requires all conceivable efforts to search for radically new methods of inquiry.

Finally, in terms of the ideological implications of social science, some behavioral scientists have taken the position that the recognition and clarification of their own biases will be sufficient to place such biases in perspective, enable them to then get on with the pursuit of science. This view is rightly attacked by Heinz Eulau, a well-known behavioralist.[48] Eulau's argument is that one's science is either value-free or it is not. It "is a problem of fact," exhorts Eulau, "that can be answered only through empirical research into the nature of science as a form of human activity."[49] The only quibble I have with Eulau, whose view is representative of most behavioral thought, is the assumption about the value-free study of politics he makes. In reference to policy science, Eulau writes: "The policy science approach does not assume that a value-free scientific study of politics is impossible because men pursue values through politics. Indeed, it sharply distinguishes between propositions of fact that are believed to be subject to scientific-empirical inquiry, and propositions of value for which empirical science has as yet no answer."[50] Accordingly, the policy scientist can avoid violating the canons of scientific method by recognizing the existence of both facts and values and keeping a subtle balance or distance between them. Therefore, Eulau concludes, this approach "does not deny that scientific research on propositions of fact cannot serve policy objectives; indeed, it asserts that political science, as all science, should be put in the service of whatever goals men pursue in politics."[51] But the keynote of Eulau's position gives a telling commentary on all three approaches when he asserts that science is still value-free even if "there is nothing in his science that prevents its being used for ends of which he disapproves."[52]

Despite his claims of value-neutrality, Heinz Eulau's conclusions could not be more insightful. Social science is always used by societies which generally determine what knowledge will be used and how knowledge will be used. The purity of knowledge is meaningless as long as that knowledge is used by social institutions for certain prescribed purposes. Hence, social knowledge, whether it be scientific or not, has a value for that society and plays a function which can most often be called ideological. Alas, we have come full circle back from the Persuasive Neutralist to the New Mandarin and Public Advocate. The differences could not have been very significant from the start.

Toward a Radical Social Science

American society is in need of a radical reorganization of social priorities. To achieve that end may call for a reconstruction of its dominant institutions, but at the least requires a redistribution of power and wealth as well as a redistribution of knowledge.[53] The need for radical change grows as America's institutions find it increasingly difficult to meet the rising social demands of its most needy, most powerless, most alienated members. The vision of a white, liberal power structure bent on exploiting and repressing the poor and black at home and fighting counterrevolutionary, imperialist wars abroad is becoming more evident to the underclasses, left intellectuals, and students. What they envisage is the rationalization of bureaucracy, the monopolization of power and wealth, the tailoring of knowledge and technology, and the manipulation and control of the people in the interests of self-serving elites—managerial, corporate, political, and intellectual. To argue to the contrary is of no avail since this generation has experienced (and is becoming more conscious of) its own poverty, powerlessness, alienation, and knows how these feelings relate to the reality of American power and ideology in Vietnam and Santo Domingo, Watts and Detroit, Chicago and Columbia University. To plead for reason, detachment, objectivity or patience in the face of abject poverty, political repression, and napalmed women and children is absurd. Along with the power structure, reason, they will tell you, is what gets us into Vietnam and keeps us there, produces a war on poverty but curtails funding, calls for "law and order" instead of freedom and justice. Moreover, what I have argued in this essay is that in spite of all claims to objectivity, rational, intellectual output, whether in the form of policy programs at home or pacification programs abroad, tends to reinforce the established order. That this may occur was underscored even by Heinz Eulau. In fact, the meaning of so much rational model-building, statistical data, theorizing, planning and programming can be viewed—as it is viewed by many of those most affected—as an elaboration of new, sophisticated techniques for "keeping the people down." This is the ideological significance of so-called "objective" or "scientific" knowledge as many have come to know it or experience its results.

Of course, this undercurrent in American society is merely the "knowledge by acquaintance" or felt knowledge of some Americans, certainly not the prevailing viewpoint, or the majority opinion. It is no wonder, then, that the rulers of both power and knowledge with their pluralistic, empiricist traditions find it so difficult to respond. For each of these two worlds of reality the other is incomprehensible, alien, quixotic. The situation is becoming more chaotic as these two worlds move farther and farther apart, demands become intolerable, and each side appears to be increasingly intransigent.

While the methods and uses of social science criticized in this chapter demonstrate behaviorialism's intellectual and political incapacity to come to terms with this social reality, recent developments in existentialism and phenomenology have provided a radical alternative, one which, I contend, is more conducive to a critique of existing social institutions as well as to a theory of social change. At the same time, existential phenomenology provides a methodology for the social sciences which is no less rigorous, no less concerned with the verifiability of knowledge, and no less concerned with empirical inquiry.

The primary concern of existential phenomenology is the description of the life world *(Lebenswelt)* of everyday, common sense reality. It is a way of looking at the world, or describing its social reality, and disclosing, therefore, its human and social meaning. Starting with the human situation, the primordial condition of man's being-in-the-world *(in-der-Welt-sein)*, phenomenology sets out to explore the different regions of human existence, the foundations of which are to be discovered in the everydayness of existence itself as it is experienced. In the language of phenomenology, the primacy of human existence is in the perception of the lived body (corps vecu) which is thrown into existence (Heidegger) with others and the world. According to phenomenology, human existence is pro-jective and intentional: through man's course of action new meaning is given to the world, history is made, and a new human and social *praxis* becomes possible. Man is condemned to history, said Merleau-Ponty; man, therefore, is condemned to be that being through whose actions the meaning construction of the world and of social relations is formed, deformed, reformed or transformed. Phenomenology, in short, is nothing less than a bold attempt to recover the primacy of human social existence, to reestablish human action as the motor of social forces and social relations, to reassert the social value and meaning of what William James called "the world of the street" in which every man and woman's actions have meaning in themselves as well as for others *(pour autrui)*.[54]

In regard to its methodological approach to social reality, phenomenology conforms to neither classical modes of subjectivism (irrationalism, solipsism) nor to classical modes of objectivism (rationalism, behavioralism). Phenomenology transcends both by establishing what Husserl, and later Merleau-Ponty and Alfred Schutz, called *intersubjectivity,* by which is meant the fundamental interconnection between the external, objective world including other people *(être-en-soi)* and the internal, subjective world of consciousness *(être-pour-soi).* This philosophy denies neither the world nor man, neither social structures and ideas nor human action, but rather attempts to describe the ineradicable link between the two, and establish thereby the primacy of coexistence or *human* sociality. Hence the importance of phenomenology rests on its radical approach to social reality, its ability to describe the existential presence of man and his actions within the objective conditions of the world which are already established prior to his existence (i.e., man is thrown into the world). But equally important is the concept of *intersubjectivity* which lays the foundation for a new socialism based on its claim that all existence is coexistence and consequently all action is coaction, and a new humanism since "... a society is not the temple of value-idols that figure on the front of its monuments or in its constitutional scrolls; the value of a society is the value it places upon man's relations to man."[55]

Phenomenologists and existentialists, moreover, such as Merleau-Ponty, Schutz, and Sartre argue for a dialectical unity of thought and action which seeks the meaning of *praxis* for social existence. Thus, following Marx, existence is meaningful only insofar as we "connect ourselves with history instead of contemplating it."[56] For, what Marx calls *praxis* "is the meaning which works itself out spontaneously in the intercrossing of those activities by which man organizes his relations with nature and other men."[57] In other words, the root of existence is consciousness; yet consciousness is always consciousness of something, i.e., involved consciousness, or a way of organizing projects of action based on the intentions of men or social classes in order to give meaning to their concrete, historical situation.

This concern for social *praxis,* for the unity of thought and action, establishes existential phenomenology as a critical theory of radical political action, and represents a significant step toward reconciling Marxian socialism and existential humanism. These two movements share an awareness of the importance of a critical, humanistic, and existential attitude toward those petrified social forces and their ideological justifications which deny human existence, enforce patterns of social injustice, and alienate man from society itself. However, the key to the synthesis of these theoretical movements is the recognition of what Merleau-Ponty called the "dialectics of ambiguity." Briefly put, man is the motor of world historical forces, the being through whose actions social meaning, social change, and freedom are possible, but at the same time man is born into a world which he did not create and is always subject to others (coactors) as well as to the existing ideas, institutions, and social processes which dominate his milieu. The dialectic, therefore, is an open-ended process, never restricted to either human action in itself or the social order in itself.

Finally, this approach to social science eschews value neutrality. It agrees with Marx that "philosophers have only interpreted the world in different ways; the point is to *change* it." While recognizing the central role of value and ideology in the quest for a free, open, and humane society and culture, existential phenomenologists and Marxists alike invite a sense of social commitment on the part of intellectuals, informed by a critical vision of the existing social world as well as a critical view toward transforming it. This approach is ideological in its quest for that historical truth by which man becomes the motor of the dialectic, enabling him to create the conditions under which he can make history and overcome both the resistance of the world and the institutional predilections of the political status quo to his projects for action.[58]

In conclusion, existential phenomenology aligned with a humanistic vision of social change is a radical alternative to behavioralism. First, because its vision of the world comprises the whole of social reality, including the common-sense reality of the man in the street, which the rationalistic universe of behavioralism tends to overlook. Second, because its vision of the social world is based on a critical attitude toward the status quo rather than the apolitical description of and compliance with established political power so predominant among behavioralists. This radical methodology of social science offers some hope that from the seemingly mindless rationalism of America's political and intellectual elites and the seemingly mindless irrationalism of America's underclasses might emerge a new sense of reason and social purpose.

NOTES

NOTE: I want to thank Hwa Yol Jung for suggesting the title and also for making available to me his unpublished paper, "Existential Phenomenology and Political Theory."

1. Maurice Merleau-Ponty, *Sense and Non-sense* (Evanston: Northwestern University Press, 1964), p. 4.

2. *Ibid.*

3. *Ibid.*

4. *Ibid.*

5. *Ibid.*, p. 5.

6. Noam Chomsky, *American Power and the New Mandarins* (New York: Pantheon Books, 1969).

7. See Charles McCoy and John Playford, eds., *Apolitical Politics: A Critique of Behavioralism* (New York: Thomas Y. Crowell, 1967).

8. See Peter Bachrach and Morton S. Baretz, "The Faces of Power," in *ibid*.

9. See Peter Bachrach, *The Theory of Democratic Elitism: A Critique* (Boston: Little, Brown, 1967).

10. See Francis Wormuth, "Matched-Dependent Behavioralism: The Cargo Cult in Political Science," *Western Political Quarterly*, 20 (December 1967): 809–840.

11. Bert Rockman, "A 'Behavioral' Evaluation of the Critique of Behavioralism" (Presented for the Caucus for a New Political Science, American Political Science Convention, September 1969).

12. *Ibid.*, p. 40.

13. Though I agree, I am not at all sure how one goes about determining the point at which science begins and ideology leaves off.

14. Rockman, *op. cit.*, p. 41.

15. *Ibid.*

16. Moritz Schlick, "Meaning and Verification," in Herbert Feigl and Wilfrid Sellars, eds., *Readings in Philosophical Analysis* (New York: Appleton-Century-Crofts, 1949), pp. 146–170.

17. David Gelman and Beverly Kempton, "The Trouble with Newspapers: An Interview with Murray Kempton," *The Washington Monthly*, 1, no. 3 (April 1969): 26.

18. Ithiel de Sola Pool, "The Necessity for Social Scientists Doing Research for Governments," *Background*, 10 (August 1966): 111.

19. *Ibid.*

20. Cited in Chomsky, *op. cit.* p. 36 *ibid.*, p. 49.

21. Cited in *ibid.*, p. 49.

22. Pool, *op. cit.*

23. Daniel Bell, "Notes on the Post-Industrial Society: Part I," *The Public Interest*, No. 6 (1967): 24–35.

24. Zbigniew Brzezinski, "America in the Technetronic Age," *Encounter*, 30 (January 1968): 16–26.

25. Daniel P. Moynihan, *Maximum Feasible Misunderstanding* (New York: Free Press, 1969).

26. Daniel P. Moynihan, "The Professors and the Poor," *Commentary*, 46, no. 2 (August 1968): 28.

27. *Ibid.*

28. *Ibid.*

29. Lee Rainwater and William Yancey, eds., *The Moynihan Report and the Politics of Controversy* (Cambridge: M.I.T. Press, 1967), p. 24.

30. Moynihan, *op. cit.*, p. 28.

31. *Ibid.*, p. 42.

32. In a perceptive article, William Ryan criticizes the Moynihan Report for drawing inexact conclusions from weak and insufficient data; encouraging a new form of subtle racism which he calls "Savage Discovery," i.e., the belief that it is the weaknesses and defects of the Negro himself that account for the present status of inequality between Negro and white; and for interpreting statistical relationships in cause-and-effect terms. See "Savage Discovery: The Moynihan Report," in *ibid.*, p. 458.

33. "The Moynihan Report," in *ibid.*, p. 443.

34. *Ibid.*

35. Ryan, *op. cit.*, p. 465.

36. Julius Lester, *Look Out, Whitey: Black Power's Gon' Get Your Mama;* (New York: Grove Press, 1968), p. 54.

37. Heinz Eulau, *The Behavioral Persuasion in Politics* (New York: Grove Press, 1968), p. 54.

38. *Ibid.,* p. 9.

39. William James, *Principles of Psychology,* 1 (New York: Dover Publications, 1950) 222.

40. Eugene T. Gendlin, *Experiencing and The Creation of Meaning* (Glencoe: Free Press, 1962), pp. 9 and 139. Cited by H. Y. Jung, "Existential Phenomenology and Political Theory" (unpublished paper).

41. *Ibid.*

42. "Foreword," In Maurice Merleau-Ponty, *The Structure of Behavior* (Boston: Beacon Press, 1963), pp. xv–xvi.

43. Wormuth, *op. cit.,* p. 816.

44. Max Weber, *The Theory of Social and Economic Organization* (New York: Free Press, 1966), p. 88.

45. Maurice Merleau-Ponty, *Phenomenology of Perception* (London: Routledge and Kegan Paul, 1962), pp. viii and ix.

46. "Knowledge is Power," *The Nation* (April 14, 1969), p. 458.

47. Elinor Graham, "The Politics of Poverty," in H. Gettleman and D. Mermelstein, eds., *The Great Society Reader* (New York: Random House, 1967), p. 230.

48. Eulau, *op. cit.,* p. 136.

49. *Ibid.,* p. 135.

50. *Ibid.,* p. 136.

51. *Ibid.,* pp. 136–137.

52. *Ibid.*

53. McDermott, *op. cit.*

54. A brief bibliography of the relevant major works of these authors is listed below. I omit Søren Kierkegaard for obvious reasons. Where available, English editions are cited. Martin Heidegger: *Being and Time* (New York: Harper and Row, 1962). Edmund Husserl: *Ideas* (New York: Collier Books, 1962), *The Crisis of European Sciences and Transcendental Phenomenology* (Evanston, Ill.: Northwestern University Press, 1970). Maurice Merleau-Ponty: *Les Aventures de la dialectique* (Paris: Gallimard, 1955), *Humanism and Terror* (Boston: Beacon Press, 1969), *Phenomenology of Perception* (London: Routledge and Kegan Paul, 1962), *In Praise of Philosophy* (Evanston: Northwestern University Press, 1963), *The Primacy of Perception* (Evanston: Northwestern University Press, 1964), *Sense and Nonsense* (Evanston: Northwestern University Press, 1964), *Signs* (Evanston: Northwestern University Press, 1964), and *The Structure of Behavior* (Boston: Beacon Press, 1963). Jean-Paul Sartre: *Being and Nothingness* (New York: Philosophical Library, 1956), *Critique de la raison dialectique* (Paris: Gallimard, 1960), *Literary and Philosophical Essays* (New York: Collier Books, 1955), and *Search for a Method* (New York: Alfred Knopf, 1963). Alfred Schutz: *Collected papers,* 3 vols. (The Hague: Martinus Nijhoff, 1962, 1964, 1966) and *The Phenomenology of the Social World* (Evanston: Northwestern University Press, 1967). John Wild: *Existence and the World of Freedom* (Englewood Cliffs, N. J.: Prentice-Hall, 1963).

55. Merleau-Ponty, *Humanism and Terror,* p. xiv.
56. Merleau-Ponty, *Sense and Non-sense,* p. 79.
57. Merleau-Ponty, *In Praise of Philosophy,* p. 50.
58. This formulation was suggested to me by Robin Blackburn.

2

BEYOND REPUBLICANISM:
THE SOCIALIST
CRITIQUE OF
POLITICAL
IDEALISM • *David Kettler*

I

An expanding critical literature shows that most American political study during the past twenty years has been dominated by an ideology which systematically diverts the attention of political scientists (and their readers) from major shortcomings in American political and social arrangements. Events of the last few years have compelled all but the most deluded to acknowledge that these shortcomings exist. That the dominant academic ideology, commonly identified as "pluralism," cannot diagnose the problems and cannot offer an adequate strategy for change has been persuasively argued in many places. The danger now is that critical political thinkers will expend too much of their intellectual energy in elaborating this critique. Exposure of the old ideology has been an essential task; the time has come to move on.[1]

Several dangers attend an exclusive emphasis on the unveiling of ideology. There is, first, the danger of supposing that the ideology screens truths which are self-evident. Recognition that the system of competition among groups interested in various policy outcomes does not have the openness and flexibility claimed for it by pluralist apologists does not itself validate Trotsky's account of political democracy in *Terrorism and Communism,* for example. Second, there is the danger of losing ourselves among those who make the critique of ideology an occasion for abandoning all efforts to develop their own rationale of political conduct and judgment. Conduct and judgment then become only matters for irrational or at least nonrational decision, and rigorous inquiry becomes a game or a production of techniques. Third, there is the danger of confusing the intellectual demolition of ideology with the transformation of the conditions which it serves to obscure.[2] Fourth, excessive attention to one ideological formulation will distract attention from the emergence of new ones. While critics are still busy with Galbraith's "countervailing powers," he has sought greener fields in the technostructure and the educational estates. Finally, the definition of the situation in social and political science as a polarized confrontation between the ideologists-who-are-pluralists and "the critical temper" inhibits the work of unstinting mutual criticism among the critics which is a prerequisite to the development of an adequate critical social and political theory.[3]

In this essay, I presuppose the intellectual demise of this pluralism and I do not feel obliged to do more than to assert three propositions in opposition to fundamental tenets of that doctrine:

1. The political arrangements of the Western nations, with their prominent patterns of bargaining among certain groups and characteristic formal institutions, represent one way of managing a modern society; they are not the actualization of the generic and universal solution to the problems of modernization.

2. This Western way of ordering a modern society exacts harsh human costs which cannot be shown to be necessitated by "the human condition," "culture," "civilization," or even by industrialization as such.[4] And these costs also press hard on inhabitants of other societies, who receive little if any compensation in return.

3. The political arrangements of Western nations must be understood as systems of power sustained by force as well as by authority, and the "equilibrium" must be seen as markedly biased in favor of those who possess certain power resources and against those who lack them.[5] Corollary to these propositions is the recognition that alternate regimes are possible and may be necessary, desirable, or both.

This paper undertakes to evaluate the alternative vision of American political life which most strongly appeals to American political traditions and which has regained influence as the inadequacies of pluralism (and of the system which that doctrine defends and sustains) are recognized. I shall refer to this alternative as "republican constitutionalism" or "republicanism." Numerous writers have remarked on the continuities between Madison's liberal interpretation of the constitutional scheme and recent pluralism. A contrasting and at times competing American tradition has also been identified, but the character of this alternate theme has not always been clearly specified. In a valuable and original essay, Norman Jacobson has compared the constitutionalism of the *Federalist* with the radical individualism of Tom Paine, who hoped to replace authoritative order with fraternal cooperation.[6] But this statement of the case is probably mistaken. Paine's radicalism expresses a style of action, a militancy, and a utopia. It does not offer a comprehensive vision of the political world capable of orienting sustained action or detailed criticism—as does republican constitutionalism. Paine politicized hitherto passive elements in the population; he mobilized and vitalized the activists—liberal, republican, or proto-socialist—but he became irrelevant when the time for inspiration passed in America, England, and France. An adequate conception of republican constitutionalism will encompass many of the phenomena to which Jacobson refers but will place them within a framework of greater theoretical interest.

The republican strand of constitutionalism places far more stress on ideas derived from Aristotle and Cicero than does the liberal. The contrast between them can be epitomized by saying that the one sees constitutional government as a school for disciplined virtue and the other as a machine for civilized and prosperous order. In the work of many constitutionalist writers, the two strands have often been intertwined, but never without serious tension within the argument. In practice, moreover, the classical argument has often served as a toga incongruously wrapped around the engine. We are not intent upon tracing the history of the interrelationship, however; rather, we are concerned to assess the revival of republican constitutionalism which has been fostered by a judgment that the pluralism which derives from liberal constituttionalism is inadequate.

Among contemporary political scientists, Theodore Lowi makes the most vigorous and politically concrete effort to effect a change in political science and to secure a renovation of American political life through a renewal of the republican tradition.[7] In order to observe the powers and limits of the alternative approach, then, we shall begin with a fairly detailed review of Lowi's latest book, *The End of Liberalism*. To see more deeply into the premises and structure of the argument, however, it will be necessary to turn next to a philosophical account of republican constitutionalism, which can be found, I will argue, in Hegel's *Philosophy of Right* and in the revisions of Hegel undertaken by his followers of more democratic persuasion. The subsequent critique of contemporary revivals of republican constitutionalism will therefore build upon the criticisms applied by Karl Marx to Hegel's work and to his own first political essays. Out of such a critique, it is hoped, will emerge an interpretation of our situation and a strategy for change which will incorporate the insights made available by the republican constitutionalist perspective but which will also transcend the limitations of that view.

The main contentions of the essay can be briefly summarized. The republican tradition, I shall argue, is an important theoretical resource. From the standpoint of its idealism, the abuses of the political order which is defended by pluralist doctrine are revealed as modern counterparts to feudal privilege, thereby exploding cant and complacency of at least one sort. Even where republicanism sees a constitutional state in the true sense and not a "new feudalism," it retains at its best a critical edge because it constantly reveals stark contrasts between the promise of a genuine public life and reality. But republican constitutionalism cannot account for departures from its ideals except finally by condemning a lack of disciplined idealism in the society. Its strategy of change ultimately depends on rhetorical exhortation, dependence on a real or figurative Cato the Censor to restore virtue, and, most dangerously, reliance on the spurts given to patriotic dedication by crisis, war, and confrontation with an enemy. I am satisfied that we must look elsewhere for the sources of our problems and that we must move from the diagnosis and strategy propounded by republicanism to a "socialism" appropriate to our time. The essay will close with a preliminary sketch of such a move.

One major objective of this paper will have been achieved if it succeeds in establishing direct contact between the literature of radical socialist criticism and the world of political discourse in which we as Americans are at home. Michael Oakeshott may well be right in his contention that political thought within a culture properly involves continuity within the framework of one scheme of political education. He is mistaken in supposing that this continuity takes the form of a genteel conversation instead of a dialectical encounter. The critical account of republican constitutionalism to be presented here means to help recast our present disputes in political theory into a form appropriate to such dialogue.[8]

II

The work of Theodore Lowi begins with a concern for the shape of public policy and constantly returns to it. He sees fundamental irrationalities of governmental conduct in many important spheres of life and concludes that these irrationalities result from basic deficiencies in the organization of public power. What he refers to as "value-free political science," corresponding to "pluralism" as the term is used here, fails to appreciate these irrationalities and consequently fails to recognize the deficiencies. More than that, in his view, "value-free political science" celebrates and fosters the "interest-group liberalism" which has displaced properly constitutional rule of law in American life and which lies, in his view, at the root of most incoherencies in public policy. The current political science sees the unceasing interplay among competing and informally bargaining groups as the basic reality of political life; and the current pattern of legislation and administration tends to conform to such a view, at the cost of denigrating the formal authoritative institutions and procedures. Lowi maintains:

In a vitally important sense, value-free political science is logically committed to the norm of delegation of power because delegation of power is the self-fulfilling mechanism of prediction in modern political science. Clear statutes that reduce pluralistic bargaining also reduce drastically the possibility of scientific treatment of government as simply part of the bundle of bargaining processes and multiple power structures. A good law eliminates the political process at certain points. A law made at the center of government focuses politics there and reduces interest elsewhere. The center means Congress, the President, and the courts. To make law at a central point is to centralize the political process. If this is too authoritative for interest-group liberalism it is too formal for modern political science.[9] *

Proceeding through a survey of major trends in the organization and work of administrative agencies, followed by a closer look at recent government actions in the cities, Lowi builds up to the following indictment:

The decline of Congress, the decline of democracy, the decline of independence among regulatory agencies, the general decline of law as an instrument of control are all due far more than anything else to changes in the philosophy of law and prevailing attitudes toward law. Admittedly the complexity of modern life forces Congress into vagueness and generality in drafting its statutes. Admittedly the political pressure of social unrest forces Congress and the President into premature formulations that make delegation of power inevitable. But to take these causes and effects as natural and good, and then to build the system around them, is to doom the system to remaining always locked into the original causes and effects.

No present-day liberal is prepared to propose that a government of laws is impossible or undesirable, just as no politician would propose that we do without the Constitution. But the system the present-day liberal would build is predicated upon just such propositions. Statutes without standards, policy without law, will yield pluralism throughout the system—just as political science predicts and liberalism prescribes. Overlooked and neglected is the converse proposition, which is also axiomatic; yet peculiarly enough the converse proposition does not yield opposite results: Policies that are real laws do not destroy pluralism but merely reduce its scope to those points in the system where decisions on rules can be made or reformed. If this proposition is true, then it obviously follows that its application could revitalize Congress, and sever agency-clientele relations. The effort to regulate . . . immediately attaches a morality to government. When that morality is a criterion for the regulatory act, it is bound to have a characteristic influence of some sort on the political process. When the regulation is done permissively and in the deliberate absence of the morality implied in the very use of coercive language, the result can only be expected to be demoralizing to the agency, the law itself, and the

*Reprinted from *The End of Liberalism* by Theodore J. Lowi, with the permission of W. W. Norton & Company, Inc., New York, New York. Copyright © 1969 by W. W. Norton & Company, Inc.

clientele. The group process is dynamic and cumulative when groups have institutional structure against which to compete. Without that formal structure the group process is not truly pluralistic at all. It is merely co-optive. And it is ineffective. Worse, it converts mere ineffectiveness into illegitimacy. Liberal sentiments remain, and indeed they may be the best sentiments. . . . The interest-group method was an ideal means of achieving a bit of equity. Its day is done, for equity is no longer enough. It has proven itself unequal to the tasks of planning and achieving justice. A grant of broad powers to administration is not a grant of power at all. It is an imposition of impotence. [P. 156]

Quoting this long summary instead of discussing the fascinating detail of his argument does Lowi a certain injustice, because his book has great value even for those who cannot accept his stark version of its teachings. But it helps us to consider Lowi's project for an alternate regime.

Pluralist political scientists describe the political regime of "interest-group liberalism" which they have helped to establish in the United States: they are among the prime contributors to the dominant ideology, a new public philosophy, and they promote its teachings in their work. The ideology in bankrupt, however, Lowi contends, and the system in crisis. There is a breakdown in legitimacy; people do not respect power wielded in the name of public authority because it is put at the disposal of agencies and groups to which people do not stand in the relationship of citizen and because that power is divorced from fair and prompt adjudication and coercive enforcement. There is no public planning because governmental agencies lack sufficient authority to coordinate, to make hard choices, to regulate and redistribute. There is no justice, because decisions in public matters without responsible authorities relate to equilibrium, not moral principle: "Consideration of the justice in or achieved by an action cannot be made unless a deliberate and conscious attempt was made by an actor to derive his action from a general rule or moral principle governing such a class of acts" (p. 290).

As contrasting model, Lowi has a vision of a restored Constitution, functioning in a manner pretty close to that described in civics textbooks. As will become clear, I don't say that slightingly. He contends that power must be exercised in accordance with laws which define norms instead of initiating processes, and that details must be spelled out in explicit administrative rules and not by case-by-case bargaining. In somewhat different language, he can be said to claim that rationality and morality both are far more likely to inhere in the formal actions of formal governmental institutions like those established by the Constitution than in the process of partisan mutual adjustment institutionalized under the regime of interest-group liberalism.

It makes no sense to apply a term like "conservative" to Lowi's argument, because it has very little to do with the talk to which such terms are normally applied in American discourse, as the following items make clear. Lowi urges the dissolution of all municipal and other local corporations because they too are wielders of powers improperly delegated by sovereign states and because they are not properly civic bodies and therefore politically incapable of dealing with their tasks. He argues that the War on Poverty represents a betrayal of the black revolution for full civil equality, that it was a subterfuge imposed by liberal Northern politicians frightened of their racist urban constituencies. With the lawless and futile War on Poverty replaced by a liberalized welfare program under legislation like the Social Security Act, the revolution must begin again in earnest. School districts must be drawn in pie-slices radiating out from the center city into the outermost suburbs; and obedience to laws requiring attendance and civil conduct must be coerced by legitimate force. "If middle-class mothers in Queens or Cicero or Berkeley have no respect for law, they can be garrisoned far more easily than the angry mob in Little Rock . . . or the mindless rioters in Newark" (p. 271). Lowi is talking about a major change in the regime of the United States and he sees that change as an instrument of basic social justice for at least some segments of the population.

Since he contends that the revolution which instituted the present regime was carried out or at least solidified by the new ideology of interest-group liberalism, sustained by political science, it is not surprising that he calls for another shift in ideology, transformation of the public philosophy, to establish the proper public order which he calls juridical democracy.

Lowi addresses his call for renovation to several political agencies. First, he speaks to "men of influence" in general. He says that "at the moment they continue to search for distant sociological causes of American distress. But ultimately they must come to see that they and their belief system constitute the pathology" (p. 297). Then "all leaders . . . will begin to search for new goals" and "they will need a new paradigm"; the platform for juridical democracy is designed to meet that need (p. 297). Second, he exhorts to courage and morality the men who occupy formal positions of authority, especially in the Congress. So, for example, he writes:

When regional variation is not desirable it is usually because some problem uniformly distributed across the country has been identified and is well known—as, for example, civil rights, military service, tax liability, access to the airwaves, obligations of contracts, free speech and petition—in which case *there is no barrier, except fear,* to prevent enactment of statutes in which clear and effective standards can accompany delegations of vast public power. [P. 306; emphasis supplied]

The political support for the change he sees in the moral character of many people *in their capacities as citizens.* This conception is not carefully developed, but underlies the whole emphasis on the states as political units to which individuals properly relate as citizens. These capacities are frustrated and left dormant under interest-group liberalism; they can be fostered and made a major political factor under a proper constitutional scheme. In the course of his telling attack on the "war-on-poverty" approach to civil rights and on fair housing legislation, he questions the political viability and morality of requiring the most disadvantaged part of the white population to make sacrifices so that the community can in some measure compensate blacks for injustices from which the prosperous and immune benefit. This is the effect, after all, of expanding welfare services financed by harshly regressive local taxes, stressing quotas in employment, integrating contiguous black and white school districts, emphasizing open housing, increasing subsidies to public institutions of higher learning, and the rest. Lowi would have the Congress enact laws to enforce justice, as he puts it, instead of compensating for injustice, and he would have those laws build upon civic virtue in the community:

If we truly seek to bring about a revolution through law [in the position of blacks] we should at least exhaust first of all the possibilities of pursuing it through *those people in the community most likely to respect the law,* and perhaps ultimately to come to see the actual necessity of eliminating all differences in human relationships due solely to indefensible and outmoded social criteria. [P. 269; emphasis supplied]

His most immediate appeal, however, is to the courts.

In his view, the Supreme Court has the power and authority to bring the other agencies into a position where they will have to make the shifts demanded. Political science sustains but does not generate the existing system, and it probably lacks the capacity for striking out in a new direction. He writes contemptuously:

Interest-group liberalism's focus on equilibrium and the paraphernalia of its establishment is apology. The focus on the group is commitment to one of the more rigidified aspects of the social process and is, there-fore, another kind of apology. The separation of facts from values is apology. [P. 313]

This is not to say that there can be no political science appropriate to a new regime:

Rules of law and their consequences—rights, justice, legitimacy—are just as susceptible of scientific generalization as their behavioral equivalents—bargaining, equilibrium and opinions. [P. 314]

The difficulty is moral, not epistemological. In any case, according to Lowi, "In the United States the history of political theory since the founding of the Republic has resided in the Supreme Court" (p. 314). Moreover, the Supreme Court made this regime through its decisions since the late 1930's, and it can unmake it by refusing to allow the kinds of delegations upon which the whole system turns. Lowi wants the Court to reinstate the rule announced and applied in *Schechter Poultry Corp. v. United States* (295 U.S. 495), where the whole system of self-regulating codes established by the National Industrial Recovery Act of 1933 was declared unconstitutional on the grounds that the act delegated too much power to the President (which he then put at the disposal of trade associations and the like). Such action by the Court would compel Congress to face problems seriously enough to translate their response into laws, and this central governmental process would authoritatively reestablish the system of juridical democracy.

Although terms like "conservative" or "liberal" do not help much, it is not so difficult to locate Lowi in the context of recent political commentary. He calls attention himself to similarities between his argument and that of Friedrich Hayek, on one side,

and of Walter Lippmann, on the other. He resembles Hayek in his
analysis of the consequences of abandoning rigorous legal norms;
and he resembles Lippmann in the stress on "public philosophy"
and in the expectations of rationality from responsible governors
who cannot hide from themselves and others that they are making
hard and authoritative choices which will be backed by coercive
force.[10] As he notes himself, he differs from Hayek in denying that
rule of law implies or creates a negative state: "Historically, rule
of law, especially statute law, is the essence of positive government.
A bureaucracy in the service of a strong and clear statute is more
effective than ever" (p. 299). His departure from Lippmann is less
consistently maintained throughout the book. He certainly rejects
Lippmann's contention that rampant Jacobinism and parliamentary
hubris are causing a crisis of authority, but he is less consistent
in replacing Lippmann's confidence in a rational universal class
located in the executive with confidence in the legislative process
as in other formal institutions. But that is the main thrust of his
argument. Once placed in this way, it is tempting to dismiss his
whole argument as merely another incarnation of the old continental liberalism (democratized a little, to get it past Bedloe's
Island), a position which arises out of a nostalgic misrepresenta-
tion of rule by public-spirited elites, supported by civic-minded
middle classes, and proceeding through firm and authoritative law.

And there are enough evident shortcomings in Lowi's book to
strengthen such temptations. In the first place, Lowi offers no
serious evidence to substantiate his contention that the regime of
"interest-group liberalism" has been created by the ideology or is
sustained by it. The new order, on his telling, can be seen to gain
strength from the time of the Wilson administration and to come
into its own with the New Deal and with the post-*Schechter* court,
with massive increments of strength added by the Kennedy administration. There are several difficulties with this chronology and
with the inferences drawn from the parallels between the rise of
the new order and the rise among political scientists and intellectuals of the variant of corporatism which Lowi calls interest-
group liberalism. The laws which the Court strikes down in
Schechter antedate by several years the Social Security Act of
1935, which Lowi cites repeatedly as the very model of proper
legislation. In the field of foreign affairs, Lowi repeatedly praises

the cherishing of the federative power by the very Kennedy administration which is elsewhere said to be permeated with the new
ideology. Such inconsistencies are clearly reconcilable with almost
any explanation for the new development except an explanation
building on the prevalence of a new public philosophy.

Lowi offers case studies and refers to others to provide empirical
(or experiential) support for the claims he makes on behalf of
responsible authoritative rule. Much of his evidence indeed backs
his charge that something is fatefully wrong in governing according to the rules which constitute the contemporary regime; but it
does not in many cases support his own contrasting model. Two
of these cases in fact throw doubt on Lowi's case; the third is
devastating (at least in one crucial area). As a very minor contributor to the work of the Commission on Money and Credit in
1959, I was astounded to read Lowi's statements about fiscal policy.
Lowi contends that "fiscal policy [is] . . . a model of responsibility
in comparison both to subsidy programs and to regulatory programs," and offers in support a table comparing "legislative crea-
tivity of Congress on subsidy bills and fiscal bills" and showing
that committees exercise much less control over the latter. Without
challenging the accuracy of the figures, it is certainly possible to
question the conclusion that "fiscal policy is really the only type of
policy that can achieve a high degree of rationality through the
incremental approach so dear to pluralists" (p. 309). The work
of Michael Regan and others, as well as the Report of the Commission on Money and Credit itself (especially the last chapter),
stress the extent to which fiscal policy is a function of a parallelo-
gram of forces and is not subject to rational coordination either in
Congress or in any part of the Executive. Economists ceaselessly
bemoan mutually offsetting uses of fiscal devices and other commentators note the frequently antisocial character of the uncon-
trollable structural bias revealed by that policy. Lowi has shown
elsewhere that he knows a good deal about these matters, but he
gives no clear sign that his curious interpretation of evidence in this
case is anything but a response to the challenge he sets himself:
the challenge to find properly legislative techniques for planning.

To support his contention that the absence of properly authoritative law fosters injustice, Lowi shows that existing federal housing programs serve as an instrument for the achievement of

apartheid in a city he calls Iron City, as well as elsewhere. That
the programs have this effect appears clear enough; that they have
it because of a political vacuum is controverted by the story itself.
In an earlier part of the book, Lowi speaks of the "political dissolution of the city"; he argues that municipal corporations should
be formally dissolved because they have already effectively dissolved themselves and because, in any case, they lack the formal
character of sovereignty upon which a proper authority can be
built. He writes:

Reform was based on an assumption that the city needed to make
no hard policy choices but only to set up a process by which agencies
and clientele would make the laws. The public interest would emerge
from interactions between elites of skill and elites of interests. The
actual result has been stalemate, because in the process of reform no
care was taken for preservation of ultimate authority. [P. 205]

But, whatever might be the situation in the federal government, it
appears clear from Lowi's story that authority in Iron City was by
no means dissolved or stalemated. The authorities in that community organized massive community resources, developed a
"rational" and authoritative plan, and they carried it through. Their
plan was racist. Now it is true that Iron City possesses the formal
disabilities cited by Lowi; but Lowi knows that the burden of
proof is on him and that he must show that the formal disabilities
make a difference. In the case of Iron City, he cannot show this.
It met all of his criteria, except that its actions were unjust. Perhaps the injustice there as elsewhere has roots different from those
he identifies and perhaps it cannot be met by his proposal. In
his own conclusion on the Iron City story, Lowi uses ambiguous
language:

The case shows how national legitimacy can be tarnished to the degree
that it is loaned to the cities for discretionary use, and how a crisis
of public authority was inevitable as long as the virtue made of an
untutored public process ended in the abuses catalogued in Iron City.
[P. 264; emphasis supplied]

The emphasized phrase could simply refer to that process of bargaining among private and public actors which has been Lowi's
main target throughout; but it could also allude to some unspecified
way in which national formal institutions can be said to be more

"tutored" than the local. Lowi's discussion of sovereignty and citizen gives some clues (although it is clear that Lowi has little enough confidence in the state governments to which he cannot deny these attributes); these clues will be followed up shortly.

But first I want to consider the failure of judgment which calls into question Lowi's whole thesis in the most striking way. It occurs in his discussion of the "federative power," which follows Lippmann very closely. The conduct of foreign affairs is seriously harmed, in this view, either when control is dispersed among diverse agencies or when the "plebescitary President" is compelled to manipulate public opinion in order to gain command of affairs— and these two circumstances are intimately bound together in a regime according to "the interest-group liberal, quasi-egalitarian requirement" (p. 187). The fatal course of policy in Vietnam, Lowi maintains, has resulted from this fault. There was an "escalation of meanings" because the President was compelled to generate enthusiasm among the broad public for the limited steps he considered necessary, and that enthusiasm then made it impossible to preserve the limits. "The peace marchers," he writes, "were only availing themselves of rights accorded them by the behavior of the leaders in the irresponsible ways they went about creating consensus and justification for their actions" (p 187). Combined with this unsubstantiated contention, then, there is exasperation "that there could be no proper conspiracy among leaders in the pursuit of the national interests of the United States" (p. 177). Spared from this general assault against presumed structural defects is American behavior in a situation of "crisis." Quite the contrary: according to Lowi, "a crisis does tend to bring out the very best in Americans. Postwar examples of exemplary behavior in crisis include Greek-Turkish aid and the Truman Doctrine, the Berlin Airlift, the response to the Korean invasion, the 1956 Arab-Israeli intervention, the Cuban Missile Crisis of 1962, Dienbienphu in 1954" (p. 159). What is distinctive in these situations, in his view, is that decisions in the national interest were made effectively and secretly by men holding formal governmental office, and, in his judgment, these decisions were "good foreign policy" and "rational" (p. 159n). I will not enter into any detailed comment on these judgments, especially since Lowi simply announces them as his "value-judgments." But I will say, first, that there is mounting evidence that American policy during the Cuban missile-crisis represented irresponsible risk-taking in pursuit of question-able objectives, and second, that the attempt to distinguish Vietnam from the whole complex of policy of which it forms an integral part is specious. Lowi's confidence in the rationality inherent in the rule of properly constituted, authoritative, foreign-policy makers, when they are not corrupted by the need to accommodate conflict-ing influences or to manipulate a mass public, seems much less well-founded than C. Wright Mills' terror in the face of the "crackpot realism" of the "power elite."

Despite these objections, and others like them, I have taken Lowi's book very seriously in this essay, and I shall want to look at his basic position some more, at a different level. This is because I consider his work to be one of the very few expressions today of a major intellectual tradition whose insights and failures both can contribute to an adequate theory and strategy of change. It is not clear from his latest book how deeply Lowi himself has pondered that tradition or even whether he is familiar with its masters. But that is little to the point, because I am not concerned with the study of "influences." With the help of some classics, I want to explicate and then criticize the premises underlying Lowi's argument. Out of that experience, we shall be able to move more purposefully back into the contemporary literature and look for answers to the questions which we shall have come to see as critical.

III

A comprehensive account of the republican tradition would have to begin with Aristotle and Cicero. Note the important modifications of the doctrine in the post-Renaissance revival which begins with Machiavelli and carries through writers like Thomas Harrington, and examine especially closely the high place accorded by the renewed doctrine to the rule of law in the work of Rousseau and Kant. Unfortunately, such an historical examination would not be appropriate at this time. Instead I shall turn to the political philosophy of Hegel which serves, in this respect as others, to continue as well as to criticize the work of Kant. The sense in which Hegel is a "republican," although he strongly upholds a monarchical constitution, is a sense already established by both Rousseau and Kant, who both distinguish between the form of government —which may be republican or despotic—and the constitutional form, the way in which offices and powers are arranged.

Except for the democratic component as such, all the key suppositions underlying Lowi's argument for a renovation of constitutionalism can be studied in Hegel. And the missing parts are supplied in the work of Hegel's democratic disciples—of whom Karl Marx is the best known. In Marx's critical reformulations of republican constitutionalism, written between 1840 and 1843, appear all the remaining elements of Lowi's position; in Marx's work of self-criticism, beginning in 1843, appear the key objections which will take us beyond that political theory (and which will, incidentally, help to account for the specific shortcomings noted before in Lowi's work). The importance of Hegel to an understanding of constitutionalism has been often underrated in American and English discussions for a variety of historical and political reasons which need not be discussed here; but it is worth recording that this misjudgment has been abetted by the fact that the highly regarded translation of the *Philosophy of Right* by T. M. Knox is guilty of very serious errors in translation which are consistently biased against an adequate understanding of the text on the points central to this theme.[11] This cannot be the place for a detailed treatment, but I will state in summary some of the problems which, according to Hegel, a proper constitutional scheme is supposed to solve, and some of his major reasons for supposing that a regime which would in Kant's language be described as republican in form and monarchical in constitution solves these problems.

Hegel derives his picture of social life from the accounts of civil society presented by British and French moral philosophers and political economists (p. 189)—except that he awkwardly sticks into the story provision for a landed aristocratic estate. His basic problem in the third part of the *Philosophy of Right* is to work out the relationship between this "civil society" and the formal institutions of the constitutional state. This is a critical problem, first, because in contrast to the older classical republican doctrine, he is determined to respect the rights and activities which constitute this sphere of "particular freedom" even though he also recognizes that they work against the political education required for a just political order (p. 185) and, second, because in contrast to liberal or Madisonian versions of constitutionalism, he is persuaded that civil society gives rise to practical and ethical problems which its own institutions cannot meet. It is this recognition of the claims of interest, subjective preference, private pleasure, expanding productivity, and similar values combined with overriding concern for universal claims of justice, morality, and a public interest separable from the sum of private interests which gives Hegel's work its modern quality and brings it, despite all changes in philosophic style, so close to an essay like Lowi's.

Civil society is the complex of activities and relationships through which individuals meet their needs, develop their faculties, and generate new needs. It is a social process of competitions and interdependencies and has a logic of its own which compels men to contribute to the prosperity of society even when they mean simply to serve themselves. But the effective supremacy of this logic is not given by nature: it depends on a certain level of civilization within society, so that men have been educated to play the roles required by the system of interests. This social education takes place over time, through a series of stages; but can be presupposed for purposes of this analysis (p. 187). Hegel is probably following David Hume and Adam Ferguson here, or their German disciples, like Christian Garve, because Adam Smith's treatment of these matters was not known at the time. Difficulties inhere in this system: the logic drives the system to steady expansion of wealth and wants and this in turn creates extremes of luxury and misery, both leading to "physical and ethical degeneration" (p. 185). Moreover, the social education cannot suffice to overcome the self-assertion fostered in each interested person. And the division of labor inherent in the system means that different strata of society receive different levels of education, while the radically unequal distribution of rewards (in part by virtue of criteria like birth irrelevant to the logic of the system) complicates the problem.

Hegel sees these difficulties countered first of all through a system of justice which secures private property. The fundamental premise of the whole logic is to be secured by a kind of public authority. In discussing the system of rights and administration of justice, Hegel carries on a sustained polemic against the historical school of jurisprudence which would seek law in the customs of particular societies. Throughout, he stands with liberal rationalism in demanding that the character of true law must be deduced from the place it must occupy in a society of free men, and that particular laws must be judged by those criteria, having regard for the concrete circumstances in different societies. Justice at this level is still an institution of civil society, according to Hegel; it implements the long-term and steady interests of the participants in the economic process, and it is sustained by their own collective agreement. But this important activity does not really meet a number of fundamental issues.

Punishing crimes against property preserves the system but does not help the individuals harmed. Moreover, even rightful uses of property can have harmful consequences. The police power exists to counter these circumstances, seeking to prevent crime and to regulate actions so as to prevent harm. Hegel includes among the public services to be rendered by police agencies a list of tasks which everyone requires and upon which all depend, but which private interest will not or cannot perform: in addition to the work of police in the modern sense, he includes supervision of market weights, measures, and the like, currency, protection of consumers in matters of necessity, safeguarding the supplies of industries dependent on foreign materials (!), shortening the time and softening the impact of market-adjustment processes through regulation (!), and public education (pp. 235–239). Special problems arise because civil society creates a class of poor who know that their condition is against right, but whose own civil qualities are so damaged that they come to lack even the capacity for maintaining themselves in their penury (pp. 243–245). He sharply rejects the idea of leaving these matters to private charity and ironically congratulates the English and Scots for turning their poor out into the streets as beggars. Two kinds of responses appear adequate: first, civil society is driven beyond itself to foreign expansion and colonization, because in colonies at least some citizens are returned to a simpler social setting more like the family than like civil society where moral recuperation can take place and expansion stimulates and invigorates everyone in the society (an economically "irrational" and yet economic explanation for imperialism!) (pp. 246–248); second, the corporations which group people according to profession or locality take on the family's responsibility for promoting the welfare of the members. If society itself simply gave wherewithal to the poor, it would go counter to the principles of civil society—principles of individual freedom and the dignity of work; if society gave work, there would be overproduction, Hegel says, and the evil would be intensified (p. 245). Help given in the context of the corporations differs from this, because it is associated with a whole complex of family-like ties of affection, mutual regard, encouragement, and education for useful tasks (p. 252).

Although it is possible to identify these problems through analysis of civil society alone because they are what Hegel calls "shared particular interests," and although it is also possible to prescribe on the basis of that analysis a platform capable of solving them, it is not possible to understand from this analysis alone how it could happen that the needed steps might be taken and the needed arrangements established. This is less true, in Hegel's view, for the activities assigned to courts of justice and corporations than it is for the remaining regulatory and service activities, but all the agencies described depend in the last analysis on an institutional force moved by considerations other than those evidenced in civil society. This is the state.

The state is governed by general laws administered by an impartial permanent estate of professional officials. From the standpoint of internal government, the prince has a symbolic function, embodying the ultimate fact that his power expresses volition but does not have a material base. The superior ethical character of the state is secured by several structural features familiar from the republican constitutional literature. The state speaks through law, which necessarily has the form of thought. Lowi asserts this by arguing that lawmaking inevitably involves debate, discussion, and reference to general moral principles. The universal class of administrators must be constituted so that its entire interest is focused on its career and so on its duty: this can be done by securing its livelihood while denying it all other sorts of income. This way administrators are neither knights-errant working for private pleasure, which introduces arbitrariness, nor servants bound by need (p. 294). Hierarchy and responsibility are supplemented by complaints from corporations and extraordinary intervention by the sovereign as controls on abuses of power by officials. But cultivation and training are the ultimate sources of their ethos; Hegel also notes a crucial situational factor: the greater the state, the more weighty its affairs, and the less likely the diversion of officials by lesser influences and passions (p. 296). Some such consideration, doubtless generated in Hegel by his view of the lesser German principalities, clearly underlies Lowi's deference to national against local and state governmental processes. Most importantly, the rational state rests on the public-spiritedness of the citizens, their favorable disposition to the state. In turn, the constitution and the government undertake to establish justice by raising the level of civic consciousness to the level required by a state ruling under law. This corresponds to the notion of public philosophy in Lowi and Lippmann.

With the help of formulations closely patterned on Rousseau's descriptions of the general will, Hegel can fairly easily characterize the standpoint of the state as transcending the various goals and aspirations of men in their private, interested capacities and constituting them into a unity focused on the solemn moral responsibility entailed by the very fact that mankind organizes itself with the help of coercion and that its separate communities war against one another (p. 258). The answer that Hegel or Lowi must make to those who charge them with deifying the state must be that unless the state does in fact have the highest moral claims and aspirations, it can never be shown to have a right to do what it must and does do. But a general formula on that level does not begin to solve the problem of relating the actual social activities of men to the ordering principles and powers of the state. For Hegel, as for Lowi, this problem involves above all the relationship between corporations and the formal institutions of the state.[12]

As we have seen, Hegel assigns an important part to corporations in promoting the welfare of victims of civil society. In relation to the state, however, it becomes clear that the independence of these agencies must be severely constricted. Civil society is a scene of battle between conflicting private interests, between private interests and shared particular interests (like education and

police), and between these social interests together and the higher
interests of the state. All the interests have their good right, but
they must ultimately accommodate themselves to the broader
context and authority. This is done in two ways: first, the state
retains the power to set legal conditions upon the franchises it
grants to corporations, and, second, the granting of these franchises
confirms the members in privileges which they know depend on
and bind them to the state: "That is the secret of the patriotism of
burghers . . . they recognize the state as their substance, because
it protects their particular spheres, their justification and authority"
(p. 289 Rem.). One type of corporation which Hegel always has
in mind throughout these discussions is the university. Now it
appears that the rights of corporations are as much devices to
strengthen the authority of the state as anything else. He points
out that the activities turned over to the corporations will almost
certainly be botched because the local officials lack the qualities of
the administrative estate: they will have no grasp of the broader
issues, and they will be too close to, or even dependent on, those
they are to govern. But he points out that these are useful play-
grounds for the passions and vanities of small men, and that the
matters they bungle will not be too important anyway (welfare!),
while flattering the gratification and self-esteem of the burghers
provides an important support to the state. Lowi doesn't consider
this rationale for the present scheme of local governments, but it
is suggestive.

This denigration of corporations becomes even clearer when
Hegel turns to a discussion of the lower house of the legislative
estates (the upper house comprises the hereditary landed estate,
whose important role in Hegel's overall constitutional scheme is
not of interest here; this exclusion is the more justified in that the
whole dimension of the argument—doubtless important to Hegel—
can readily be isolated as a special local feature without seriously
affecting the main development of his republican doctrine). The
members of the lower house are emissaries from corporations and
officials of government. Legislation is enacted there, on the advice
of the government, and complaints and requests are delivered, but
the major function of the estates is to mediate between government
and people. Mediation here means above all that rule is made
comprehensible and acceptable to the ruled. In a properly con-

stituted legislature of this sort, such conflict as will arise concerns narrow personal matters, primarily the pursuit of high office (p. 302 Rem.); the members chosen will be men possessing an administrative and political sense empathetic to the needs and perspectives of decision-makers (p. 310); a primary consequence of deliberation will be the education of the general public to the standpoint of the state: it will be a place for public officials to demonstrate their superior information and mastery of problems, so that subjective opinions in the press and elsewhere will appear stupid and uninformed by contrast (pp. 315, 319). This posture is certainly considerably more hostile to the influence of private groups tied to the particular interests making up civil society than anything in Lowi. There is something similar in Lowi's discussion of "untutored political processes," and the notion of the legislature as a place where grievances are aired, officials recruited and most importantly, governmental authority is enhanced, has an important function in the kind of aristocratic republican constitutionalism which is represented by Walter Lippmann in the United States but is more common in Europe. It may also have a good deal to do with reality, especially where legislative bodies are established in institutions like universities and commercial enterprises. For Hegel, in any case, the public order and its instrumentalities must prevail over private interests in the event of conflict, although the primary objectives of the public order are measures to secure and enhance the world of private interests. It may be said that Hegel has the highest regard for the claims of private interests, but contempt for those who present themselves as claimants.

But Hegel believes that this state of affairs is inherently unstable despite its high ethical character and rationality. Men will abuse the freedom granted by the constitution and will replace their patriotic and loyal disposition with subjective opinions and preferences about public matters. The breakdown of public-spiritedness can only be countered by external war, which provides the ultimate experience of the bonds between the individual and the state. This is the portion of Hegel's teaching which has historically roused the greatest revulsion among liberals who do not reject war but are repelled by the only kind of rationale which could conceivably make sense of obedience to the point of murder which national armies require as a matter of course (pp. 323, 324). But

if the integrity of the state ultimately depends on war, it appears
clear to Hegel that the claims to rationality of the state are not
the highest claims. War subjects the life of states to the power
of myriad accidental factors which cannot be comprehended or
mastered by reason, and so the philosophic quest must go beyond
the philosophy of right. We are not concerned to follow Hegel
in this course, but simply to register this denouncement of his
analysis. His assessment of the relationship between war and a
republican constitution is much more common in the tradition
than the sharply contrasting view of Kant, although in much of
the literature the topic is somewhat disguised behind the theme
of a militia. It is by no means farfetched to interpret Lowi's discussion of the federative powers and his admiration for American
"response to crisis" in the context of this tradition.

IV

Hegel's version of republican constitutionalism was sharply attacked and vigorously amended by a group of his followers, and
their important corrections bring the doctrine closer to Lowi in
some key respects. As editor of the *Rheinische Zeitung* in 1842,
Karl Marx was an important spokesman for this group, and his
contributions to that journal apply the revised position to a number
of important political issues. His detailed commentary on paragraphs 261 to 313 of Hegel's *Philosophy of Right* carries the
critique still further; but his work beginning with the "Essay on
the Jewish Question" of 1844 breaks with democratic republicanism on a number of basic points. There is no possibility of
pursuing this argument in any detail in this already overlong survey. I shall simply quote from the newspaper essays to show the
continuity between Hegel, Marx, and Lowi, then summarize the
most important changes made in the Hegelian doctrine, and finally
indicate the fundamental reason leading Marx to abandon this
approach (or, better, to revise it so sharply that the focus shifts
from state to society).

Marx's earliest political essays appeared as commentaries on debates in the provincial estates, and their major themes were rule of law and public interest. Commenting on a proposed law to establish and define freedom of the press, he attacked the contention that such a law would set greater limits on freedom of action than the prevailing system of licensing journals and journalists during "good behavior":

Judicially recognized freedom exists in the state in the form of law. . . . Laws are the positively clear, general norms, in which freedom has won an impersonal, theoretical existence, independent of the arbitrary will of any individual. A legal code is a people's testament of freedom. . . . Where law is genuine law, i.e., the embodiment of freedom, it is the real free existence of man. Laws cannot restrict the actions of men, because they are themselves the inner vital laws of his action, the conscious mirror images of his life. Law then does not interfere with a human life which is life of freedom; it is only when a man's actual conduct reveals that he has ceased to heed the natural law of freedom that law, in the form of state-law, forces him to be free.[13]

Of course, the laws on whose behalf such claims can be made are not to be asserted under the influence of an interest other than the public interest, otherwise the theory would vindicate every form of repression, and such a state of affairs requires a people immersed in public affairs, not a *Privatpöbel* (private rabble). This is why a free press under law is so essential, according to Marx. It serves to educate the population both by its information and analyses as well as the fact that it proceeds under law (p. 156). A defense of a free press in the name of freedom of trade, however, is no better than the attacks upon it by urban spokesmen worried about possible agitators. In both cases, the argument derives from "the *bourgeois* and not the *citoyen*" (p. 158). The public interest in a free press has nothing to do with the private interest of the businessmen who own presses: "the first freedom of the press consists in not being a branch of commerce" (p. 165). The Rousseauist language would doubtless make Lowi squirm, but the emphatic assertions in behalf of genuine law as a source of direction radically different in its impact upon human life from any other sort of constraint or influence are echoed in the more cautious later language as well. And it was John Locke, after all, who wrote:

Freedom of men under government is to have a standing rule to live by, common to every one of that society and made by the legislative power erected in it, a liberty to follow my own will in all things where the rule prescribes not, and not to be subject to the inconstant, uncertain, unknown, arbitrary will of another man; as freedom of nature is to be under no other restraint but the law of nature.[14]

Where Marx departs from Locke and the liberal tradition of constitutionalism most clearly is not in the praise of law but in the sharp distinction between the activities constituting the private sphere and those which are truly public, and in this matter, Lowi is doubtless closer to Marx than to Locke. Marx describes the work of political education carried on by the state:

The genuine "public" education pertaining to the state is the rational and public existence of the state. The state itself educates its members by transforming purposes of the individual into public purposes, primitive drives into ethical inclinations, natural independence into spiritual freedom, by the fact also that the individual fulfills himself in the life of the whole and the whole fulfills itself in the loyal disposition of the individual.[15] [P. 185]

Marx's comments on the debates in the Rhenish provincial legislature concerning a proposed law to penalize the taking of wood from private estates cover a number of points not central to our present discussion, but develop at eloquent length an indictment of putting public authority at the disposal of private interests, especially when this involves turning over any public powers. A crime, Marx insists, is punishable insofar as it is a violation of a right essential to the freedom which the state is to serve. Damage to private interest is not as such punishable, since private interests are not secured against all loss by the state, and penalties may not legitimately take the form of reparation (the law in question proposed to compel offenders to render to the owners not only the original value but also the profits lost). Interest sees only damage; it fears and hates those who threaten it. "The character of laws dictated by cowardice is terrorism (*Grausamkeit*), because cowardice can only be energetic in being terroristic. But private interest is always cowardly, because its heart and soul is an external object, which can always be taken and damaged, and who does not tremble at the danger of losing his heart and soul" (p. 224)? Marx contrasts with this the perspective of a genuine state:

The state must see more in a wood-scavenger than an enemy of wood. Is not each citizen attached to the state by a thousand live nerves and may it cut all of these nerves simply because the citizen has himself voluntarily severed one: The state will also see in the wood-scavenger a human being, a living member in which its own blood flows, a soldier who is to defend the nation, a witness whose testimony is to count in a court of law, a member of a local community, who is to perform public tasks, a father of a family whose existence is sacred, and above all a citizen—and the state will not lightly exclude one of its members from these attributes, for it amputates itself each time that it makes a criminal out of a citizen. [P. 223]

A legislature bringing together agents for diverse private interests cannot make public law. In these essays as well as in his commentaries on Hegel's *Philosophy of Right,* Marx inveighs against representation by corporations or estates. Genuine representation, he argues at this point, represents individuals in their capacities as citizens drawn from geographic constituencies, as in France, England, and the United States. Such representatives, meeting in open assembly, controlled by the public spirit which they themselves foster, can create and sustain a legitimate state. Hegel affirms these principles in the most general terms, Marx contends, but denies them in his account of the state.

Marx's critique of the *Philosophy of Right* occupies more than two hundred closely printed pages and addresses a number of important philosophical issues as well as the political ones. I will simply summarize what seems to me to be the central point. Marx rejects categorically all the concessions which Hegel makes to such Prussian institutions as estates, corporations, landed aristocracy with entailed properties, and monarchy by divine rights. Marx believed that Hegel had correctly discerned the most general principles of political "idealism"; a contemporary formulation might paraphrase Marx's point by saying that Hegel has identified the values which ought to be subserved by a just or rational political order. But, Marx contends, "the idealism is not developed into an explicit, rational system" (p. 282). The political order recommended by Hegel fails to embody the principles. When the order which Hegel has portrayed is at peace, Marx says, "it appears as nothing more than an external compulsion emanating from the dominating power and forced upon private life by means of 'direct intervention' from above"; or whatever order may exist is the "blind, unconscious result of self-seeking" (p. 282). In Hegel's scheme, the principles of idealism are actualized "only under conditions of war or destitution in the state" (p. 282). Marx states his important conclusions in paradoxical language. He says that Hegel's idealism has as its essence the experience of "war and destitution" within the presently existing state; and that this state under conditions of peace is the arena for the "war and destitution of self-seeking." In other words, Marx argues that the constitutional state portrayed by Hegel recognizes genuine republican principles only when it is at war or in crisis, and that the operating principles of that order under normal conditions are the destructive principles of greed and lust for power.[16]

Marx denies that Hegel has actually provided for the universal interest: he pokes bitter fun at the pretensions of the universal administrative class (p. 322), denies the coherence of the relation between the sovereign volition of the prince and the rational complex of actions which he supposedly empowers, and portrays Hegel's constitution as a state of unresolvable conflict between two irrational forces: the private interests expressed in the corporations and in the economic life of society and the despotic and arbitrary will of the prince, with the universal class, so-called, caught between these two forces. The sole constitutional form corresponding to a society liberated from the privileges of feudal times is democracy, Marx argues; only when the people govern themselves is the state recognized as an expression of acting men and not fancied as the creator of men (p. 292f.).

But at this point Marx's argument takes an important turn away from any conception of democracy which contemporary political writers would recognize, and in this turn he raises several objections which, I believe, cut deeply into the republican constitutionalist case, including Lowi's formulations of it. Marx does not question the historical fact that the democratic political movement culminating in the French Revolution seriously and sincerely projects the public sphere as a realm where men function as citizens and not as denizens of civil society, where action is to be directed toward both the general public interest and toward private gain. He argues, instead, that this conception of the situation is untenable. It envisions a division between a private and a public sphere, which means a bifurcation of each individual into two beings, one doing what must be done to maintain himself and his family and the other dedicated to the public weal. But these beings are fundamentally unequal: one has to do with real needs and real relations and concrete activities day after day; the other pursues ideal objectives only abstractly related as moral imperatives to the concrete world of experiences:

The political constitution has been the religious sphere, the religion of the people's life, the heaven of its general interest in contrast to the earthly existence of its actuality. [P. 295]

Marx does not simply condemn this abstract conception of man's situation; he sees its emergence as a progressive step in comparison with the principles predominating before the modern bourgeois age. During the middle ages, he contends, factors which must be identified as "political" impregnated all aspects of social life; there was no separation between civil society and political state:

There were serfs, feudal possessions, craft corporations, scholarly corporations, etc.; i.e., in the middle ages, property, trade, society, person are political. . . . In the middle ages the political constitution is the constitution of private property but only because the constitution of private property is political. . . . Man is the actual principle of the state, but it is *unfree* man. It is thus a "democracy of unfreedom." [P. 296]

The language is again irritatingly paradoxical, but the basic conception is enormously fruitful. Marx uses the word "political" to describe the sphere of life marked by domination, by volitional control over the actions of men through coercive power and authority. He speaks of "democracy" in the broadest sense as an arrangement in which the commands which may be given directly serve the needs and wants of the men living and working in the community, and not the particular interests or preferences of some political class or power-wielder. His view of feudal society as a "democracy of unfreedom," then, points first to the fact that governing functions are not separate from the functional regulation of daily life: authority attends the organizing of economic activity, social welfare work, scholarship and education, religious services, etc. This is the element of "democracy." His view then points to the second central fact: that the institutions of daily life are marked by fundamental arbitrariness, unjustifiable dominations by a few over the many. Supremacy within these institutions rests on force and other power resources, and not on free or rationally necessary concessions of a functionally specific authority. This is what Marx means by speaking of the political impregnation of the society and by designating the constitution as a "democracy of unfreedom." When critics today characterize the political pattern celebrated by pluralism as a "New Feudalism," they can be usefully understood as countering claims made in behalf of "polyarchical democracy" with evidence of its unfreedom (which need not entail a *political* elite). The modern conception of the state, Marx says, represents the liberation of the private sphere from the political factors which had dominated it, especially when that modern conception is given its systematic and consistent formulation in democratic republican constitutionalism of the sort he himself expressed in his earliest journalistic efforts. The abstraction of a public domain arises together with the abstraction of a private domain.

The conceptions have a certain meaning insofar as they refer to the process of liberation, the elimination of the powers which had shaped the old society. But this is not a constitutional situation or established public order. The essential unreality of this abstract state and its abstract citizens has already been remarked. The establishment of a modern state, according to Marx, will have one of three outcomes, and none of them will correspond to the vision of the political democrat. There will be political despotism; there will be domination over the state by civil society and its requirements—a new "democracy of unfreedom"; or there will be socialism, a "democracy of freedom." Let us consider each of these prospects in turn.

1. If the state actually attempts to dominate civil society, it must proceed despotically, continuing the techniques of revolutionary terrorism. The prime example here is Napoleon: although he recognized that the modern state rests upon a commercial society and sought to foster it, "he still thought of the state as an end in itself and thought of civil life as his commissary and his subordinate, which was to have no will of its own. He carried through the terror by putting permanent war in place of permanent revolution."[17] He satisfied national ambitions but came to ride roughshod

over the interests and rights of civil society. Marx contends that this cost him his position, that the delays which led to the Russian defeat resulted from bourgeois resistances. This fate points to the most common and fundamental pattern in the modern state, the supremacy of civil society over the state.

2. Marx writes:

In the last analysis, it is as member of civil society that man counts as the genuine man, as the *homme* in contrast to the *citoyen,* because this is man in his experiential (*sinnlich*), individual, most immediate existence, while the political man is merely an abstracted artificial man, man as an allegorical, moral person. The actual man is given recognition only in the character of the egoistic individual, but the *true* man is recognized only in the abstract *citoyen.* [P. 479—"Zur Judenfrage"]

Specifically, the modern constitutional state comes to devote itself to the rights of man and not to the rights of the citizen; John Locke triumphs over Jean-Jacques Rousseau. And the rights of man are the prerequisites of that civil society which Hegel and others have shown to be antithetical to fundamental claims of justice, morality, and genuine human freedom.

In this connection, then, Marx wrote a commentary on the question of abolishing pauperism which is so close to the central issues in Lowi's book and in our contemporary discussion overall that I will reproduce a lengthy excerpt:

The Convention had for a moment the courage to order the abolition of pauperism. . . . What was the result of the Convention's ordinance? Only that there was one more ordinance in the world, and that one year later the Convention was besieged by starving weavers.

Yet the Convention represented a maximum of political energy, power and understanding. . . . In so far as States have concerned themselves at all with pauperism, they have remained at the level of administrative and charitable measures, or have sunk below this level.

Can the State act in any other way? The State will never look for the cause of social imperfections in "the state and social institutions themselves." . . . Where there are political parties, each party finds the source of such evils in the fact that the opposing party instead of itself is at the helm of the State. Even the radical and revolutionary politicians look for the source of the evil, not in the nature of the State, but in a particular form of the State, which they want to replace by another form.

The State and the structure of society are not, from the standpoint of politics, two different things. The State is the structure of society [according to the political thinkers] in so far as the State admits the existence of social order, it attributes them to natural laws against which no human power can prevail, or to private life which is independent of the State, or to the inadequacies of the administration which is subordinate to it. Thus in England poverty is explained by the natural law according to which population always increases beyond the means of subsistence. From another aspect, England explains pauperism as the Consequence of the evil disposition of the poor, just as the king of Prussia explains it by the unchristian disposition of the rich, and as the Convention explains it by the skeptical, counter-revolutionary outlook of the property-owners. Accordingly, England inflicts penalities on the poor, the king of Prussia admonishes the rich, and the Convention beheads property owners.

In the last resort, every State seeks the cause in adventitious or intentional defects in the administration, and therefore looks to a reform of the administration for a redress of these evils. Why? Simply because the administration is the organizing activity of the State itself.

The contradiction between the aims and good intentions of the administration on the one hand, and its means and resources on the other, cannot be removed by the State without abolishing itself, for it rests upon this contradiction. The state is founded upon the contradiction between public and private life, between general and particular interest. The administration must, therefore, limit itself to a formal and negative sphere of activity, because its power ceases at the point where civil life and its work begin. In face of the consequences which spring from the unsocial character of the life of civil society, of private property, trade, industry, of the mutual plundering by the different groups in civil society, impotence is the natural law of the administration. These divisions, this debasement and slavery of civil society, are the natural foundations upon which the modern State rests, just as civil society [of another sort] was the natural foundation of slavery upon which the State of antiquity rested. The existence of the State and the existence of slavery are inseparable. The State and slavery in antiquity—frank classical antithesis—were not more intimately linked than are the modern State and the modern world of commerce—sanctimonious Christian antithesis. If the modern State wished to end the impotence of its administration it would be obliged to abolish the present conditions of private life. And if the State wished to abolish these conditions of private life it would also have to put an end to its own existence, for it exists only in relation to them. . . .

The more powerful the State is, and therefore the more political a country is, the less likely it is to seek the basis of social evils and to grasp the general explanation of them, in the principle of the State itself, that is in the structure of society, of which the State is the active, conscious and official expression. Political thought is really political thought in the sense that the thinking takes place within the framework of politics. The clearer and more vigorous political thought is, the less it is able to grasp the nature of social evils. The classical period of political thought is the French Revolution. Far from recognizing the source of social defects in the principle of the State, the heroes of the French Revolution looked for the sources of political evils in the defective social organization. Thus, for example, Robespierre saw in the coexistence of great poverty and great wealth only an obstacle to genuine democracy. He wished, therefore, to establish a universal Spartan austerity. The principle of politics is the will. The more partial, and the more perfected, political thought becomes, the more it believes in the omnipotence of the will, the less able it is to see the natural and mental limitations on the will, the less capable it is of discovering the source of social evils.[18] *

3. The replacement of the state with a "democracy of freedom" can only be achieved if the separation between man and citizen is eliminated. Following a lengthy quotation from Rousseau, taken as a correct portrayal of the ideal political man, Marx says:

Only when the actual individual man brings back into himself the abstract citizen and becomes a being corresponding to the essence of the species, in his empirical life, in his individual work, only when man has recognized and organized his "forces propres" as social forces and therefore no longer divorces social force from himself in the guise of political force, only then has human emancipation been achieved. [P. 479]

Such a movement beyond politics may begin with a political step, and in some sense must do so. The third possibility, then, which arises with the establishment of political democracy, is that the revolution which brings it about sets off a social chain reaction, so that the State organization which has been shattered can never properly reform while men throughout the society assert themselves as true men in their social capacities, and not simply as citizens. For Marx, of course, this came to mean above all that the subjugated working class claimed a life of fellowship, or socialism, in place of the life of slavery and this entailed the destruction of private property:

A social revolution has thus a universal aspect, because, though it may occur in only one manufacturing district, it is a human protest against an inhuman life, because it begins from the single real individual and because the social life, against his exclusion from which the individual reacts, is the real social life of a man, a really human life. The political aspect of a revolution consists in the movement of the politically uninfluential classes to end their exclusion from political life and power. Its standpoint is that of the State, an abstract whole, which only exists by virtue of its separation from real life, and which is unthinkable without the organized opposition between the universal idea and the individual existence of man. A revolution of a political kind also organizes, therefore, in accordance with this narrow and discordant outlook, a ruling group in society at the expense of society. . . .

Revolution in general—the overthrow of the existing ruling power and the dissolution of existing social relationships—is a political act. Without revolution socialism cannot develop. It requires this political act as it needs the overthrow and dissolution. But as soon as its organizing activity begins, as soon as its own purpose and spirit come to the fore, socialism sheds this political covering.[19]

Marx's lifelong effort to specify the ways in which the processes of civil society do violence to men and to foster the work of liberation within the class he believed called to the task need not concern us here. His political writings as a whole (especially his journalistic work during 1848) and his comments on British elections for the *New York Tribune*) make it clear that he never seriously revised the position developed in 1844.[20] In the classical language so important to Marx and to the republican tradition out of which he sprang, it may be said that he came to deny the possibility of a political sphere removed from and superseding the economic relations—those of the household between master and slave, and those generated by that all-pervasive economic preoccupation which Aristotle himself had called chrematistik and considered antithetical to the formation of a genuine polis. Marx's constant reference to slavery should not be seen as hyperbole: it expresses his conviction that the normal operation of economic life has everywhere required that some men at least meet the conditions which define a slave for Aristotle: they are by their nature (i.e., their social destiny, for Marx) not their own man, but another's; although men, they are articles of property, which means that they are instruments intended for the purpose of action. They do not project; they do not shape their lives; they are resources in the plans of others. If the realm characterized by these relationships dominates the formally political realm, then the promises and strategies of the republican constitutional tradition must be adjudged irrelevant, on the authority of its founder, Aristotle.

I do not intend in this paper to pursue further the line of Marx's own attempt at clarifying and solving the problem here raised. There are many reasons for this, but chief among them is a strong sense that the intellectual issues have all become so bogged down in formula and counterformula that it is very hard to follow along and still remain concrete and relevant. As his prognosis and the strategy attending it has come to be understood, it does not self-evidently make sense of our experience and situation. If he has been misunderstood and is, after all, right, we shall have to discover his truth anew. Perhaps this is only autobiographical, but I shall in any case attempt to draw from his critique of the political tradition some points of departure for a direct encounter with the contemporary versions of that tradition and shall not conduct myself in any other sense as a "Marxist."

Marx and Lowi agree on the "impotence of the administration," when it comes to social problems. They also agree on the supreme weight to be attached to the qualities of individual and social life stressed by the writers of the republican tradition, although Marx scorned to conceptualize this situation in the language of "morality" and Lowi would probably seek more place for qualities which Marx consigns to bourgeois society. Lowi perceives the problem in terms very similar to those which Marx first employed against Hegel and the reality he was justifying: public authority is squandered because public power is an instrument of particular private interests, because there is no real law, because the state is part blustering force and part patsy, because there is no political education worthy of the name. In Marx's later language, he would have us move (once more) from the "democracy of unfreedom" to the level of the "state." Marx sees a situation closely comparable in the Germany of the 1840's and concludes that a move to a real democratic republic can certainly eliminate some important irrationalities (the privileged estates, etc.) but that the basic change must be in the sphere of civil society whose fundamental structure denies the realization of republican virtue.

This throws in sharp relief the extent to which Lowi calls on the presumed moral will of the public agencies: the Black Revolution will proceed once it is restored to its moral character and public decisions are made in a setting generating moral awareness, for example. Moral and rational decisions will be made in the international sphere once the public processes are freed from corrupting necessities to bargain or oversell. The question raised by our consideration of Marx is whether there might not be, after all, influences in the basic pattern of social life apart from the political sphere which set the limits beyond which constitutional renovation cannot bring us. And if that were shown to be the case, the question would be whether there are forces in sight—actual ones and not the abstract imperatives of good intentions, as Marx says—likely to counter or revise this pattern, so that the political aspect of their activity would be as meaningful as Marx believed democratic developments (most revolutionary, but not invariably) to be when the political activity builds upon the kinds of activities within other spheres of society which Marx calls socialist activities. We want to consider what practical work today most nearly approximates socialist work so understood, what work builds toward alternatives in the realm of "civil society" where the "democracy of unfreedom" is steadily generated and sustained despite the hopes and efforts of political idealism.

V

First it must be understood that a socialist alternative is in no sense inevitable. Aristotelian teleology is endemic among all political thinkers. The hope that "nature" somehow collaborates with the highest human aspirations resists every kind of epistemological onslaught. One major symptom of this condition is the expectation that a political system antithetical to human freedom and justice cannot really survive. If there is any objective possibility at all for integrating the society in a better way, such a system will inevitably succumb to crisis. Since the time of Aristotle, this view has been applied particularly to the prospects of despotism. A regime resting on fear, coercion, terror, it is said, simply cannot maintain itself, unless the human materials in the society are wholly passive anyway. This conception plays an important part in the republican tradition, as well as in the liberal one, although writers like Montesquieu, Ferguson, and even Marx stress the fact that a despotic and terroristic system is the ever-threatening alternative to a rational management of political tasks. But even in these cases, despotism is said to be the nemesis for failure because it is inherently unable to sustain life in a civil society above the level of barbarism. Corresponding to this is the expectation that the logic of events will itself point the way to rational management and that natural processes will come to a crisis within society and polity so that attention is focused on the basic problems of the day and toward their solution. Contemporary radical commentators frequently count on the pervasiveness of such crisis not only to give their views a hearing but also to give them influence; this also tempts them to be "optimistic" in their assessment of crisis.

The very important book by E. V. Walter must help cure us of this misconception, because he challenges such assumptions precisely at the point where they appear most secure: the viability of terroristic regimes.[21] He shows that establishment of a terroristic regime may be a matter of choice, although alternate solutions appear available, that the political need for sharing power with officials may create an organized force in support of the terror and not a check, and that a terroristic regime has at its disposal techniques of control which can, in some societies at least, sustain its own authority and secure the necessary social cooperation needed to keep a civil society of sorts going. This is not a Machiavellian counterorthodoxy, according to which power can do all things at all times; it is rather a sober plea for empirical assessment of the conditions under which one or another range of possibilities remains open. Marx portrayed the careers of the first and second Napoleons as partly instrumentalities of the prevailing social imperatives and partly anecdotal accidents (as tragedy the first time and as farce the second, it will be recalled). Marxists understood the Fascist experience in the same way. And the literature on "totalitarianism" rests on such assumptions. Walter does not prove that these assessments were wrong; he simply calls their self-evidence into question. Walter is relevant here both because he puts soberly before us the possibility of terroristic responses to whatever crises may shake our society and because he undermines more generally the confidence in an intellectual and political strategy of crisis-mongering. More specifically, it means that we cannot rely upon the "situation" to pose "problems," as the pragmatic tradition suggests; we have to attend to the processes which transform hurts into problems, as C. Wright Mills said. Moreover, we cannot assume that "solutions" which appear irrational from a critical humanist standpoint (or however one wants to label the congeries of presuppositions which underlie and animate all our theoretical work) cannot work or must be self-defeating "in the long run." In strategic political terms, what follows is that it is simply not true that whatever hurts "them" helps "us": a strategy for radical social and political change cannot disregard the front against despotism. Things can get worse and can stay worse.

The first task then is to understand the signs of "crisis" which have doubtless erupted in American society. Lowi's view is clear: we are experiencing symptoms of a crisis of authority which will be eliminated when the source is removed, when a legitimate public authority is restored, and the remedy is at the disposal of public officials. We have stated many reasons for seeking a social explanation, instead of one so exclusively "political."

The German sociological literature, at least since the time of Max and Alfred Weber, offers a theoretical approach which promises to clarify the situation. Writing out of this tradition in 1935, Karl Mannheim offered an explanation of the events in Germany which led up to the Nazi seizure of power and warned that comparable crises would grip other Western societies unless appropriate countermeasures are taken. He argued, in brief, that civil society can no longer be regulated by the automatic controls described by liberal theorists, that the scope and importance of what Hegel called the "police" must now be vastly increased to create a "planned society." Failure to do this leads to a rise of social irrationality and anxiety so profound that a despot is found who will meet this social need in a barbaric and inherently self-destructive way. Mannheim contended that a constitution of "planning for freedom" would at once serve society and fulfill the requirements of the republican tradition. A new universal class, skilled in the techniques of physical and sociological technology, will work to implement the inherently rational will of a democratic or aristocratic public sphere. It is probably accurate to characterize this as a neo-Hegelian scheme, except that Mannheim attempts to meet the Marxian objection by assigning key importance in the process to the concrete experiences and skills of intellectuals and managers. They experience the capacity for managing complex situations in their concrete, daily work; planning for freedom simply implements at a national level what they are already building and doing within segments of society. The planned society is no mere moral imperative.[22]

If Herbert Marcuse is to be believed (or John Kenneth Galbraith), the planned society is no longer a prospect, but a reality.[23] But it is simply a new and more terrible dominion by civil society over man; it is not a new republic. The logic of civil society has been changed from the largely implicit one (although neither Locke nor Hegel ever doubted that there had to be specific elements of control) to an explicit, technological one, with the imperatives and dominations characteristic of this sphere dictating the actions of states. Marcuse sees this system as massively established and characterizes it as a "totalitarian" antithesis to the whole critical humanist tradition: techniques of social control and integration are so demonic that the very tension between the "idealist" rationale for the State and the "materialist" reality of the social sphere can be liquidated. What Marcuse calls "one-dimensional thought" makes it unnecessary and impossible to think about alternatives. From this standpoint, then, it follows that the conflicts and eruptions which do take place make no sense at all in terms of the system; they represent forces wholly alien to it which may, in some unspecifiable way, bring about collapse of the old and transformation to a new. Here Marcuse's projection becomes sybilline and many have read out of it whatever they wanted.

It is not necessary to accept the thesis of the technological state as all or nothing. The interesting question is whether there is an important trend in that direction and whether and how that trend affects the political questions we have been discussing. Jurgen Habermas has been developing a more careful statement of the case. But his most recent studies come very close to the views of Marcuse: it appears that the rules of conduct and inquiry appropriate to the production sphere increasingly serve as surrogates for rules of quite a different sort than had historically prevailed in cultural and political spheres, with a consequent inestimable impoverishment of human faculties.

If this is indeed what is happening, then the signs of crisis which provoke Lowi's call for renovation and which others see as harbingers of revolution may be nothing more than isolable and manageable reactions to a process of change, controllable frictions which arise while the regime switches from the liberal constitutions idealized in the theory of pluralism to the new authoritarianism which will be able to dispense with idealization. In such a case, Lowi's appeal to the republican virtue inherent in our civic *personae* and truly public institutions of state becomes ludicrously irrelevant. But if the process were as far advanced as Marcuse sometimes suggests, the prospects for socialism would also appear as little more than a pious hope. The terrible drama of the fundamental social changes here under discussion tempts us to proceed by painting pictures instead of raising questions which admit of answers specifying the degrees and rates of change. But such temptations must be resisted. There are clear signs that the development dramatized by Marcuse is in fact underway; there are also clear signs of resistance.

In keeping with the socialist intellectual tradition which was given its highest expression in the work of Marx, we shall take the first steps toward a socialist understanding of our situation by seeking to identify those resistances within society which give substantial signs of opposing the most marked manifestations of oppression and unfreedom. If we can find social entities which meet this general standard, we can then proceed to a truly adequate account of social reality by looking at it from the point of view of their practical struggle. This is far less a metaphysical or even epistemological principle than it is a strategy of inquiry. We must have some approximate notion of what is wrong in order to speak sensibly about various possible loci of creative opposition, but the intellectual process is one of steadily refining the approximations, and this in turn depends upon discovering a strategic perspective for study. The concluding portion of the essay, then, will attempt to distinguish among the resistances which many of us see about us—to identify the resistances which can be easily controlled to which counterresistant concessions can easily be made, and those which give promise of leading toward a "democracy of freedom." Three elements of what has been called "the Movement" can get some attention here.

1. The "New Politics." On one level, this can be diagnosed in terms of our discussion of republican constitutionalism. On another level, however, it may be that our demonstration of its incapacity to affect the outcomes of political actions does not seriously trouble its proponents. Michael A. Weinstein[24] has claimed that "new politics" must be understood in relation to a search for "personal consciousness," as a counter to the distrust so pervasive in the culture as to break down the integrity of self-relationship as well as relationship with others. He extends the term to include the campaign of George Wallace as well as the campaign of Eugene McCarthy, and celebrates both as events in which life-styles and personal responsibility were put on the line. What was involved for the participants was involvement in an occasion with demonstrable personal significance. The New Politics as described quite plausibly by Weinstein represents the bankruptcy of republican constitutionalism. But although the tendency in this direction appears clearly present in these movements, it is not out of the question that many within them can be brought to a critique of republicanism and a move to something more.

2. "Revolutionary Action Movements." Insofar as violence is not merely verbal (where it helps to break down the possibility of strategic resistance without affecting the system of power— although it may also serve the kinds of objectives ascribed to New Politics), its use may be clarified by comparison with medieval jacqueries, where violence was often a plea to good and great men to remedy suffering. But the location and character of the violence make it possible to respond to it by constituting a "zone of terror." Some proponents of violence imagine that repression will radicalize other segments of the society, as it becomes clear that a reign of terror is being established. What they fail to see is the possibility of government ruling in radically different ways in different spheres of the society, so that the middle-class householder who supports his local police may be acting quite appropriately in terms of his own situation. He is not being in any way subjected to terror, but is provided with law and order.[25] The authority-deflation upon which the revolutionaries count will under these circumstances simply not take place.

3. "New Left." This is a residual category for the "movement" that is centered around some such slogan as participatory democracy. The need here is to distinguish sharply between applications of the slogan which, in Marx's language, serve the "democracy of unfreedom" and those which serve the "democracy of freedom." This is a distinction which Lowi is naturally unwilling to make. The former sort of self-rule involves the self-administration by existing social units as they are now structured and inwardly biased. The latter sort involves processes of socializing the corporate organizations as they now exist. This is sometimes confusingly described as "organizing" them. Otherwise it is described as "politicizing" organizations which have been professional, civic, efficient, etc. Lowi is certainly right in attacking the first sort of participatory democracy, and he is also right in saying that the latter kind is antithetical to the principles of a rational state. The question is whether those principles can be more than the scholasticism of a repressive society. But such a general brief for the New Left may soon have little more than historical interest, since it appears that resistances of the first two types have all but consumed this earlier surge. John McDermott has recently advanced a number of hypotheses which suggest that the development of technological society will produce new social sources for the kind of political conflict which may produce a wholesome environment for man.[26]

McDermott raises the prospect of the rise of oppositions within the technical structure. He speaks, for example, of the conflict between the intense degree to which individuals must be disciplined and the limited authority of the disciplining powers. In the technological and scientific fields themselves, for example, this conflict may arise from the "generation gap" between the level at which the teachers work and the level at which the students know the science to be moving. He also cites the disparity between the skills inculcated into the new technological worker and the severely limited use to which these acquired powers are put in the normal technological process. Perhaps out of these conflicts—for which some aspects of the present struggles in the elite universities may be paradigmatic—may unfold a pattern of oppositional actions which will be "socialist" in Marx's original sense. Action in the strictly "political" sphere—whether it be electoral work or a protest-initiating movement relating to a great issue, or some other kind of political action,[27] would secure its *meaning* and not simply its *support* from these developments in society and would, in turn, help to provide a focus and direction for them.

The experience many had in the university-based antiwar movement is directly relevant here. There was a steady interaction between the growing discomfort with our "professional" roles and the campaign against an outrageous war. The area specialists who came to feel in 1964 that they should have enough control over their own skills to be able to devote them to the public discussion of the war within the place of their work (the Teach-In movement) did not foresee or intend a time when their colleagues' defense contracts—or their own—would be challenged. But some of them and more of their students came in time to do just that. The present resistances within a number of academic professions are a direct outgrowth of the "political education" generated by those experiences. And, insofar as the "New Politics" ventures, especially the McCarthy campaign, were not wholly sustained and directed by the moral-psychological energies discussed above, they had some measure of reality on the basis of that work.

These experiences were inconclusive, of course. They didn't end the war; they haven't transformed the universities; they may not change the professions. But they have already made differences in the lives of those who were involved in them. Not at the level of "personal consciousness" and private integrity alone—they have in fact often challenged and unsettled those and have posed new dilemmas. Far from making the participants "feel good," they have created awareness of moral problems and moral ignorance where there was none before. The changes in our lives have to do with rigid role-definitions cast aside, new relationships between some teachers and some students, new agendas for action, new theoretical work ventured. The nature of these accomplishments is that they do not satisfy; they demand more. That may be what socialism in Marx's sense is about: that we act together insofar as we can as "true men" in our actual circumstances in order to learn what we need, to become the men who are able to need.

At the moment this movement in the universities is in serious danger, if it is not already dead. There has been a demand that all talk be in language that Marx would call merely political, that all action be directly geared to the "revolutionary seizure of power" —what Marx called the "political aspect" of socialism, which has no meaning whatever except in relation to an ongoing socialist movement. And there is no such movement in most parts of the society. Out of such demands come the escalation of rhetoric, the soaring into a purely political empyrean so lofty that it can no longer be described as the heaven of our everyday world, but as a hashish-dream of heaven: the politics of the trip. Any issue of Andrew Kopkind's journal *Hard Times* or *Ramparts* will bring reports of good, kindly "revolutionary" people wandering off into isolated communes and corners of New Mexico and California and getting at least part of their kicks from "rapping about the revolution."

Some of this dispersion might yet make a socialist sense, but it will do so only if people will make their actual lives in the new situations (including their livelihoods), earn the right to be taken seriously by their neighbors and work-associates, and do socialist work while working. That is a life-time commitment. Socialism is struggle to make ourselves and others whole in the concrete circumstances in which our basic education takes place, the settings in which we must work to support ourselves. The Wallace movement, the Black Power Movement, the Women's Liberation Movement actually have some such impact on the constituencies within which they work. Wallace workers ask why the employer extorts "voluntary" contributions to United Funds which support "liberal" and "Commie" causes; the demand of black workers that the reality of their experience as blacks gain some special treatment does not extend to the work-place. If there were socialist workers on the scene they could have things to say to these situations which might redefine them and foster change in the form and content of the work-place. In this sense, these mutually antithetical types of resistances can contribute to socialist change. But the idea that these movements in their political capacities can play a "revolutionary" role because they will help to topple the "system" through talk about shooting pigs or general assaults on liberals and establishments is wild delusion.

The idea that rational change in a system can come from those who are "altogether outside" the system, as Marcuse suggests, is a form of the political fantasy Marx counters so tellingly. It is simply another version of the ideal republic of virtue dominating crass civil society—Robespierre or Napoleon. The point is not that the actions of such men or movements have no consequences at all; it is that the consequences are not what the actors intend. Rational change derives from participants within the system, actual men, who oppose the dehumanizing impact of the system while remaining in active contact with its work. This implies, for example, that students and professors, active in one of the central productive institutions in the society, must go about their training and their disciplined work even while struggling to bring their full humanities into these situations—as women, youth, blacks, but also as compassionate men and fellow-sufferers. Socialism does not say that the moral impulses of men make no part of their reality. At least Marx doesn't say that. He says that they cannot become a genuine factor when assigned to some special roles and institutions—churches or republican states. They become unreal, mere ideology, when they are not integrated into the work which consumes and sustains our actual lives. The *qualities* which the republican tradition ascribes to publics are never derided by Marx and should not be derided by Socialists. The point at issue is that these qualities cannot be fostered in an education which is merely political; they must find expanding expression and development in all of our activities.

This discussion has concentrated on the oppositions and has not addressed itself to the power system. Within each of the institutions there are controls, controllers, and institutionalized directions. I do not imagine that these controllers can be somehow converted or humanized in the course of socialist organization. Their identity and being are forged by the circumstances of enjoying power, and their effect will have to be countered by power-techniques of resistance appropriate to the character and objectives of the movement. The vast store of counterresistance techniques and resources at their disposal and their successful employment in recent years make understandable the escalation of political language among resisters. But premature talk of seizing control instead of building resistance is bravado; replacing one boss with another or putting everybody out of work usually serve little defensible purpose.

Such a conception of New Left is implicit in many of the things that were done, but a poor theory has helped to demoralize the

actors, to raise preposterous expectations which in turn lead to
desperate violence and quiescence. When there are left committees
among engineers and machinists as well as among social workers
and students, questions of political party or other modes of political
organization can become prominent again. With a broadly based
socialist movement under way, it would then make sense to talk
about the "political aspect" once more.

N O T E S

1. Influential early formulations of pluralism (in the sense intended
throughout this essay) include Robert Dahl, *A Preface to Democratic Theory* (Chicago: University of Chicago Press, 1956), Joseph Schumpeter,
Capitalism, Socialism and Democracy (New York: Harper, 1947). The
works of Dahl, Lindbloom, Shils, Downs, Schumpeter reward study and
merit criticism; much of the pluralist literature, however, cannot be taken
seriously. See, e.g., Reinhold Niebuhr and Paul E. Sigmund, *The Democratic
Experience: Past and Prospects* (New York: Praeger, 1969). Early characterization of pluralism as ideology can be found in the work of C. Wright
Mills, especially *The Power Elite* (New York: Oxford University Press,
1956) and *Sociological Imagination* (New York: Oxford University Press,
1959), and in P. H. Partridge, "Politics, Philosophy, Ideology," *Political
Studies,* 9 (1961): 217–235. For examples of critical literature and a useful
selected bibliography consult William B. Connolly, ed., *The Bias of Pluralism*
(New York: Atherton, 1969) and the essays by Crenson and Parenti in
this volume.
2. I have argued my position on these questions in "Political Science
and Political Rationality" in David Spitz, ed., *Political Theory and Social
Change* (New York: Atherton, 1967) and in "The Vocation of Radical
Intellectuals" in Godfried van den Bergh and David Kettler, eds., *Reason
Against Power* (Amsterdam: Vangennep, forthcoming).
3. The expression "critical temper" is used in this way by William E.
Connolly, "The Challenge to Pluralist Theory," in William E. Connolly,
op. cit. In an introduction to such an anthology, the concept has a certain
limited value. I am concerned now to stress the limits.
4. A literature building on Sigmund Freud, *Civilization and Its Discontents* (New York: Norton, 1962) claims to show just such necessity.
For an extreme example of this literature, see R. E. Money-Kyrle, *Psycho-
analysis and Politics* (New York: Norton, n.d.); the most persuasive formulations can be found in the writings of Benjamin Nelson. Among American
social scientists, the work of Talcott Parsons and Edward Shils on the
"values" of modern societies has probably been most influential in under-
pinning the view that Americanism corresponds to the objective needs of

complex and advanced society. But see also the writings of Robert MacIver. Niebuhr performs the same intellectual service with the help of orthodox Christian categories. To see how finished this whole argument was already in the eighteenth century, see David Kettler, *The Social and Political Thought of Adam Ferguson* (Columbus: Ohio State University Press, 1965).

5. This paper builds on an earlier effort, "The Politics of Social Change: The Relevance of Democratic Approaches" in William Connolly, *op. cit.*, where these contentions are elaborated.

6. Norman Jacobson, "Political Science and Political Education." *American Political Science Review*, 57 (September 1963): 561–569.

7. Different aspects of that tradition are invoked by very diverse schools of thought. Leo Strauss, Harry V. Jaffa, and others emphasize the classical republican concern for "virtue," but have a dangerous weakness for the Caesarism which often accompanies that concern. See Charles Norris Cochrane, *Christianity and Classical Culture* (Oxford: Oxford University Press, 1940), Part I. Franz L. Neumann, Otto Kirchheimer, and others stress the positive consequences of rule by general law in a way more reminiscent of republicans like Rousseau and Kant than of Locke. Citation of these influential writers underlines the importance of the issues to be discussed. But none of them represents as complete an approximation of the republican model as does Lowi.

8. Michael Oakeshott, *Rationalism in Politics,* (New York: Basic Books, 1962). Cp. David Kettler, "The Cheerful Discourses of Michael Oakeshott," *World Politics,* 16 (April 1964): 483–489.

9. Theodore J. Lowi, *The End of Liberalism* (New York: Norton, 1969), p. 127. The comparison to Dahl refers to *Preface to Democratic Theory, op. cit.*

10. Friedrich Hayek, *The Road to Serfdom* (Chicago: University of Chicago Press, 1944). Lowi is right, in my judgment, in referring to the essay on rule of law as superb, although much else in that book is absurd. Walter Lippmann, *Essays in the Public Philosophy* (Boston: Little Brown, 1955).

11. As far as I can determine, the serious errors arise in the section where Knox must deal with concepts which Hegel takes from the literatures of political economy (especially the Scots) and jurisprudence, i.e., in the section on ethical life. The following lists paragraphs where I have identified translation errors which change the meaning in important ways: 169, 195, 197, 207, 211, 229, 233 (where a discussion of police powers of the state quite consonant with American constitutional law is made to appear like unlimited license to a police state), 243, 248, 249, 253, 255, 258, 260, 270, 273, 280, 281, 288, 302, 306, 307, 239, 241. Number in parentheses refer to paragraphs in Georg Wilhelm Friedrich Hegel, *Grundlinien der Philosophie des Rechts,* ed. Johannes Hoffmeister (Hamburg: Felix Meiner Verlag, 1955). I will not comment here on the translation problems. George Romoser alerted me some years ago to the fact of weaknesses in the Knox translation. It is surprising that Walter Kaufmann, in his popular and sensible attempt to counter Anglo-American Hegel-myths, did not see this symptom/source of the problem. Walter Kaufmann, *Hegel* (Garden City: Doubleday, 1965).

12. Hegel's account of corporations is ambivalent, but tends very clearly away from the Genossenschaft idea associated with Justus Moser and the

historical school of jurisprudence and toward an idea so modern as to make the parallel between Lowi's "interest-groups" and Hegel's "corporations" not at all far-fetched—especially since Lowi includes local governments and similar groupings in his own listing. For an introduction to the topic, see the introductory essay in Z. A. Pelczynski, ed., *Hegel's Political Writings* (Oxford: Oxford University Press, 1964), ix f.; F. W. Maitland's introduction to Otto Gierke, *Political Theories of the Middle Ages* (Cambridge: Cambridge University Press, 1900; Boston: Beacon Press, 1958), xix–xii; Otto Gierke, *Natural Law and the Theory of Society* (Cambridge: Cambridge University Press, 1934; Boston: Beacon Press, 1958), 62–92, 162–198, with notes; Introduction in Ernest Barker, ed., *Social Contract* (New York and London: Oxford University Press, 1960). Hegel's ambivalence comes to the fore most clearly in an early essay. "Positivity of Christian Religions" in G. W. F. Hegel, *On Christianity: Early Theological Writings* (Gloucester, Mass.: Peter Smith, 1948), pp. 104–110.

13. Karl Marx, "Debatten über Pressefreiheit," Hans-Joachim Lieber and Peter Furth, eds., Karl Marx: *Frühe Schriften* (Stuttgart: Cotta Verlag, 1962), p. 148.

14. John Locke, *The Second Treatise of Government,* ed. Peter Laslett (Cambridge: Cambridge University Press, 1967), p. 302. I have followed Thomas Cook in modernizing the punctuation. This side of Locke is greatly illuminated by Philip Abrams, ed., *John Locke: Two Tracts on Government* (Cambridge: Cambridge University Press, 1967). A measure of ambivalence about the republican or commonwealth tradition runs through all important liberal texts. Marx closes the paragraph quoted earlier with a parallel to man's relation to physical laws of nature. Note the significant fact, however, that Locke speaks of civil *or* political society.

15. Cp. Marx's comment thirty years later: "Elementary education through the state is altogether objectionable. . . . The state has need, on the contrary, of a very stern education by the people." *Critique of the Gotha Programme* (New York: International Publishers, 1938), p. 21. The difference is not quite as great as it might appear.

16. As part of his circumspect critique of the republican constitualist tradition, Montesquieu tells the story of Roman history as a story of tragic self-contradiction: republican virtue required and fostered military expansion which in turn enlarged the territory and generated new interests so that republican virtue became impossible. *Considerations on the Causes of the Greatness of the Romans and Their Decline,* tr. and ed., David Lowenthal (Ithaca: Cornell University Press, 1965). Adam Ferguson stretches this thesis over a five-volume history in the course of which he acts out the characteristic modern conflict between the appeals of Roman idealism and the hard-headed appreciation for social imperatives.

17. Karl Marx, "Die heilige Familie," in Lieber and Furth, *op. cit.,* p. 817.

18. Karl Marx, Article I in *Vorwärts,* 1844. Translated in T. B. Bottomore and Maximilien Rubel, *Karl Marx: Selected Writings in Sociology and Social Psychology* (London: Watts and Co., 1956), pp. 215–218.

19. Karl Marx, Article II in *Vorwärts,* 1844, in Bottomore and Rubel, *op. cit.,* 238.

20. Cp. also Karl Marx, *Critique of the Gotha Programme,* p. 18 and *passim.*

21. E. V. Walter, *Terror and Resistance: A Study of Political Violence* (New York: Oxford University Press, 1969), esp. pp. 205 and 289f.

22. Karl Mannheim, *Man and Society in an Age of Reconstruction* (New York: Harcourt, n.d.).

23. Herbert Marcuse, *One-Dimensional Man* (Boston: Beacon Press, 1962); John Kenneth Galbraith, *The New Industrial State* (Boston: Houghton Mifflin, 1967). For important critical comments on Marcuse, see Jurgen Habermas, ed., *Antworten auf Herbert Marcuse* (Frankfurt: Suhrkamp Verlag, 1968) and Habermas, *Technik auf Wissenschaft als 'Ideologie'* (Frankfurt: Suhrkamp Verlag, 1968). I draw on both of these works in what follows. Galbraith does not share Marcuse's pessimism, of course; he is much closer to Mannheim.

24. Michael Weinstein, "A Normative Theory of Social Action (Mimeographed paper presented to the Midwest Political Science Association, May 1969).

25. The distinction between regime of terror and zone of terror is in Walter and has broad possibilities.

26. John McDermott, "Intellectuals & Technology," *The New York Review of Books,* 13 (July 31, 1969): 25–35. Contemporary German discussion bears on what follows. I have learned something about that from essays in *ad lectores. 8,* published by the social science editors of the German publisher, Luchterhand (Neuwied, 1969). They tend to formulate the issue in the Marxist terms, whether students, editors, the technical intelligentsia constitute a "proletariat." I think that this is a misleading formulation, but that the discussion is worthwhile. I am not myself familiar with the most recent French discussion, but have the impression that they are moving in similar directions.

27. On an important aspect of this question, see George Lukacs, "Legality and Illegality," in *Geschichte und Klassenbewusstsein* (Berlin: Malik Verlag, 1923; Neuwied: Luchterhand, 1967). His "Methodological Contribution to the Question of Organization," *op cit.* is also valuable.

3

THE VIOLENCE
COLONY • *Marcus Raskin*

> A tacit contract! That is to say, a wordless and consequently a thoughtless and will-less contract: a revolting nonsense! An absurd fiction! An unworthy hoax! For it assumes that while I was in a state of not being able to will, to think, to speak, I bound myself and all my descendants —only by virtue of having let myself be victimized without raising any protest—into perpetual slavery.
>
> —MIKHAIL BAKUNIN

> No generation can bind the next generation to commit suicide.
>
> BENJAMIN V. COHEN

Since the eighteenth century modern political thought has attempted two difficult tasks. One task was to justify the importance of the nation-state to the individual. The other was to show what obligations a citizen owed to the nation-state and what services he could expect from it. Because a new class, intent upon redefining its rights and obligations, emerged by the eighteenth century, the philosophers of that class needed to investigate the basic question of allegiance and authority. Until that time, there had been very little reason for the peasant, the worker, or the bourgeois to pledge allegiance to the nation-state. They had few rights and many obligations. The people internalized the rights of kings and palace others. According to the reactionary Joseph De Maistre, anything was better than a society in which men returned to their animal nature. If society had to be held together by the guillotine in which a king and/or an elite set the order, so be it. For De Maistre, all organized society rested on the subordination of the people to fear of the executioner.[1] While the violence of the guillotine and the whip were (and are) very much in evidence, the first line of defense for the ordered society in De Maistre's time (and now) is respect for authority. The grandeur and power of the kingly class and the whipholders had to be respected and followed. If obeisance were paid by the individual to the king or elite class as an ordinary matter of psychological or physical fear, using the whip would not be necessary; the hierarchic other or characterization would do the job of brute force.

De Maistre's view fitted well with the Prussian idea of the state. There was law in the idea of the Prussian state; indeed, its existence was identical with what law was. There was no law outside of the state and outside of the hierarchic structure of the state. Those who needed the notions of social contract to justify the existence of the state came to understand that the individual gave up all rights once he became part of the social contract. The state, therefore, was the highest Authority and those who ran the state through the armed forces, the churches, and the landed gentry were the highest authorities. The forces of the state were to be represented in governing through acceptance of the Law of Authority and Order. This was a Lutheran view of the state.

On the other hand, political thinkers of disparate views held certain conceptions common in the Age of Enlightenment that contradicted the authoritarian mode of statecraft. The power of the state was not absolute, nor was the power of those who ruled it. The views of Machiavelli, in which the state was concerned merely with power and its extension, were challenged by the more democratic-minded philosophers who were concerned with the question of how the state was to be controlled and how the citizen would live with authority as defined in practice by the bourgeois class. Thus, while Machiavelli was correct in his static description of the operation of states and the men who administered them, because the power-wielders could dictate the external actions of men, by the eighteenth and nineteenth centuries, the views of Locke,

Rousseau, and Jefferson had changed the frame of reference to the aspirations of justice and the self-governing community. Laws and obligations gave new meaning to the idea that people were a self-constituted community, not objects of the few who ruled it. Even in the Hobbesian scheme of the state, the individual citizen could act in his own behalf if the sovereign coveted the life of the citizen. The citizen was protected through the social contract, which in the eighteenth century had an extraordinary effect on governing. For example, the social contract was widely accepted by the Puritans in seventeenth-century New England. As Gough has pointed out, contract theory was enshrined in the American State constitutions. Consent of the governed as spelled out by Locke and Paine found its way into the constitutions of Delaware (1776); Pennsylvania (1776); Vermont (1777); Maryland (1776); Massachusetts (1780); and Tennessee (1796).

The themes of social contract and limited control over the individual were primary in the preparation of the American constitution. St. George Tucker, a prominent constitutionalist, stated in his commentaries on Blackstone that the Constitution "is an original, written federal and social compact, freely, voluntarily and solemnly entered into by the several states, and ratified by the people thereof respectively; whereby the several states have bound themselves to each other, and to the Federal government of the United States, and by which the Federal government is bound to the several states and to every citizen of the United States."[2] Jefferson supported this view. He believed that the states entered into a constitutional compact by which they agreed to become a single government.

While less idealistic motives can be found and indeed were present in the choices which were made by the handful who accepted the invitation to write an American constitution, certain important general assumptions applied. Those opposed to the Constitution were afraid that governors would emerge as a separate and despotic class representing only their own whims and wishes. According to Charles Beard, some influential revolutionaries like Patrick Henry, who refused to attend the Constitutional Convention, argued that any "strong government might end in a monarchy or that it would mean, in any case, big armies, big navies, heavy taxes, mountainous debts, and interference with personal liberty.

. . ." The people feared a government which might, either by its form or through its actions, transform itself into an unquenchable militaristic despotism, or become enamoured of abstract concepts which would be Prussian in outlook and purpose to the point where a man was paying obeisance to the state for his life and livelihood. These fears were generally held and the author of the Constitution, Alexander Hamilton, found that it was politically necessary to address himself to the fears of the "extremist antiauthoritarians" if the Constitution was to be ratified by the states. Hamilton pointed out that the power of the Congress to provide for a military force in times of peace was absolutely essential because the United States was encircled by British settlements, "savage tribes on our Western Frontier," and shared interests between Spain and Britain which posed a threat to the United States.[3] But his argument for the right of armed forces during peacetime was based on the idea of control over the armed forces and the actual operational working of constitutional control by Congress. He rejected the argument that "We must expose our property and liberty to the mercy of foreign invaders and invite them by our weakness to seize the naked and defenseless prey, because we are afraid that rulers, created by our choice, dependent on our will, might endanger that liberty by an abuse of the means necessary to its preservation."[4]

In his analysis, Hamilton assured the doubters that there was no time in the foreseeable future in which the "federal government can raise and maintain an army capable of erecting a despotism over the great body of the people of an immense empire. . . ."[5] As we shall see, that situation, the apprehension of which Hamilton thought to be a "disease, for which there can be found no cure in the resources of argument and reasoning . . ." has now come to pass.

In any case, whether one favored the Constitution or was opposed to it, the primary concern which occupied the minds of its proponents and opponents was the fear of the absolute power of a ruler of a military class which could wage war without the consent of the people, reducing them to objects. The solution which such men as Hamilton found to provide for the common defense (but not to build a military class) was through two methods of governance. One solution was the belief that sovereignty rested with the people and not with the state; the second, that a system of continuous control would operate over the governors and the military. Administrative control over the military would be exercised through a system of fractionated and dual power measures shared by the President and the Congress. On the other hand, the gratuitous use of power was to be controlled by dividing authority between the several branches of government. During the period of writing the Constitution, revolutionaries and their supporters argued the question of the Constitution on the basis of how much sovereignty would remain with all of the people or the more "responsible" property holders. Those who favored the kingly or military form *per se* fled to Canada, the Indies, or England.

In the eighteenth century the idea of sovereignty residing in "the people" was a provocative idea which seemed to sum up the revolutions in England, the United States, and later, in France. Although each had different roots and purposes, as Hannah Arendt points out, the fact is that they all assumed as the minimum purpose of revolution the ideological need for sovereignty of people over monarch. As Ranke has pointed out, "There is no political idea which has had so profound an influence in the course of the last few centuries as that of the sovereignty of the people. At times repressed and acting on opinion, then breaking out again, openly confessed, never realized and perpetually intervening, it is the eternal ferment of the modern world."[6]

But sovereignty of the people and by the people, while it had the political effect of removing legitimacy from one particular class or person which could call on that legitimacy as a way to keep the people objects, did not in practice have the effect of controlling the powers of those chosen by the people, who might act from avarice and usurpation. Once a group began to think that it had unlimited power, they might begin to use the people any way they desired. The method of control to be exercised by the people was similar to a contract in which the obligation of support of the government was given by the citizen in exchange for the provision and guarantee of his protected and peaceful existence. These latter assurances were to be buttressed by the continuous right of choice

for those officers of the government who would be responsible
for upholding such obligations. But in Hamilton's conception of
its authority, the seeds of contradiction were set as to the power
of such a government. Certainly, enemies could always be found
to justify the extension of state power. "And as I know nothing
to exempt this portion of the globe from the common calamities
that have befallen other parts of it, *I acknowledge my aversion to
every project that is calculated to disarm the government of a single
weapon, which in any possible contingency might be usefully employed for the general defense and security.*"[7] (Emphasis added)
Although in this context Hamilton's view relates to the particular
embattled situation of the proposed United States, there is sufficient
evidence to note that already the definition of security, general
defense, threat, and other such concepts would result in very different interpretations, and hence, in very different sorts of governmental purposes. It seemed that threats of the moment would be
used as the pretext for expansion and bellicosity. Such interpretations could only result in the derogation of the social contract since
some special group or class would have to act for everyone in
interpreting when to risk the life of the society. For a long while,
this risk was run without adverse consequences. Americans
thrived on wars and expansion.

The activists who administered the United States intended that
the imperialist impulse of an aggressive people be satisfied. Parts
of the *Federalist Papers* make clear that the United States was
to be an empire with imperial designs, weak now but not for long.
The imperial design took on its most immediate and brutal meaning through the decimation of the American Indian and his continued removal from place to place, much in the manner that the
United States is now using the Vietnamese peasant and removing
him. Of course, the other brutal meaning of the American empire
was to be found in the system of slavery and its attempts to
"liberate" the slaves. The most important and immediate contradiction to the social contract in America was slavery. From
our constitutional beginning it was clear that the "pox of slavery"
would force a redrafting of the compact if the idea of humanity
as basic to the compact were to exist in this country. Beyond these
instances of imperial action, there have been the approximately
125 conflicts in which the United States has engaged. All of them

have been imperial; and the leadership class has grown richer, more aggressive, and more truculent.

What we see, therefore, is a people who began an ideology of liberty with great energy and with the idea of becoming an important imperial power. Its leaders would be clever, and when necessary, bellicose. The leadership class would decide when to buy, when to be politic, and when to make war. This stance of statecraft operated on two assumptions: that military power was merely a tool for the political-economic leadership class because the military man could always be controlled, and that technology did not bring with it another group of challengers who then would try to acquire political leadership. Beginning as an instrument for the leadership class, the military by the mid-twentieth century became the system upon which the leadership class depended to uphold its power and the "order" of the society. Power and military action were no longer mediated through law. They were rationalized through self-deceiving rhetoric and propaganda. Thus, we see two important conditions which pervade the Violence Colony. One strain is that of militarism *per se*. The national security bureaucracy, as Richard Barnet has shown, is an important rationalizing organization within which militarism fits. The violence-colonizer who controls or works within that bureaucracy enjoys the fact of excellence of his military organization. He views the military organization as efficient, privileged, and with powerful instruments for use. It appears to be precise, efficient, and paramount. No doubt as the democracy and the ideology of the society reduce all questions to function, efficiency, and violence, militarism will increase its influence in all areas of life.

In a government the mode of efficiency through militarism shows itself as a function of command. For example, if the President wants ten thousand troops sent to Thailand tomorrow, or if he wants a staff paper today on options for use of weapons on American cities tomorrow, he knows that the necessary papers will be presented on time, and if he requests military actions, they will occur. Yet it does not follow that the President has the power to stop covert and military actions once they have begun. In comparison, the civilian side of the government, as President Kennedy was fond of pointing out, seems lumbering and inefficient. Because of its enormous efficiency, militarism is rewarded with a greater number of assignments and tasks. Its ideology and adherents begin to pervade more of the society as the assumptions of militarism engulf other activities.

The other strain is bellicosity, the heroic warlike stance. This strain is generally supplied by civilian leaders who want to see themselves remembered in history as great leaders. They are prepared to risk and court war as an instrument of personal and state aggrandizement. For example, President Roosevelt risked war prior to World War II; President Johnson made war in Southeast Asia; President Kennedy chanced war in Asia and during the Cuban missile crisis; President Truman made war in Korea; and yet, President Eisenhower, the militarist, avoided war. Finally, the civilian leadership, because of its own glory or foolish sense of purpose and efficiency, is swallowed by the militarist tradition of efficiency. This tradition is related to the model for the modern economic organization of the industrial state.

The average citizen has accepted the military system and the judgments of the leadership class because he believes that his security and well-being are protected by the military and provided for through the judgments made by an elite. In the last generation, for example, the citizen accepted the establishment of a Department of Defense which has spent over $1,400 billion since World War II, while allowing incursions on himself through military conscription and an extraordinarily high tax for the idea of common defense. Given the historical ethos of "protection" which the military class sells and citizens have been in the habit of internalizing, it has been difficult for Americans to see that the defense they were offered was merely a new version of the old empire builders and pharaohs who used the defenseless for their greater glory whether they were part of one's own state or had yet to be conquered or absorbed.

The difference between the use of force externally (*in* other nations) on those yet to be absorbed or subjugated, as against those who are already absorbed and thought of as citizens, generally disappears when a nation's internal economic and political instabilities make clear that there is no legitimacy of action except force. The technology used externally, as well as the people who use such technology, are now called upon to perform domestically in the same way they performed in the imperial wars or in imperial administration. For example, the use of the same techniques in Saigon, Berkeley, and Chicago has had the effect of internationalizing the confrontation of the colonizer and colonized, especially because the American imperium is so powerful. It is now viewed as the world's primary enemy by the poor and the young. The hierarchic, pharaohistic relationship is under attack in the twentieth century as a result of a world egalitarian and democratic rhetoric in which the socialists and capitalists, the Maoists and the liberals, vie with one another in showing the importance of the people's rights and the people's power. Such rhetoric is used by leadership for the purpose of keeping and extending their authority. It is, of course, self-delusive, and has the effect of causing delusion among the citizens as to the purpose of their leaders. In the United States, it is the democratic ideal which people fight for and believe in. However, when they realize that the rhetoric no longer reflects anything near the reality, and this contradiction is presented to them through television, or in deprivations and depredations which they suffer, it is only a matter of time before the people realize they are not citizens, but are themselves colonized. They then begin to examine the value of imperialist adventures in which young men are called upon to pay the price of protecting the colonizing class. The conservatives doubt the state structure because they begin to see that those who run the state do so according to whims and fancies. In the areas where the legislature should have power, they see it eroded into a nondeliberative, rubber-stamp body which ratifies the growth of overseas commitments and an imperial bureaucracy virtually without question. Such ventures as the American war in Vietnam are advanced, even though they destroy the monetary system which the conservative covets. The young men, the colonized, view the military from a different perspective than the pomp and efficiency seen by the colonizer. They see the inefficiency of the militarist, the doing and redoing of the same activities for no purpose while waiting to be called upon to fight for unexplained purposes. People wondered but they were silent. As George Bernanos wrote in *Tradition of Freedom:*

I have thought for a long time now that if some day the increasing efficiency of the technique of destruction finally causes our species to disappear from the earth, it will not be cruelty that will be responsible for our extinction and still less, of course, the indignation that cruelty awakens and the reprisals and vengeance that it brings upon itself—but the docility, the lack of responsibility of the modern man, his base subservient acceptance of every common decree. The horrors which we have seen, the still greater horrors we shall presently see, are not signs that devils insubordinate, rather that there is a constant increase, a stupendously rapid increase, in the number of obedient, docile men.[8]

Bernanos' fears were not misplaced, but the mask is now lifted. What is the face?

The national security state emerged from conditions of the economic depression. The first contracts awarded in 1938 were to Navy yards as a means of getting into the world imperial game and employing workers. Ideologically, the New Deal had run out of ideas and therefore blamed the organization of the Congress. Liberals believed that the legislative branch of the government could not perform those functions necessary to right the economy or move quickly enough to deal with crises and opportunities to which the leadership could react. Furthermore, liberals saw themselves as collaborators with the more decent and empty-headed of the corporate establishment. Their power plus that of the bureaucracy under executive leadership could provide the necessary active force to deal with depressions and capture world leadership. In this process, Keynesian espoused the theory that the economy could operate to the general benefit with some state guidelines while remaining under private control and direction except where it was necessary to get together through the Federal Reserve system, or through Business Advisory Councils to act in concert for their interests. Meanwhile, the state itself would expand its activities. First, there would be a strong bureaucracy which would operate as a force that had to be bargained with because it would be staffed with people who had new sorts of knowledge and could assess information. Second, there would be a strong emphasis on force and control to fight authoritarianism and totalitarianism. This view was mediated through a constructive strainer.

To the authoritarians the national security state would see internal threats to itself which it would control through an internal security network. It would chip away at pluralism while praising its existence and would build the internal power of the military and economy groupings which appeared to reflect its stability and growth. The cosmetic elements of pluralism which the liberals had thought were necessary for their security—free speech, for example, would be guaranteed so long as free speech had no effect on the political life of the country; that is to say, on how it was ruled and who ruled it. Where free speech became a threat to the pyramidal structure, to those at the top of the structure who made deals with each other and brokered huge interests within the national security state, then free speech would be eliminated, curtailed, or flooded by other information until people had no choice but to tune out.

Nuclear weapons took the national security state system outside of a more classic analysis of an authoritarian-totalitarian state which was held together by rhetoric and National Guardsmen who were called to defend property of industrialists. (As one of the Violence Commission reports points out, the Guard was established to deal with labor, at the insistence of the capitalist class.) Military technology changed the nature of the national security state from the systematic genocide characteristic of Naziism or Communism where a particular class or race was destroyed over a period of time. Instead, planning in advance was necessary to bring about nuclear genocide which could occur in one moment of Götterdämmerung. By this I do not mean that an important aspect of the Vietnam genocide was not the attempts by the military and civilian bureaucrats to see if they could fight a brush-fire genocidal war by quickly moving communications networks, bombs, whole administrative teams across the world in an imperial show of force and organization. This methodology, of course, is the more classic way of the modern security state with imperialist designs. The report of General Westmoreland and Admiral Sharp showed the imperial war as a colossal success for such forms of organizational "rationality." The difference is in the nuclear weapons.

To put this matter another way, the history of the cold war and great power politics has been an exercise in using millions of people as hostage. Stripped of pretense and rhetoric, the cold war has been nothing more than a situation in which a group of people who have the keys to nuclear destruction brandish nuclear weapons because their views of interest or ego say that that is what must be done. They offer others for slaughter on their own authority, self-inspired and self-initiated, in order to assert their power or personal prestige. Thus in a rich, technologically advanced mass society, politics is reduced to the ability of small groups of people to dictate suicide for the rest. In the summer of 1961, I was a member of the special staff of the National Security Council. The nation was caught up in the Berlin crisis and the cry for civil defense. The latter notion was initiated by those who saw the possibilities of using nuclear weapons as first strike threats to be carried out against the other side, provided we had some civil defense. The "policy-maker," the President, was to be armed with what was called "will stiffeners," i.e., more missiles and shelters. During the Berlin crisis, the President asked that a paper be written on how to perform a first strike against the Soviet Union. Five people were privy to the plan, which outlined the methods of attack, how many would be killed if we hit them first, how we would use S.A.C., etc. I was given a copy of the paper by one of the five and after reading it I went to see him. The paper was to my way of thinking quite mad, and morally bankrupt. I came into the office and said that the paper was morally bankrupt, foolish, etc. We yelled at each other and screamed, *and cried*. I said that we were no different than the planners who worked out the train schedules and the movements of Jews into concentration camps. Who were we to "tear up" the Russian people, or East European people, or any people at all?

In 1962, fifteen men in the entire world at the time of the Cuban missile crisis played out their nuclear poker hands while 500 million people waited to find out whether they themselves would live or die. In 1967, the ruling junta in the United States bombed on the border of China while the world waited to see whether it would be plunged into nuclear war. In 1967 an unctuous Undersecretary of State, Nicholas Katzenbach, announced that the Congress has no power to stop unauthorized wars, and the senators were flabbergasted. Aren't these examples of the end of one politics and the need for another? They are the stark illumination of how hierarchic structures, coupled with a massive war technology, turn people into things and objects, if those at the top of the pyramid so decide.

What we see here is a double reality, one political, the other technological. The political structure has broken down, since operationally there is no control which the Congress or the people is able to exercise over the bellicose and the militaristic. Second, the nation-state cannot protect its citizens because of runaway technology and an unaccountable corporate-defense structure. In this situation, we will find the military-political leadership expecting and demanding total obeisance to its will. To command such obeisance it will become even more arrogant and take more risks in order to bring about a populace which will bend to its needs and purposes. Consonant with this demand will be greater reliance on force and violence in the American society. The Dream Colony will serve the purpose of bringing forward an immobile mass that fantasizes about personal violence as an heroic act.

The violence-colonizers who control the state (and those to whom they have given the keys) have now arrogated to themselves the right to commit suicide for everyone in the society. Their ability to foster a political situation in which the power of suicide is given to the violence-colonizer stems from the belief on the part of the colonized that the hierarchic structure acts according to the interests of the colonized. Accepting the idea of function, role, and specialized knowledge, the people are easy prey for the argument of superior information and intelligence. The colonized assume that the choices of the colonizer are based on superior information and intelligence which the colonizers have in their possession. Existentially, people give their allegiance or accept their passive situation because they are led to believe that they are secure and protected by the colonizer.

But the roots are now exposed. The national security state system can no longer keep the social and political pieces in place. All people in American society tremble at the possibilities of revolt in their cities, and they cannot imagine any apparent way to handle such revolts. They are stunned by a war in Southeast Asia in which the average soldier is befuddled and demoralized by what he is doing, and they are beginning to sense the probability of continued imperialist wars in nonwhite countries as a result of American commitments and games of nuclear chicken. Furthermore, controls over the armed forces are loosened as each grouping gets its own nuclear weapons to control. For example, once MIRV is in place, each submarine and crew will be able to destroy 180 cities, and there is no way to know whether the submarine commander can or cannot, will or will not, once he undertakes his threat. It is virtually impossible for people to internalize the idea that the state technology and bureaucracy know what they are doing. The "facts" which seep to the top of the pyramid through the bureaucracy appear as mass delusion when exposed. Historically, the colonizers of violence play the kingly game of superior "intelligence" and information to justify their wars, mistakes, and power. The colonized in this view are like children who are not expected to understand the sorts of choices leaders have to make. Furthermore, they are not expected to have the information, technical knowledge, or intelligence to pass judgment or comprehend decision-making. The leaders use locked doors, guards, electric fences, and quantities of hearsay and other forms of make believe in order to help them think and encourage others to think that they have important intelligence and objectively found information which cannot be shared. "If only you knew what we in power know," says the colonizer. In a statement before the House Armed Services Committee, the madness of this situation was unfolded. The Secretary of the Air Force was testifying on the Vietnam War Budget with specific reference to the Air Force bombings and their success:—

MR. LEGGETT. Yes. Thank you, Mr. Chairman.

[Deleted.] I wonder if you could just give us a thumbnail sketch of how that aircraft is doing, what additional capability does it give us out there, and what are the nature of the missions that are being run?

SECRETARY BROWN. We are using a variety of [deleted] aircraft [deleted] out there, Mr. Leggett. I would like to go off the record and then put as much of it as I can into the record, because I know you will want some of it in the record.

MR. PRICE. Yes.

SECRETARY BROWN. May I go off the record?

MR. PRICE. Yes, off the record, Sam.

(Further statement of Secretary Brown off the record.)

SECRETARY BROWN. I wanted to go off the record on that because it is a quite sensitive subject.

MR. PRICE. We are off the record, Mr. Secretary.

(Further statement of Secretary Brown off the record.)

SECRETARY BROWN. Maybe I should now go back to the record.

[Deleted.]

SECRETARY BROWN. Yes.

MR. BATES. It says that. These things are not very closely held at this point in time.

SECRETARY BROWN. It is one thing for him to say it and it is another thing for me to say it.

MR. BATES. Yes, you will confirm it, I think is your point.

SECRETARY BROWN. That is right. I think Mr. Bray made that point very, very well. And I would like that statement off the record.

MR. BATES. We all have that same problem. Every time you have information, people ask you, even though it might be common knowledge. There is a question of confirmation.

SECRETARY BROWN. Let me see what I can do about determining how much of this information can be legitimately declassified. It will so appear in the record and can be so used.

(The following information was received for the record:)

> Additional information, which could expand the subject under discussion, cannot be provided in unclassified form.

MR. LEGGETT. [Deleted.]

SECRETARY BROWN. Well, I definitely want this off the record. [Deleted.]

THE CHAIRMAN. Yes.

(Further statement of Secretary Brown off the record.)[9]

But now those who subjectively feel their dissonance between what is told to them and what is obvious answer the colonizer by announcing that it is he who is imprisoned in his temples of power. An extraordinary dialectical trick is played: the colonizer who profiles others ends up as the profile because his ways of living and obtaining knowledge are so abstracted.

The fact of knowing only the profile of the body politic does not mean that the colonizer has no power to destroy. The power of destruction has been deeded to him by technology, hierarchy, and the mandarin intellectual. As I have suggested previously, the pyramidal structure is buttressed by the rationalizers of colonized knowledge. During the administration of President John Kennedy, leading professors from Harvard, MIT, the RAND Corporation, and other institutions spent their time computing ways to destroy the Soviet Union and other communist countries through a series of nuclear strikes. The same habit of mind and in some cases the same people developed our stance for brush-fire wars. They are also developing technological methods and economic controls to work with the military and the police in putting down revolts in the slums. The nation-state structure (and now the universities) finds itself reduced to an arm of the Violence Colony, specifically the militarized caste, in its attempt to put down internal rebellion, not only in terms of research input but also in terms of methods of dealing with dissenters of the university who object to its research for war on the campus. The People's Park at Berkeley where the university president sent in 2500 Guardsmen, armed and shooting, is an example. To keep power the militarized civilian caste will protect itself by giving more power to the police and military to deal with internal rebellion. Consequently, they will lose power to the military-police group as well as any controlling authority over them.

In its foreign relations, the nation-state becomes an anomaly because of technology.

The physical security of its citizens can no longer be provided by it. Each nation-state at best mythically protects its citizens. In the present nuclear arms race world, the national security of the United States is dependent on the Soviet Union, while the national security of the Soviet Union is dependent on the United States. And further, both societies are dependent on the whims and rationalities of military and civilian strategists; that these specialists in violence will not use the nuclear weapon to threaten or blackmail their own societies.[10]

The nation-state has reduced itself to an arm of military power, and its leadership ends up as destroyers of community. The habits of mind are bellicose and military.

Some time ago my wife and I had dinner with an American ambassador, a man who had thought often of becoming Secretary of State. In our discussion about nuclear war and weapons he said that such a war was absurd and impossible. No one wanted to use such weapons in Vietnam, or anywhere else. "Quite so," I responded, "and I am sure that no rational man such as yourself, if you were Secretary of State, would use nuclear weapons." "That isn't what I said," he replied. "If I were Secretary of State, perhaps there would be instances in which I would have to use them."

By allowing the leadership every option, including the ultimate one, we have allowed ourselves no option at all. Where "everything is permitted," in Dostoievski's phrase, nothing is possible. By allowing a leader the right to destroy us if he ever gets the technical and political power to do so, we have put ourselves in the position of the exploited and oppressed. The people are instruments who are dependent on the leader's wish to keep open options of our destruction. Our existence is dependent upon someone's mask of rationality. In the elementary, secondary, and university schools, the mandarins develop the attitudes and knowledge which give leaders violent options. The case of civil defense is pertinent in this regard. While it was sold as a measure to protect people, the mandarins viewed civil defense as a necessary instrument to strengthen the will of the people so that they would be more willing to allow the leaders to take risks in their name. Herman Kahn and others talked about the evacuation of cities to strengthen the policy-maker's hand at the bargaining table.

While submission to this perverted view of Hobbesianism might be thought of as a way for a state to operate which explicitly started from the assumption that there was no social contract between the people and their government, the American experiment assumes and acts on the basis of a social contract. This social contract rejects the idea that man can give up his uniqueness or his own personality in such a way as to become a plaything in the hands of others.

This fundamental right, the right to personality, includes in a sense all the others. To maintain and to develop his personality. It is not subject to freaks and fancies of single individuals and cannot, therefore, be transferred from one individual to another. *The contract of rulership which is the legal basis* of all civil power has, therefore, its inherent limits. There is no *pactum subjectionis,* no act of submission by which man can *give up the state* of a free agent and enslave himself. For by such an act of renunciation he would give up that very character which constitutes his nature and essence: he would lose his humanity.[11]

It may appear surprising to think of the social contract in strictly negative terms. After all, the social contract was not merely a political contract. By the eighteenth century, it was a primary instrument for the individual to seek his humanity. One hope was that it could be found through community. But the tragedy and the hope of the moment are that the positive aspects of the contract cannot be fulfilled through a hierarchic and authoritarian structure of society.

Historically, the social contract has had two separate meanings.

On the one hand, its terms may be viewed as those of a community which binds itself together based on reciprocity and the presupposition of equality. It is an agreement of equals who associate themselves together in a relationship of equality. The Greeks referred to such a relationship as that of nonrule or no ruler (*isonomy*). The second meaning of social contract emerged from the most minimal notion of relationship to a sovereign. It was, of course, the idea of obeisance in exchange for protection.

It is obvious that the latter definition of the contract was most easily opened to a nonconsensual view of relationship. In both cases, however, once one leaves the framework of face-to-face communities, the daily effect of the state and large organizations on the lives of individuals invariably favors the idea of obeisance for protection as the way for people to live. The contradiction is manifest when the governors are no longer able to give protection for themselves or security. If they do, the objects and institutions which they once accepted as the means for those protections will go unsupported, and new modes of institutional arrangements will come into being to supply protection. This is especially true in the case where the stronger presupposition of the social contract as it is understood in America—at least theoretically—is that it reflects the coming together of an association of equals. Consequently, demands and practice will require that people find ways of fulfilling that definition of the social contract once it is clear that the idea of obeisance for protection no longer operates in practice. The redefinition of the social contract will most likely emerge from the seeming inability of the present Constitution to deal with either national defense or face-to-face relationships.

There are some who hold to the uniqueness of the individual as the basic premise of the social contract and therefore believe that individuals must be protected against majorities. We find, however, that given the present structure of technology and authority, the question we seek to answer is much more mundane. How do we protect ourselves from elites who use us, the majority, as hostage for their whims and purposes?

Because the terms of allegiance for protection are shattered, the contract between the individual and those who arrogate sovereignty to themselves ceases to exist. The *de facto* termination of the contractual obligation forces people to define different contractual relationships which assert new legitimate objects of authority *in themselves*. We shall not deal here with the search for new legitimate objects of authority. However, it should be noted that the replacement of the social contract with a theory of elitism and hostage holding, as mediated through the national security state, is not a stable mode of governing, although this theory has been an important countertheme in American history. The problem of hostage holding and elite control has been consistently attacked by a vocal minority in the United States since its inception. For example, in the mid-west the prospect of war has never been taken lightly. Led by Senator Robert La Follette, the Progressive Movement had as one of its cardinal principles the idea that war should not be declared either by the President or the Congress. According to the Progressives, war was a matter of such basic interest to each of the citizens that it should only be declared through popular referendum. Whether or not the method which the Progressives put forward was the perfect way of deciding the question of war or peace for the body politic, it assumed the rights of citizens to know and make known their will on basic questions of their existence. It is difficult to fully appreciate the importance, for example, of Senator Borah's resolution (December 12, 1927) in the United States Senate as a way of protecting the people against the follies of government and reestablishing their legitimate authority. His resolution stated that as war had been a lawful institution among states, he wanted the Senate to resolve:

that it is the view of the Senate of the United States that war between nations should be outlawed as an *institution or means for the settlement of international controversies by making it a public crime under the law of nations,* and that every nation should be encouraged by solemn agreement or treaty to bind itself to indict and punish its own international war-breeders or instigators and war profiteers under powers similar to those conferred upon our Congress under Article I, Section 8 of our Federal Constitution, which clothes the Congress with the power to define and punish offenses against the law of nations. . . .[12]

Such ideas do not die easily. At first they may be used rhetorically, and then worn as the clothes of vengeance. The United States pressed Borah's argument in the allied case against Japanese leaders who were successfully tried for war crimes after the Second World War. In the latter part of the twentieth century, it is likely that many people in the name of a national community will insist that the people as a community, not the rulers, should decide questions of war and peace and punish those who arrogate authority over others. Were such a position to be taken by dissenters and resisters who believed that the social contract had ended unless the leadership could be held to account, they would personally enter a period of grave personal risk, because their position would bring them into direct confrontation with a military class which views war as the basic activity of the state.

Attempts by the students and faculty of the academic community to resist the military conscription system suggest a first step in challenging part of the structural foundation of the national security state. How this confrontation will resolve itself and what the results of such a confrontation will be cannot be predicted. While the confrontation will continue through an entire generation, that is, through the last part of the twentieth century, as increasing numbers of people and institutions discover how they have become hostage, positive alternatives will be tried which will attempt, in a pragmatic way, to redraft the social contract in all life areas which are interdependent and shared. New places of authority outside of the state will emerge.

There are certain necessary requirements to the redrafting of the social contract. One primary requisite is to find the way in which the participation of the individual citizen and the corporate unit of which he is a part may be democratized so that he will not feel himself to be part of the powerless and alienated masses. The project in reconstructing the social contract requires new attention to boundaries between the individual and the community. Not only are there constraints which the individual accepts in the community and vice versa, but it is also the case that the leadership of the community will have to deny itself certain tools and sanctions whose use would be self-destructive. The hubris of the leader who reserves to himself the right to destroy whole cities for his good and sufficient reasons is an example of one who can be controlled only through the horizontal group which specifically reserves rights of uniqueness to individuals and the right of finding ways to join their uniqueness with others. We are required to change leadership and the function known as leadership. This view now requires a new politics of participation and control.

I suggest one mode hesitantly and only in the hope that we may begin to find ways of reasserting control over the fundamental political parts of our existence. There is a stubborn and irremediable fact. The national government now collects resources, men, and wealth, which are used to make the basic human problems of our society greater. These irrational choices by the colonizer force those in politics to suggest the necessity of returning to first principles, to principles of definition about such matters as the social contract. No doubt they present themselves in ways which at first appear to be disrespectful of "law and order"; this phrase becomes the way for many in the society to insist on protecting the colonizer by whatever means or cost. But protection of the state or of allowing it colonizing power is not the concern of the young. Some refuse to fight in colonial wars; others flee. Within the society those who accept its pyramidal structure cannot abide expenditures on military intervention abroad. Those who are elected to public political office on a local level begin to see the contradiction of huge expenditure for irrelevant and mad items while their constituencies are deprived and their geographic areas decay at an exponential rate. Is it a dream which says that the United States spends 700 million dollars a week destroying another nation while not finding ways to spend 10 million dollars to clean up rats? The contradiction is too great and obvious. It is one with which a society will not be able to live.

By the very nature of the situation with which we are presented, it becomes necessary to face the ominous question: When may the people dissolve their government? This is not a trivial matter, nor should one who raises it do so in arrogance or superiority. It can only be raised without being considered a jest when it is done from a sense of felt need and attention to the obvious. It is important in discussing this question to remember the basis of democratic action. As John Locke has said, there is a great difference between the dissolution of the society and the dissolution of the government. A society dissolves itself when it is conquered by a foreign invader. In that case, the individual has no choice according to Locke but to shift for himself. Governments, whether they are free or totalitarian will invariably fall to the conqueror. Obviously, in our time a resistance would form itself. On the other hand, governments may and should be dissolved either when a single person or prince sets himself above the laws and authorities, refuses to carry out the laws, or "when the legislative or the prince, either of them, act contrary to their trust."[13] The people always reserve themselves the right to act against a legislature which causes the people to be reduced to slavery. When the annoyances are not petty but clear and major, the people who are willing to accept a great deal of mismanagement and even minor treachery will exchange murmur for mutiny. However, the people do not have to wait until a general catastrophe has occurred, for example, nuclear destruction, or a nuclear "accident" which destroys an American city, to act. Where the design is clear, according to Locke, the people should rouse themselves and "endeavor to put the rule into such hands which may secure to them the ends for which government was erected. . . ."[14] People are absolved from further obedience when governments are able to put themselves into a state of war with the people. They are "left to the common refuge which God hath provided for all men against force and violence." To the black man, his choices seem clear. Those of us characterized by the choices of men who undertook to build nuclear weapons in secret without the permission of the people, and who finally built a military force which can destroy a whole civilization in a few hours while cities suffocate from pollution and inaction, are left to conclude that the American government finds itself in jeopardy because we are characterized as hostages.

Whensoever, therefore, the legislative shall transgress this fundamental rule (of not making its citizenry slaves to arbitrary power) of society, and either by ambition, fear, *folly* or corruption endeavor to grasp themselves, or put into the hands of any other, an absolute power over the lives, liberties and estates of the people, by this breach of trust they forfeit the power the people had put into their hands for contrary ends, and it devolves to the people, who have a right to resume their original liberty and by the establishment of a new legislative (such as they shall think fit), provide for their own safety and security, which is the end for which they are in society.[15]

NOTES

1. This principle of governing later came to be applied by Europe and the United States in the poor countries of Asia, Africa, and Latin America —children to be spanked and intimidated, or women to be bought, towns to be destroyed which had to be taught a lesson, or to comprehend that stability-making subordination to the grandeur of the civilizers, set the terms of reference for the world. I am reminded of Simone Weil's discussion of the Roman Empire and her quotation from Polybius on the destruction of Carthage:

"Some people killed themselves without motive; others fled from their towns through deserted parts of the country, with no definite aim in their wanderings, from the panic prevailing in the towns. People denounced one another as having been hostile to the Romans; they arrested and accused their neighbors, although as yet, no one was being called to account for anything. Others went to meet the Romans with supplicants' branches, confessing their political transgressions and asking what penance they were to pay, although no one as yet had made any inquiries about them. Everywhere there was a fetid smell, because so many people had thrown themselves down wells or over precipices. So dreadful was the situation that, as the proverb says, 'even an enemy would have pitied' the state of Greece. . . . The Thebans fled from their city in a body and left it entirely empty."—Simone Weil, "The Great Beast," *Selected Essays* (London: Oxford University Press, 1962), p. 110.

2. St. George Tucker, *Blackstone's Commentaries*, 5 vols., 1803.

3. Alexander Hamilton, *Federalist Papers*, no. 24.

4. *Ibid.*, no. 25.

5. *Ibid.*, no. 28.

6. Leopold von Ranke, "Ferment of the Modern World," *History of England*, vol. 3. (New York: AMS Press, 1875)

7. Alexander Hamilton, *Federalist Papers*.

8. George Bernanos, *Tradition of Freedom*.

9. U.S. Congress, House Committee on Armed Services, *Hearings on Military Posture* and *An Act, S. 3293,* To Authorize Appropriations During the Fiscal Year 1969 for Procurement of Aircraft, Missiles, Naval Vessels, and Tracked Combat Vehicles, Research, Development, Test, and Evaluation for the Armed Forces and to Prescribe the Authorized Personnel Strength of the Selected Reserve of Each Reserve Component of the Armed Forces, and for Other Purposes, p. 9663.

10. Marcus Raskin, *Journal of Psychiatry* (1964).

11. Ernst Cassirer, *Myth of State* (New Haven: Yale University Press, 1946).

12. U.S. Congress, Senate (see p. 133), 90th Cong., 1st sess., December 12, 1967.

13. John Locke, *Of Civil Government* (New York: Dutton, Everyman), p. 228.

14. *Ibid.*, p. 231.

15. *Ibid.*, p. 229.

II

POWER IN AMERICA: CRISIS IN THE STATE

AN extensive reevaluation of the location and use of power in the United States has recently begun. *The conclusions reached by the writers in this section—that power is not located in roughly equal proportions among all groups and that there are crises in the way power is used—run the risk of seeming totally obvious to the lay reader. Such is the difficulty of dealing with optimistic pluralism as a description of, rather than a prescription for, American politics. The two authors deal so meticulously with liberal assumption after liberal assumption, presenting empirical support for each of their criticisms, that the reader must wonder what all the fuss was ever about. That is the contribution this section makes; it shows that the fuss was not worth it. Pluralism and optimism as description can hardly be taken seriously. By proving that to most people's satisfaction—we admit that some, with intellectual vested interests will hold out—the contributors have prepared the way for a more rational investigation into the questions of how power is distributed and used in American society. Hopefully, that investigation will now proceed more grounded in reality —and therefore as scholarship will be more intellectually exciting— than previous disagreements between pluralists and nonpluralists.*

4

POWER AND
PLURALISM:
A VIEW FROM THE
BOTTOM • *Michael Parenti*

In the absence of its natural defenders,
the interest of the excluded is always
in danger of being overlooked.
—JOHN STUART MILL

Was he free? Was he happy? The question is absurd!
Had anything been wrong, we should
certainly have heard.*
—W. H. AUDEN

It is said we live in a pluralistic society, and indeed a glance at the
social map of America reveals a vast agglomeration of regional,
class, occupational, and ethnic associations all busily making claims
upon state, local, and national governing agencies. If by pluralism
we mean this multiplicity of public and private interests and
identities, then America—like any modern society of size and
complexity—is pluralistic. Used in this broad sense, the term is
not a particularly arresting one for those political scientists interested in determining the extent to which power is democratically
operative in America. However, if by "pluralism" we mean that
the opportunities and resources necessary for the exercise of power
are *inclusively* rather than exclusively distributed and that neither
the enjoyment of dominance nor the suffering of deprivation is the
constant condition of any one group, then the question of whether
ours is a pluralistic society is not so easily resolved.

*Reprinted from *The Collected Poetry of W. H. Auden* with the permission of Random
House, Inc. Copyright © 1945 by W. H. Auden.

I

The protracted debate between "pluralists" and "antipluralists" is testimony to the difficulties we confront. After investigating "concrete decisions" at the community and national levels, the pluralists conclude that participation in decision-making is enjoyed by a variety of competing groups operating in specific issue-areas often in response to the initiatives of democratically elected officials. No evidence is found supporting the claim that a corporate "power elite" rules over an inarticulate mass. If there are elites in our society, they are numerous and specialized, and they are checked in their demands by the institutionalized rules of the political culture and by the competing demands of other elites, all of whom represent varying, if sometimes overlapping, constituencies.[1] Conflict is multilateral and ever-changing, and the "bulk of the population consists not of the mass but of integrated groups and publics, stratified with varying degrees of power,"[2] and endowed with a "multitude of techniques for exercising influence on decisions salient to them."[3]

Not long after this theory became the new orthodoxy of American political science, antipluralist critics began voicing certain reservations. The antipluralists remain unconvinced that influence and benefits are widely distributed, and that political and administrative officers operate as guardians of the unorganized majorities and as the controllers, rather than the servants, of important interests groups.[4] While not defending the idea of a monolithic power elite, they question whether elites are mutually restrained by competitive interaction by observing that many of the stronger elites tend to predominate in their particular spheres of activity more or less unmolested by other elites.[5] Not only are elites often unchecked by public authority on the most important issues affecting them, but in many instances *public* decision-making authority has been parceled out to *private* interests on a highly inegalitarian basis.[6] The antipluralists further criticize the pluralists for failing to take notice of the "powers of pre-emption"; is it not true, for instance, that corporate leaders often have no need to involve themselves in decision-making efforts because sufficient anticipatory consideration is given to their interests by officeholders?[7] Attention, therefore, should be directed to the nondecision, "nonissue" powers such as the power to predetermine the agenda and limit the scope of issue-conflict, and the power to define and propagate "the dominant values . . . myths, rituals and institutions which tend to favor the vested interests of one or more groups relative to others."[8]

The pluralists respond to these last few criticisms by noting that theories about unuttered anticipatory reactions, invisible participants, and hidden values cannot be scientifically entertained. We may conjure an "infinite regress" of imaginary powers operating behind the observable decisions-makers, the pluralists say, but we can study empirically only what is visible, and only those who can be seen as making decisions or engaging in activity bearing directly upon decision-making can be said to share power.

Now I, for one, have no quarrel with the dictum that we observe only the observable, but it might be suggested that what the pluralists have defined as "observable" is not all that meets the eyes of other researchers. Particularly troublesome to me is the relative absence of lower-strata groups from most community power studies and the ease with which their absence is either ignored or explained away.

Let me begin with a fundamental pluralist proposition, *viz.,* only those who participate in the decision process share in the exercise of power. If true, then it would follow that those who do *not* participate in decision-making do *not* share power. This latter proposition, however, is treated rather equivocally by most pluralists. If the nonparticipants are of the upper classes, it is concluded that they are noninfluential. But if the nonparticipants are from the lower-income groups, it is usually maintained that they exercise "indirect" influence.

The New Haven investigation conducted by Robert Dahl and his former student, Nelson Polsby, represents one of the most important of the pluralists' community studies and, for the moment, I will concentrate on what is revealed in their work. Dahl and Polsby discover that New Haven's active decision-makers are composed primarily of civic and political leaders centering around the mayor; only a few of these participants are members of the "eco-

nomic elite." For one to argue that municipal authorities are under
the power of the economic elite one must demonstrate, according
to Polsby, that upper-class members "customarily give orders to
political and civic leaders" which are obeyed, or that they regularly
and successfully block policies, or that they place "their own
people in positions of leadership." Finding to his own satisfaction
that none of these conditions obtains in New Haven, Polsby concludes that the upper class is not preponderately influential.[9] The
only way to determine whether actors are powerful, he says, is to
observe a sequence of events demonstrating their power: "If these
events take place, then the power of the actor is not 'potential'
but actual. If these events do not occur, then what grounds have
we to suppose that the actor is powerful? There appears to be no
scientific grounds for such an assumption." Those who assign "a
high power potential to economic dominants" are therefore "indulging in empirically unjustified speculation."[10]

What, then, of the lower-strata groups that do no participate in
decision-making? The New Haven study shows that only a miniscule fraction of the citizenry engage in any activity bearing directly
upon community decisions and that none of the decision-makers
are drawn from lower-income groups, white or black.[11] However,
the nonparticipant exercises "a moderate degree of indirect influence" through his power to elect officials or—if he does not vote—
through his "influential contact" with those who do vote, presumably relatives and friends.[12] The vote is an effective popular control
because "elected leaders keep the real or imagined preferences of
constituents *constantly in mind* in deciding what policies to adopt
or reject."[13] Most people, Dahl observes, "use their political resources scarcely at all," some not even bothering to vote; hence
they never fully convert their "potential influence" into "actual
influence."[14] They do not exert themselves because they feel no
compelling need to participate. To assume that citizens, especially
of the lower class, should be politically active is, Polsby says, to
make "the inappropriate and arbitrary assignment of upper- and
middle-class values to all actors in the community."[15] There are
"personally functional" and habitual reasons for lower-class withdrawal having nothing to do with political life. Polsby further
assures us that "most of the American communities studied in any
detail seem to be relatively healthy political organisms which means

that there is bound to be considerable conservatism and self-preservation rather than innovation and demand for change within the system."[16]

Here it seems we are confronted with a double standard for the measurement of power. Despite the fact that large corporation leaders and other economic notables control vast resources of wealth and property which affect the livelihoods, living standards, and welfare of the community, it cannot be presumed that they exercise indirect or potential influence over political leaders. Furthermore, it is unscientific to speak of political leaders as having anticipatory reactions to the interests of these economic elites. There must be discernible evidence of upper-class participation and victory in specific policy conflicts. But it may be presumed that the unorganized, less-educated, lower-income voters exercise an indirect influence over decisions to which they have no easy access and about which they often have no direct knowledge. They accomplish this by evoking in the minds of political leaders a set of "constant" but unspecified anticipatory reactions to the voters' policy preferences, preferences which themselves are frequently unspecified and unarticulated.

If it may be postulated, without the benefit of demonstration, that ordinary voters exercise indirect controls over decisions, then we can conclude that any community in America which holds elections is, by virtue of that fact, pluralistic. One wonders why there is any need for elaborate case studies of particular decisions since we have presumed to know, from the beginning, the very things that need to be empirically determined: to whose needs and imperatives do elected officials respond, as measured by what actual decisions and outcomes?

But if lower-class groups do not participate in decision-making activities, how can we determine the extent of their influence, if any, over actual decisions? And what meaning can we ascribe to their nonparticipation? I would suggest that instead of declaring them to be an unknown but contented entity, we allow ourselves the simple expedient of directly investigating the less privileged elements of a community to determine why they are not active, and what occurs when they do attempt to become active. Studies of policy struggles involving lower-strata groups are a rarity in the literature of American political science partly because the poor seldom embark upon such ventures[17] but also because our modes of analysis have defined the scope of our research so as to exclude the less visible activities of the underprivileged. "The case study approach to power location should not be discredited," Todd Gitlin reminds us, "but why are only certain cases studied?"[18] If it is true that one's sense of reality is partially determined by one's position in the ongoing social system, then a view from the bottom of the class structure recommends itself as a means of counterbalancing the picture of middle-class professors.

To observe power "from the bottom up" is what I shall attempt to do in the following case studies of three "issue-areas." My approach here does not involve any detailed analysis of those maneuvers and interactions within official circles normally considered a central part of the "decision-making process"; rather the focus is on actors who try to influence decisions from afar, the active nonelites who attempt to overcome the social distance that separates the subject of politics from the object by trying to participate in both the creation of an issue-agenda and in issue-decisions. Any assessment of nonelite influence should take into account actual outcomes; that is to say, in order to determine whether the protest group does or does not prevail we must look at the effects of the contested decision. A view from the bottom requires a shift in emphasis away from studying process as an end in itself which is divorced from substantive effects (who governs?) toward some empirical consideration of substantive effects (who gets what?), the presumption being that substantive effects are, after all, what make the decision process a meaningful and important topic of study. Furthermore, these effects are certainly an essential variable for political actors whose efforts otherwise cannot be properly understood.

Many questions of broad theoretical import might be entertained when investigating the limits and realities of lower-class power and participation. In the present study attention shall be directed primarily to the following theoretical considerations: is the present political system, as pluralists contend, responsive to the interests of all groups that seek to exercise influence through legitimate channels? Do the protest groups which represent the more acutely deprived strata suffer liabilities within the political system of a kind not usually accounted for in pluralist theory?

II

Early in the summer of 1964, at the invitation of a private welfare group, thirteen members of the Students for a Democratic Society went into the lower Clinton Hill neighborhood in Newark's South Ward and in cooperation with local residents formed the Newark Community Union Project (NCUP), an organization intended to assist ghetto people in the building of a social protest movement.

The lower Clinton Hill area was turning into an all-black area whose outward appearance of greenery and trees did not quite hide the underlying conditions of overcrowding, poverty, underemployment, and insufficient public services.[19] The already strained housing conditions were further aggravated by the influx of displaced persons whose previous neighborhoods were being obliterated by urban renewal projects. Nevertheless, as is the case with many large ghettos, the population was somewhat heterogeneous, including, along with the very poor, some relatively comfortable wage-earners, semiprofessional, and even professional people who remained in the South Ward because of racial discrimination or personal preference.

The NCUP organizers began making contacts with the poorer residents, hoping to find specific issues that would bring people together and involve them in community action.[20] The people who came to NCUP meetings, numbering from twenty-five to eighty on different occasions, and others interviewed in their homes or on street corners almost invariably expressed anger and distress about such problems as job discrimination, job shortages, poor wages, garbage and snow removal services, inadequate schools, rent gouging, police brutality, merchant overpricing, etc. "I am mad," said one, "I am angry when I see my people living the way they do." Coupled with these feelings was the widespread conviction that protest efforts would meet with frustration, and that the voices of the poor would not be heard, and if heard, not heeded. "What's the use?" "Nothing can ever get changed," "Why get your hopes up?" were some of the more common expressions. Nevertheless, some fifteen residents along with seven white students were resolute enough to give almost full-time efforts, staying with NCUP for the duration of its existence, ("This time the poor man's going to do something for himself," said one resident). Another twenty-five or so blacks were intensely active for periods extending from several months to half a year, and scores of others involved themselves intermittently at various times. It might be roughly estimated that as many as one hundred and fifty residents participated in some major or minor way over a two-and-a-half year period in public demonstrations, rent-strikes, meetings, and other organizational activities.[21]

The problems to which organizers could address themselves were varied and enormous. Several considerations determined priorities: first, what did the people themselves feel most strongly about?; secondly, were there visible targets and goals?; and thirdly, was there some chance of success? During a period extending from 1964 to 1966 efforts focused primarily on the following issues.

Issue 1: Housing

The poor in the South Ward area paid monthly rents ranging from $115 to $135 for the privilege of living in small subdivided apartments without proper heating or water facilities. The apartments were generally in deteriorated, ill-lit, unpainted, rat-infested buildings. Groups of tenants organized by NCUP made several trips to municipal housing authorities to complain of conditions, but won nothing more than promises to "look into things." Subsequent visits to the Human Rights Commission induced that agency to send inspectors to the buildings in question. The inspectors found evidence of widescale building code violations (as many as 125 in one apartment house), filed reports, and sent copies to the landlords in question. Lacking enforcement powers of its own, the Commission took no further action.

After two months had passed without any response from the building owners, NCUP began organizing rent strikes in some of the worst buildings in an eight-block area. This action led several of the landlords, including South Ward City Councilman, Lee Bernstein, to make minor repairs in a few buildings. But most owners did not respond during the first month of the strike and none attempted any major improvements.[22] A visit by protesters to the mayor's office in turn produced a visit by Mayor Addonizio to one of the apartment houses; the rent strike issue had by now won some passing attention in the local press. After taking due note of conditions, the mayor and his team of observers returned to city hall where, in the words of one tenant, "They made us a lot of promises but they didn't carry any out." NCUP protesters, joining forces with a local antipoverty group, resorted to picketing the suburban home of one of the worst slumlords, an action taken over the protests of Councilman Bernstein who described the peaceful picketing as "disgraceful behavior."

Two months after the strike started, landlords of the affected buildings began issuing eviction notices. One tenant, Mrs. Ida Brown, a mother of five children, was forcibly barred from her apartment by her landlord and two city detectives. When Mrs. Brown protested and attempted to enter her apartment, she was arrested and charged with assault and battery.[23] Her arrest was sufficient to persuade a number of other tenants that they had better withdraw from cooperation with the rent strike. Still other tenants, with the threat of eviction hanging over them, eventually moved out—their places quickly taken by other poor families—or complied with the law and resumed rent payments. Fear of arrest, forceful eviction, and legal prosecution, combined with a growing realization that nothing was being won except promises from public officials and threats from landlords, eventually proved effective in breaking the momentum of the rent-strike campaign. "There is," a resident accurately concluded, "no way us tenants, no legal way we can fight a landlord."[24] The ghetto residents learned what many always had suspected: some laws, such as those dealing with the collection of rents, the eviction of tenants and the protection of property, were swiftly enforceable, while other laws, such as those dealing with flagrant violations of building and safety codes and the protection of people, were unaccountably unenforceable.

The rent strikes ebbed in Newark as in other cities without winning improvements in living conditions, or creating a permanent tenant's movement, or getting the city and the courts to change their methods of dealing with slumlords. With nothing to show for their months of strenuous organizing, NCUP volunteers turned to a smaller and ostensibly more manageable issue.

Issue 2: A Traffic Light

Given the ghetto's immense needs, the desire for a traffic light on Avon Avenue might have seemed almost frivolous, but neighborhood feeling was surprisingly strong on this issue: too many children had been maimed and killed by speeding vehicles, and people found it hazardous to cross the avenue. For most residents the traffic light was literally a matter of life and death. In a few weeks NCUP collected 350 signatures on a petition, held a block rally and waged call-in and letter-writing campaigns, directed at the mayor and the City Council. Such efforts eventually earned the residents an audience with Mayor Addonizio who, confronted with a strong and well-organized community demand, agreed that a traffic light be installed forthwith, contingent only upon City Council approval. The residents departed from the meeting in a hopeful spirit. But after another month of inaction NCUP sent another delegation to city hall, this time to be told that a traffic light would cost $24,000 and therefore was too expensive, an argument which even the municipal authorities soon discarded as untenable. The protesters took to blocking traffic and picketing at the Avon Avenue intersection. On several occasions police dispersed the demonstrators with little difficulty, most participants being hesitant to force a confrontation and expose themselves to arrest. A few "Stop" signs were installed on the side street leading into Avon Avenue, a gesture that did nothing to slow down the main artery traffic, although it served to forestall further demonstrations as people awaited the impending light. Municipal officials gave repeated assurances that a traffic light would soon be installed, as one said, "If only you'll just be a little patient." After several more months of inaction and several more visits to city hall, it was revealed that the mayor had no authority to install a traffic light; the matter fell under state jurisdiction and had been referred to Trenton.

The protesters took to the streets again; this time attempts to block traffic led to the arrest of a few demonstrators. Municipal traffic officials continued to send assurances that the permit was "going through." But it remained for the State Bureau of Motor Vehicles to demonstrate how best to thwart the petitioners. State authorities informed NCUP organizers that they could not install a light until they had undertaken an extensive study of traffic conditions at the intersection. Data would be needed demonstrating that a certain number of accidents—only of a kind that a light could prevent—occurred on Avon Avenue over a given period. Since no one in the community, including police and medical authorities, had kept complete records of vehicle and pedestrian mishaps, there was no proof that a light was needed: only an independent study of forthcoming fatalities and injuries could decide the matter. Despite this professed commitment to empirical research, state traffic authorities seemed unable to indicate when they might initiate the requisite survey. (Soon after this position was enunciated, white residents in a nearby middle-class neighborhood were able to get a traffic light installed twenty-eight days after submitting a petition of approximately fifty signatures.)

Three years later, at the time of this writing, there is still no light, children are still hit by speeding vehicles at the intersection, and state officials have yet to begin their exhaustive study. More than ten months of intensive protest by lower Clinton Hill residents had produced yet another defeat.

Issue 3: Electoral Contest

"Why didn't you go to the local politicians for help on the rent strike and the traffic light?" I asked a number of the neighborhood organizers. "Are you kidding? They hate us! They call us troublemakers," exclaimed one. "They are whites, Toms, and heavies. They want to run us out of town," said another. "What could they have done?" a white student conjectured in retrospect. "They knew cooptation into the Democratic Party wouldn't silence us. We couldn't be bought off. So they were out to defeat us—even on a little thing like a traffic light." The Democratic party regulars were seen as being either indifferent or unsympathetic to ghetto needs. On the few occasions they showed themselves responsive to the poor, it was in the performance of petty favors. They might "look into" a complaint by a mother that her welfare checks were not arriving but they would not challenge some of the more demeaning and punitive features of the welfare system nor the conditions that fostered it. They might find a municipal job for a faithful precinct worker but they would not advance proposals leading to a fundamental attack on ghetto unemployment. They might procure an apartment for a family but they would not ask the landlord, who himself was often a party contributor, to make housing improvements, nor would they think of challenging his right to charge exhorbitant rents. The party regulars, be they white or Negro, seemed prepared to "look into" everything except certain of the more harrowing realities of slum life.

An opportunity to challenge them seemed to present itself in the autumn of 1965 when the United Freedom Ticket (UFT), a coalition of dissident blacks, Puerto Ricans and "civil-rights oriented whites," asked NCUP to support the insurgency candidacy of George Richardson, a black man and a former Democratic assemblyman who had broken with the party because of its unwillingness to confront the problems of slum housing and police brutality. Richardson was "sort of a politican" to some NCUP people, and "no great prize in his political views," but he compared favorably to his Democratic opponent whom one UFT supporter described as "the ultimate Uncle Tom." After some debate, NCUP decided to support the United Freedom Ticket which, along with Richardson, was running two other black candidates for the State Assembly. After the failure of the rent strike and traffic light campaigns, a frontal assault at the polls seemed like the only recourse: "We are tired of protesting and losing, so we're going right into politics," explained one organizer who hoped that NCUP's coalition with the UFT would increase the efficacy of both groups. Even if the Democratic incumbents were not defeated, a serious electoral challenge might make them somewhat more responsive to reformist pressure.

It was anticipated by some of the NCUP people that the campaign would provide an opportunity for creating a community-wide dialogue on fundamental issues. "Organizing the people" was, first of all, a matter of devising means of contacting and talking to individuals who heretofore never had been reached; the campaign seemed to offer just such an occasion. But faced with the necessity of swiftly reaching large numbers of people with limited resources, the challengers soon found themselves resorting to the traditional techniques of sound truck, leaflets, and slogans. Even so, not more than one-third of the contested area was covered and less than one-third of the voters were actually contacted by UFT volunteers.

"We've got that one thing that can take it away from [the bosses]" Candidate Richardson said, "the vote." Not many residents believed him. Campaigning for "decent housing," "more and better jobs," and "freedom," the UFT found itself burdened by the very sins it was trying to fight: too many years of unfulfilled pledges by too many candidates had left people immune to political promises. Some residents felt threatened by appeals for direct involvement: "I don't know anything about politics. I don't want to have anything to do with it," was a typical response. Many had never heard of the UFT and were hesitant about an unknown ingredient. Still others indicated their sympathy for the third party's goals but were quick to voice their skepticism: "We've had our people in there before and they couldn't do nothing." The many expressions of cynicism and distrust reported by UFT canvassers might be summarized as follows: (1) reformers were politicians, and therefore were as deceptive and insincere as other politicians; (2) even if sincere, reformers were eventually "bought off" by those in control; (3) even if not "bought off," reformers remained helpless against the entrenched powers: what could the UFT do even if it won all three contested seats? The conviction that "politics" could not deliver anything significant left many of the poor unresponsive, even if not unsympathetic, toward those who promised meaningful changes through the ballot box.

Of the blacks who voted, the majority were composed of the "better-to-do" elements: ministers, funeral directors, small businessmen, postal and clerical employees, and some skilled workers. A sizable number were beholden to, or related to those beholden to the Democratic organization for jobs and for positions within the party, thereby bringing them a modicum of social prestige. Often both resented and respected by poorer residents, the local ward politicians cultivated a wide range of acquaintances and traded on "friends and neighbors" appeals. They repeatedly stressed that a vote for the UFT might bring a Republican victory, and while many voters entertained no great expectations about the Democrats, they did fear that the Republicans might in some nameless way create still greater difficulties for blacks.[25] Furthermore, for some middle and lower-middle class blacks the act of voting

was a manifestation of civic virtue comparable to saluting the flag
or singing the national anthem, a mark of good citizenship status
reflecting well upon those Negroes who achieved it.[26]

Both the Democratic and Republican organizations provided
substantial funds for neighborhood workers who saturated the
black and white precincts with posters, party literature, and
door-to-door canvassing, and who manned the fleet of cars to
transport voters to and from the polls on election day. Even with
these efforts, less than half of the registered blacks bothered to vote
(as against almost two-thirds of the whites in the contested areas).
The UFT ticket was thoroughly defeated, running well behind
both major parties and polling less than 5 per cent of the vote.

This description of events in Newark cannot be concluded without some mention of the role played by community officials. In
the statements delivered to the press and sometimes to the protesters themselves, municipal officials voiced a dedication to the
best interests of the people. Certainly, it would have been remarkable were they to have professed otherwise, but sometimes their
behavior did betray their words. The methods they utilized to
defeat NCUP on the rent strikes and traffic light issues were
familiar ones: the insistence that the problem in question needed
elaborate investigation, the claim that the issue was not within a
given authority's jurisdiction, the posing of rigorous and time-
consuming legalistic procedures, the ritualistic appearance of a
public official to investigate the question—followed by disingenu-
ous promises that a solution was at hand, and the constant admoni-
tion to the protesters that they exercise restraint and patience.
"They just moved to go through the motions, to make us think
they were moving," said one black man. "The city," concluded a
white youth, "did a masterful job of destroying us. After a while
we didn't know who was the target. . . . We were always promised
something to take the steam out (of us). . . . They just wore us
down with a runaround."[27]

The protesters also were subjected to a series of unsavory harass-
ments. A false replica of the *NCUP Newsletter,* printed by unknown individuals and containing what purported to be admissions
of perverted sexual practices and communist affiliations—falsely
attributed to NCUP volunteers, was mailed to some 500 *NCUP
Newsletter* subscribers. NCUP was also infiltrated by at least one

undercover agent who was ejected from the organization after admitting he was in the pay of an unnamed municipal personage. It was apparently through his efforts that the newsletter subscription list fell into mysterious hands. A black detective, who quit the police force out of disgust for the racism he had encountered, confirmed the strong suspicions of NCUP workers that their telephone was being tapped by the police. On one occasion three NCUP girls were evicted from their three-bedroom apartment on the charges of maintaining an unsanitary premise, sleeping on the floors, and conducting sex orgies. The landlord's letter containing these accusations was reprinted by a City Councilman and circulated among members of the Council and other municipal authorities. NCUP itself was evicted from its original storefront office, no reason being given for the action. On another occasion threatening calls on the telephone by unidentified voices were followed by the breaking of NCUP office windows. Police repeatedly entered the office and arrested NCUP workers on disorderly conduct or loitering charges. A municipal judge once instructed one organizer brought before him to "go back to Russia." Other workers were arrested without cause while lawfully picketing a local food store accused of overpricing. Within a period of a few days, six black teenagers who assisted in routine NCUP tasks and who were planning a youth organization were arrested coming to and from the NCUP office. When Jesse Allen, a mild-mannered black leader of NCUP, went to the fifth-precinct station to inquire on their behalf, he, too, was placed under arrest. Two of the youths, having been arrested, were convicted of breaking probation, and each was made to serve two years in prison.

The only conceivably friendly gesture directed toward NCUP in the several years of its existence came in the late spring of 1967 when Mayor Addonizio and Police Chief Spina sent letters asking the organizers to help "keep a cool summer" in the ghetto. The ensuing summer riots sent a number of NCUP people into hiding because, as two of them testify, a highly placed state official sent a warning that the police would be "out to get the radicals." These precautions did not prevent several NCUP workers from being arrested soon after the disorders and charged with conspiracy to riot and arson, charges that were subsequently dropped for lack of evidence.

By the end of 1967 NCUP ceased functioning. Several of the whites moved on to SDS organizing or to community action programs in other cities: others got jobs in Newark. Some of the activist blacks became involved in running a community center set up by the United Community Corporation, an antipoverty group under OEO sponsorship. They now found their energies absorbed in minor administrative tasks and were no longer involved in protest action. NCUP dissolved without ever coming close to achieving its central objective: the building of a viable local social movement that could exercise influence and win changes in community conditions and in the system that fostered them.

In his excellent study of young radicals, Kenneth Keniston made an observation which might serve as a summary description of the white and black activists in Newark: "What is most impressive is not their secret motivation to have the System fail, but their naive hope that it would succeed, and the extent of their depression and disillusion when their early reformist hopes were frustrated."[28] Some of the people who were engaged in NCUP have long since discarded their earlier hopes about the viability of the system, thereby calling to mind an observation made by Christian Bay in 1965: "If budding Western-democracy-type pluralist institutions turn out to benefit only the middle and upper classes—as in many Latin American countries—then we should not be surprised if idealistic students and others with a passion for social justice . . . may become disposed to reject the forms of pluralist democracy altogether."[29]

III

The events in Newark provide us with a view of community power which qualifies the pluralist picture in several important respects. The following discussion attempts to summarize the findings and analyze some of the wider implications of this study.

1. For the urban blacks of Newark who had the temerity to fight city hall, there exists the world of the rulers and the world

of the ruled, and whether or not the first world is composed of a monolithic elite or of intramurally competing groups does not alter the fact that the blacks find themselves occupying the second. What impresses them and what might impress us is that the visible agents of the ruling world, a "plurality of actors and interests" as represented by the municipal and state housing officials, motor vehicle and transit authorities, the landlords and realty investors, the mayor, the City Council, the political machines, the courts and the police—with or without the benefit of conspiratorial orchestration—displayed a remarkable capacity to move in the same direction against some rather modest lower-class claims.

It is one thing to conclude that power is not the monopoly of any one cohesive power elite and another to contend that it is broadly distributed among countervailing and democratically responsive groups. The belief that lower-strata groups exercise a constant, albeit indirect, power remains an article of faith rather than a demonstrated proposition at least as regards the issues here investigated. Banfield's assertion that community decision-makers operate "on the principle that everyone should get something and no one should be hurt very much," and Dahl's view that "all active and legitimate groups in the population can make themselves heard at some crucial stage in the process of decision," do not seem to be borne out.[30] Nor were we able to detect the "multitude of techniques for exercising influence on decisions" which Polsby believes is readily available to any group willing to engage in political competition.[31]

It may be that decision-makers are responsive to lower-class pressures that are less visible than those observed in this study, but, as the pluralists would warn us, we should not embark upon an infinite regress of conjectures about covert influences. Suffice it to say that if Newark's officials were favorably influenced by the ghetto poor, it must have been in ways so subtle as to have escaped the attention of both the researcher and the poor themselves. Since the data indicate that a lower-class group exercises no successful influence when *active,* I find no compelling reason to entertain the conclusion that the group wields power through unspecified means when *inactive.*

The data on Newark are consistent with the suggestion, offered by Edelman and Lipsky, that students of power and protest make a distinction between symbolic reassurances and substantive goods; the former are almost always more readily allocated to protesters and are usually designed for the purpose of deflecting the protest.[32] The few "positive" responses which Newark's officials made cost little in time, energy, and support; they were the appropriate "reciprocal noises," to use Dahl's term, intended primarily as substitutes for more tangible allocations. The familiar delaying tactics used by public officials are, Lipsky observes, "particularly effective in dealing with protest groups because of (the group's) inherent instability."[33] And the group's instability is due, he adds, to its dependence on the political resources of "third parties." However, this study of Newark shows that even when a group demonstrates unusual durability—NCUP persisted for three years—it still may be unable to outlast the ploys of decision-makers. The latter can, so to speak, wait forever, and on many issues they would prefer to do so, while the protest group, *no matter how organizationally stable,* must start producing results if it is ever to attract a stronger following.

The idea that nothing succeeds like success is well understood by the challenged authorities. Often their unwillingness to make tangible allocations is due less to any consideration of immediate political expenditure and more to their concern that present protests are but a prelude to more challenging and more costly demands in the future. The traffic light (unlike the housing issue) hardly represented an appropriation that would have strained municipal resources nor would it have threatened the interests of more powerful groups, but a victory for the protesters might have reinforced the very kind of oppositional activity which Newark's officials wanted to see nipped in the bud.

2. One of the most important aspects of power is the ability not only to prevail in a struggle but to predetermine the agenda of struggle, that is, to determine whether certain questions ever reach the competition stage. Assertions about the impossibility of empirically studying these "nondecisions" need to be reexamined. Many "nondecisions" are really decisions of a sort, specifically to avoid or prevent the emergence of a particular course of action.[34] Much of the behavior of Newark's officials can be seen as a kind of "politics of prevention," to use Harold Lasswell's term, a series of decisions designed to limit the area of issue conflict.

More extensive study of the attitudes, actions, and inactions of municipal authorities toward lower-strata claims might reveal a startling number of instances in which office-holders avoid politically difficult responses to lower-class pressures. "The problem of politics," according to Lasswell, "is less to solve conflicts than to prevent them." Too much inclusiveness of "all the interests concerned arouses a psychology of conflict which produces obstructive, fictitious and irrelevant values," a situation best avoided when social administrators and political leaders learn to dampen by manipulative ploys those issues which they judge to be detrimental to the public interest.[35] Newark offers an example of how "the politics of prevention" is practiced in the less than antiseptic world of a municipality. Some readers will find the reality no less distasteful than the theory.

Direct observation of lower-class groups may bring to light other instances of "nondecisions" and "nonissues," specifically those resulting from the actual and anticipated discouragements suffered by people at the lower portion of the social structure. In classic democratic theory and in much of the pluralist literature, attention has focused primarily on the presumed anticipations of political leaders to the interests of various constituencies, but perhaps a more significant determinant of the conflict-agenda can be found in the anticipatory reactions of lower-strata groups toward those who govern. In Newark, for instance, no attempt was made to organize protest around a number of real grievances. "If we couldn't even get a lousy traffic light with half the neighborhood out there screaming for it," explained one NCUP worker, "how could we hope to fight the corporations and the unions . . . or even the school system?" Protest groups remain inactive in certain areas because, given the enormity of the conditions needing change and the strength of the interests opposing it, they see no opportunity for effective protest.[36] For them the agenda is predetermined by preferences and powers other than their own.

The same might be said of isolated individuals. Only a small percentage of the lower Clinton Hill residents were active in the various NCUP projects. According to one view, most sternly enunciated by Polsby, there is no reason to assume that politically quiescent people suffer deprivations unless they express actual grievances. But this ostensibly empirical position itself

harbors an *a priori* assumption, for, in fact, individuals may remain politically quiescent (1) because they feel no deprivation
or (2) because they feel real and urgent deprivations but are
convinced that protest is futile and, hence, give no political expression to their grievances. One can decide which is the case
only by empirical investigation of the social group in question.[37]
Any widely felt deprivation discovered by the investigator which
fails to become an issue because the deprived have not the ability
to force a confrontation may be considered a "nonissue"; these
"nonissues" (or anticipatory reactions) are *empirically visible* even
if, by their nature, they tend to be *politically invisible*.

The unwillingness of so many people in Newark to make any
kind of political commitment can be partly attributed to the
limitations of time and energy which the poor suffer.[38] Working
long hours for low pay, deprived of a host of services which
middle-class whites take for granted, many residents have neither
the physical nor psychic energy to engage in the demanding tasks
of community organizing. Many do not feel personally capable
and confident enough to ask their neighbors or themselves to
participate actively. In a way which most white people cannot
appreciate, fear is a palpable ingredient in the lives of the black
poor; many are deterred by fear of eviction, legal harassment,
prosecution, police assault, and by a more diffuse and ubiquitous
fear of the powers that be.

But were I to offer any one explanation for nonparticipation,
it is the profound belief held by so many ghetto residents that
there exist no means of taking effective action against longstand-
ing grievances, and that investments of scarce time, energy, money
and, perhaps most of all, hope serve for nought except to aggra-
vate one's sense of affliction and impotence. In this case, nonparticipation is an expression of what Kenneth Clark describes
as the "psychology of the ghetto with its pervasive and total sense
of helplessness,"[39] a pattern of anticipatory reactions which attempts to avoid direct exposure to, and competition against, unresponsive and unsympathetic authorities.

The contention that the poor are not really discontented else
they would register a protest vote at election time presupposes
among other things that the poor share or should share the middle-
class belief that the ballot is an effective and meaningful means

of changing the condition of their lives and their community. But, recalling Polsby's warning, we must guard against "the inappropriate and arbitrary assignment of upper and middle-class values to all actors in the community." We might also avoid treating lower-class nonparticipants as a self-generated entity, a manifestation of some innate subcultural habit or lack of civic virtue, and allow ourselves the notion that attitudes of defeatism and withdrawal are fostered by conditions within the socioeconomic system and to that extent are accurate representations of the systemic realities and everyday life-conditions faced by the black poor.[40]

With that in mind, we might question the consistency and ease with which public opinion surveys report that lower-strata individuals are more apathetic and less informed than citizens from better-educated upper-income groups. If by "apathy" we mean the absence of affect and awareness, then many ghetto blacks, while nonparticipants in the usual political activities, can hardly be described as "apathetic." Apathy should not be confused with antipathy and alienation.[41] As to the finding that lower-class people are "less informed," what impressed me most about the poor, often semiliterate, blacks I talked to (residents of Newark and also of New York and more recently New Haven) was the extent to which they had a rather precise notion of what afflicted them and certainly a better sense of the difficulties and deprivations that beset the black community than the whites in the same cities, many of whom refused to accept the legitimacy of black complaints.[42]

Whether a group appears apathetic and ill-informed depends on the kinds of questions it is being asked. Perhaps survey research, not unlike I.Q. testing, inadvertently reflects the cultural and class biases of the dominant society by focusing on those questions which are defined by the white middle-class world as "public issues." Something of the same criticism can be made in regard to the community power research of the last fifteen years. That researchers have been able to study so many American cities and find so few deep-seated grievances tells us more about their research models than about urban reality. By considering only those issues worthy of study which are pursued by politically visible interests they rarely reached the muted lower strata.[43] ". . . Rigid adherence to a conceptual schema," Charles McCoy notes in his critical appraisal of pluralism, "restricts the range of the political scientist's observable data so that he may fail to see what is taking place outside his frame of reference."[44]

3. If "inequalities in political resources remain, they tend to be noncumulative," some pluralists believe, since no one group either monopolizes or is totally deprived of the attributes of power.[45] Even if lacking in money and leadership, the lower strata still have the power of numbers. Thus it might be argued that the failure of NCUP and the UFT to mobilize sufficient numbers of poor people tells us only that they were unable to tap the ghetto's power resources and not that such resources are non-existent.

The contention that the slum constituency is ineffective because it fails to mobilize its numerical strength is something of a tautology. It is to say that the poor will have power if and when they act in such a way as to have power—presumably in sufficient numbers with sufficient energy. But the only way we can determine "sufficiency" is by noting that the poor prevail on a given issue. By that approach, they can never be judged powerless. If they win on any issue, then they have power; if they lose, they still have power but sufficient numbers have not made sufficient use of it. One cannot imagine a situation in which sufficient numbers have acted and lost; the proposition is established by definition rather than by observation and is thus nonfalsifiable.

Moreover, to contend that the lower strata have a potential power which would prevail should they *choose* to use it presumes that their nonparticipation is purely a matter of volition. The volition argument is given its more familiar and vulgar expression by those who dismiss the inequalities of opportunity in economic life: "Anyone can make his fortune if he puts his mind and effort to it." The antecedent conditions which are crucial determinants of performance merely become a matter of self-willed doggedness.[46] The argument overlooks the fact that the ability to take effective advantage of an opportunity, the ability to convert potentiality into actuality, is itself a crucial power. The actualization of any potential power requires the use of antecedent resources, and just as one needs the capital to make capital, so one needs the power to use power. This is especially true of the power of numbers, insofar as the opportunity to achieve political effectiveness by activating large numbers of people, especially lower-class citizens, within the normal channels of group politics necessitates a substantial command of time, manpower, publicity, organization, legitimacy, knowledgeability, and—the ingredient that often can determine the availability of these resources—money. Aside from its more circumspect influences, money is needed for the acquisition of elected office. "Probably the most important direct contribution" to political leaders, according to Dahl himself, "is money." The "most important indirect contribution is votes. . . ."[47] The power of numbers, then, is an influence which is highly qualified by material and class considerations.

For the poor of Newark, the situation closely approximates one of "cumulative inequalities," to use Dahl's term. If the poor possessed the material resources needed to mobilize themselves, they would not be poor and would have less need to organize their numbers in a struggle to win services which the economic and political systems readily grant to more favored groups. Can the dispossessed who desire inclusion in the decision process gain access to political office without the capital needed to mobilize and activate their numbers? There seems no easy answer to this question. The problem of "political capital accumulation" is compounded by the fact that, unlike the indigent in many other countries, the poor in America are a minority and therefore even when mobilized for electoral participation they might have only a limited impact. The power of numbers can be employed with countervailing efficacy by that majority which identifies itself with the "haves" against the "have nots."

Furthermore, in places like Newark, the one institution theoretically designed to mobilize and respond to the demands of the unorganized lower strata, the local political party, fails to do so. One of the hallowed teachings of American political science is that the political party is the citizen's means of exercising collective power; the stronger the party system, the abler will it effect the polyarchic will. But the party organization in Newark is less a vehicle for democratic dialogue and polyarchic power than a pressure group with a rather narrowly defined interest in the pursuit of office, favor, and patronage. Moved to collective activity only at election time, local politicians seem most possessed with the overriding task of securing and advancing their own positions and maintaining the ongoing equilibrium, not out of any dedication to stability as such, but because the present "equlibrium" is one that favors them.

Party politicians are inclined to respond positively not to group *needs* but to group *demands,* and in political life as in economic life, *needs* do not become *marketable demands* until they are backed by "buying power" or "exchange power," for only then is it in the "producer's" interest to respond. The problem with most lower-strata groups is that they have few political resources of their own to exchange.[48] NCUP's protest action failed to create the kinds of inducements which would have made it in the political leaders' interest to take positive measures. The withholding of rent payments, the street corner demonstrations, the momentary disruptions of traffic, and the feeble electoral challenge were treated by the politicians of Newark not as bargaining resources but as minor nuisances which were not to be allowed to develop into major threats. Concessions to the troublemakers might have led to demands for even greater reallocations and would have eventually challenged the interests of groups endowed with far more political "buying power."

4. Not only do party regulars have little inclination to entertain the kinds of issues that might incur the wrath of higher political leaders or powerful economic interests, they also try to discredit and defeat those reformers who seek confrontations on such issues.[49] Questions about poverty, urban squalor, unemployment, the tax structure, and the ownership, control and uses of private and public wealth do not win the attention of most urban political organizations. But the sins of the politician are more than personal ones, for the forces that limit him also circumscribe most of political life. The very agenda of legitimate conflict is shaped by widely accepted and unquestioned belief-systems and power distributions which predispose the decision-makers to view the claims of certain groups as "reasonable" or "essential" and the claims of other groups as "questionable" or "outrageous." The systemic norms and rules which govern political procedures operate with something less than egalitarian effects. To say that the political system is governed by "the rules of the game" is to apply an unfortunate metaphor.[50] In most games the rules apply equally to all competitors, but in political life the symbolic norms, standards,

and practices which govern traditional forms of political competition are themselves part of the object of competition. Rules that regulate procedures and priorities in any social system cannot be extricated from the substantive values and interests that led to their construction. Rather than being neutral judgments, they are the embodiment of past political victories and, as such, favor those who have "written" them. Many of the past struggles of dispossessed groups have involved actions which, until legalized as part of the rules, were treated as crimes against property and against the Constitution, including such things as collective bargaining, boycotts, strikes, sit-downs, and the demand to legislate standards for wages, hours, and other working conditions. Many of the earlier efforts in the labor movement were directed toward legalizing certain methods of protest and competition, thereby changing the rules so as to allow for more effective participation in future competitions.[51] Those who contend that a commitment to the rules is a precondition for democratic politics[52] overlook the fact that for some groups such a commitment is tantamount to accepting a condition of permanent defeat since certain of the rules as presently constituted (e.g., the rent laws) are, in fact, the weapons of a dominant interest.

5. Finally, one might wonder whether accession to office and control of municipal government by those dedicated to the black poor will do little more than transform the local political system from one which performs petty individual favors to one which performs minor collective services. To be sure, these services are no matter of indifference to the deprived but they would hardly touch the structural and systemic difficulties which the poor confront. Municipal governments are dependent creatures whose options are limited and preempted by socioeconomic forces commanding resources that extend far beyond the city limits. The black mayor of Gary, Indiana, Richard Hatcher, pointed to the problem:

I am mayor of a city of roughly 90,000 black people but we do not control the possibilities of jobs for them, or money for their schools, or state-funded social services. These things are in the hands of the U.S. Steel Corporation, and the County Department of Welfare, the State of Indiana. . . . For not a moment do I fool myself that black

political control of Gary or of Cleveland or of any other city in and
of itself can solve the problems of the wretched of this nation. The
resources are not available to the cities to do the job that needs doing.[53]

Hatcher is raising a question rarely entertained by students of community power and one which we cannot pursue in this present
discussion. It concerns itself not with the powers of the actors in
the system but with the system as a whole: is the political system,
as defined by the confines of a particular governmental jurisdiction,
capable of effecting the kinds of substantive reallocations needed
to end the plight of the lower-classes?[54]

Whatever the answer to that question, we can conclude that in
Newark and probably in many other cities even the limited resources of the municipality are not allocated in anything resembling
an equitable fashion. We can conclude further that the existence
of protest activity should not be treated as a sure manifestation of
a pluralistic influence system. Even if the thought is incongruent
with the pluralist model, it should come as no surprise to political
scientists that the practices of the political system do not guarantee
that all groups will have accessibility to the loci of decision-making,
and the ability to be heard in a debate, even when achieved, is not
tantamount to the sharing of power. To proffer an image of
democracy as a kind of debating society affording everyone the
opportunity of contributing to a free-wielding, consensual decision
process—one that is rarely troubled by zero-sum choices—is to
presume that the struggle for policy is determined primarily by
locations and that decision-makers embrace a policy more because
they are persuaded by its logic, justice, and wisdom than because
they are impressed by the strength and importance of its advocates.

If American communities are governed democratically, then let
it be said that democracy, like any other form of government, is a
power system and as such it allocates its values and priorities most
favorably to those who have the most power, those who have the
wherewithal to take best advantage of systemic arrangements. The
political order that emerges may prove to be "functional" and
"workable" without contributing to the well-being of large segments of the population. Those who suffer no severe deprivations
under such a system are most capable of counseling patience and
civility to those who do not and are most inclined to view the
present system as being beneficial to all—sooner or later. At the

same time, those who are most needful of substantive reallocations are, by that very fact, furthest removed from the resources necessary to command such reallocations and least able to make effective use of whatever limited resources they possess. If this is pluralism, who needs the power elite?

NOTES

NOTE: I would like to thank Darryl Baskin, Robert Dahl, Edgar Litt, Douglas Rosenberg, and Kenneth Sharpe for their helpful comments.

1. Robert Dahl's *Who Governs?* (New Haven: Yale University Press, 1961) remains the most intelligent and important pluralist statement, one that can still be read with profit even by those who disagree with it. Other pluralist views may be found in Arnold Rose, *The Power Structure* (New York: Oxford University Press, 1967); Edward Banfield, *Political Influence* (New York: Free Press, 1961); David Riesman, *et al., The Lonely Crowd* (Garden City, N. Y.; Doubleday, Anchor, 1955); Nelson Polsby, *Community Power and Political Theory* (New Haven; Yale University Press, 1963); David Truman, *The Governmental Process,* (New York: Alfred A. Knopf, 1953).

2. Rose, *op. cit.,* p. 6.

3. Polsby, *op. cit.,* p. 118.

4. For data and critical analysis supporting the antipluralist position see Grant McConnell, *Private Power and American Democracy* (New York: Alfred A. Knopf, 1966) and the many studies cited therein; see also, Paul Baran and Paul Sweezy, *Monopoly Capital: An Essay on the American Economic and Social Order* (New York: Monthly Review Press, 1966); Gabriel Kolko, *Wealth and Power in America* (New York: Praeger, 1964); Henry Kariel, *The Decline of American Pluralism* (Stanford: Stanford University Press, 1961); Theodore Lowi, "The Public Philosophy: Interest-Group Liberalism," *American Political Science Review,* 61 (March 1967): 5–24; Philip Green, "Science, Government and the Case of RAND," *World Politics,* 20 (January 1968): 301–326. For a collection of the best analytic critiques of pluralism see the articles reprinted in Charles McCoy and John Playford eds., *Apolitical Politics: A Critique of Behavioralism* (New York: Thomas Y. Crowell, 1967).

5. See Peter Bachrach, *The Theory of Democratic Elitism,* (Boston: Little Brown, 1967), p. 37. Some antipluralists such as G. William Domhoff, *Who Rules America?* (Englewood Cliffs, N. J.: Prentice-Hall, 1967) conclude that a power elite rules at the national level even if there may be more pluralistic elites at the community levels.

6. See Kariel, *op. cit.,* especially Chapters 5 and 6 for a development of this point; also Lowi, *op. cit.*

7. Even the pluralist Banfield seems to support the above idea. In

Political Influence he observes (p. 251): "When Mayor Daley took office, he immediately wrote to three or four of the city's most prominent businessmen asking them to list the things they thought most needed doing. . . . He may be impressed by the intrinsic merit of a proposal . . . but he will be even more impressed at the prospect of being well regarded by the highly respectable people whose proposal it is."

8. Peter Bachrach and Morton Baratz, "Two Faces of Power," *American Political Science Review,* 56 (December 1962): 950, reprinted in McCoy and Playford, *op. cit.* See also Matthew Crenson's essay in this volume. For a detailed development of the effects of myth and ritual in political life see Murray Edelman, *The Symbolic Uses of Politics* (Urbana, Ill.: University of Illinois, 1964): also Thurman Arnold, *The Symbols of Government,* (New Haven: Yale University Press, 1935). For a detailed analysis of the structure and content of a prevalent belief-system see Francis K. Sutton, *et al., The American Business Creed* (Cambridge: Harvard University Press, 1956).

9. Polsby, *op. cit.,* pp. 88–89. Yet Polsby goes on to say: "Mayor Lee's achievement in generating support from New Haven's economic and social elite should not be underestimated. . . . Economic and social leaders, who had originally been reluctant to support the urban redevelopment program, became so firmly committed to the program and to Lee that many of these lifelong Republicans found themselves actively supporting Lee for the U.S. Senate and contributing heavily to his re-election campaign against the Republican candidate. At least one businessman even suggested that the *Republican* party nominate Lee for Mayor." *Ibid.* (emphasis in the original). It seems not to have occurred to Polsby that Lee's unusual popularity with businessmen was due less to his personal seductiveness than to his having proven himself so repeatedly responsive to business interests. For a more critical study of Mayor Lee's urban renewal program and his dealings with the economic elite see John Wilhelm, "The Success and Tragedy of Richard Lee," *The New Journal* (New Haven, Conn.: October 15, 1967): 5–9.

10. Polsby, *op. cit.,* p. 60. By this approach, considerations of historical, class, cultural, and structural factors are relegated to an incidental or even nonscientific status. Here indeed is "behaviorism" in its Pavlovian-Watsonian sense.

11. Dahl, *op. cit.,* pp. 180–181. Other community studies similarly find that active participants are almost invariably drawn from professional, business, and better-income strata.

12. *Ibid.,* p. 164 and pp. 100–103.

13. *Ibid.,* p. 164; the italics are mine.

14. *Ibid.,* p. 270f.

15. Polsby, *op. cit.,* pp. 116–117; see the critical comments in Jack L. Walker, "A Critique of the Elitist Theory of Democracy," *American Political Science Review,* 60 (June 1966): 289.

16. Polsby, *op. cit.,* p. 134.

17. Actually, political activities involving the dispossessed occur more frequently than we have assumed. In recent years there have been scores of attempts by migrant workers, sharecroppers, ghetto blacks, rural whites, American Indians, indigent elderly, and others to effect specific changes in various communities and institutions. Most of these activities have yet to be studied systematically as situations which tell us something about the

dynamics and distributions of power in America. Most studies of conflict and discontent within the political system are written from the perspective of those concerned with channelizing or reducing the challenges of competing groups. See, for example, Neil J. Smelser, *Theory of Collective Behavior*, (New York: Free' Press, 1963). Note the discussion in William Gamson's *Power and Discontent* (Homewood, Ill.: Dorsey, 1968) pp. 11–19.

18. Todd Gitlin, "Local Pluralism as Theory and Ideology," *Studies on the Left*, 5 (1965), reprinted in McCoy and Playford, *op. cit.*, p. 143.

19. More than one-half of Newark's 400,000 residents are black. A third of the city's housing is substandard. Unemployment in the ghetto is "officially set at 12 per cent, unofficially as high as 20 per cent;" some 17,000 households try to exist on annual incomes of less than $3,000. See Paul Goldberg in the *New York Times Magazine*, September 29, 1968, p. 117. The conditions in Newark are bad but hardly atypical. In municipal governmental structure, political party system, racial make-up, population density, housing conditions, occupational and income distributions, and instances of riot and civil disturbances Newark is fairly representative of most good-sized American cities in the Northeast.

20. Many of the events described herein occurred before I began my research. My information is based on protracted interviews and less structured conversations conducted in the autumn of 1965, the winter of 1966, and the spring of 1968 with black activists and whites involved in NCUP, and other Newark residents. In most instances the information reported here has been corroborated by two or more respondents. A less detailed but helpful history of the events described above has been recorded in the documentary film, "The Troublemakers," produced and distributed by Newsreel, Inc., New York, N. Y. The direct quotations in these case studies are from my interviews and field observations, except for a few taken from the documentary film.

21. One of the black leaders, Jesse Allen, a former union shop steward, exhausted his life savings in order to support himself while working for NCUP. Other black activists included youths, welfare mothers, housewives, and working and unemployed men.

22. In a number of instances it was difficult to determine who owned what building. Some owners found it advantageous to use "fronts." Occasionally a building might change hands several times in quick succession only to return to the hands of the original owner.

23. The detectives charged that Mrs. Brown threw one of them down a flight of stairs. Eye witnesses gave a contrary account, testifying that it was Mrs. Brown who was thrown down the stairs. The jury chose to believe the police and Mrs. Brown was convicted and given three years probation. A subsequent grand jury investigation of her countersuit led to the conviction of one of the detectives for assault and battery. The conviction against Mrs. Brown, however, was never repealed.

24. This also seems to be the case in other communities. In Mount Vernon, N. Y., in 1965, fifteen welfare mothers submitted a petition to housing authorities protesting conditions in their apartment building. Within a week all had been served eviction notices. In New York and other cities, rent strikes when "successful" often produce results of dubious value to the tenants. After laborious legal proceedings on the tenants' part and after the numerous delaying tactics and appeals available to the landlord

have been exhausted, the city usually takes the building into receivership, uses the rent money to make repairs, and then returns the building to the landlord while allowing him to charge substantial rent increases because of the improved conditions. Frequently, the repairs are so extensive that the tenants are evicted by the city only to be relocated in slums elsewhere, far from their neighborhood friends, their jobs, and their children's schools. Today most community organizers have few illusions about the efficacy of rent strikes. See Stanley Aronowitz, "New York City: After the Rent Strikes," *Studies on the Left,* 5 (1965): 85–89.

25. The South Ward might be considered as having a "modified two-party system": The Republicans are always strong enough to raise a serious electoral challenge but seldom strong enough to win.

26. Compare to Howard Swearer's explanation of electoral participation in the Soviet Union in his "The Functions of Soviet Local Elections," *Midwest Journal of Political Science,* 5 (May 1961): 149.

27. Those who insist that more militant protest tactics should not be employed until all legitimate legislative and administrative channels for redressing grievances have been exhausted, might consider whether such channels are not, by their very nature, inexhaustible.

28. Kenneth Keniston, *Young Radicals, Notes on Committed Youth* (New York: Delta, 1968): 127.

29. Christian Bay, "Politics and Pseudopolitics: A Critical Evaluation of Some Behavioral Literature," *The American Political Science Review,* 59 (March 1965): 39–51; reprinted in McCoy and Playford, *op. cit.*

30. Banfield, *op. cit.,* p. 272: Robert Dahl, *A Preface of Democratic Theory,* (Chicago: University of Chicago Press, 1956), p. 137, but see the qualification Dahl offers on p. 138. Another pluralist, Merelman, goes so far as to argue that those who are defeated nevertheless share in power because they have been able to induce the prevailing group to expand the effort needed to vanquish them! "Even if those planning to initiate policies hostile to an 'elite' become subject to its power and are constrained to desist, they still have exerted power of their own. The elite has been forced to anticipate them and exert power in return." Richard Merelman, "On the Neo-Elitist Critique of Community Power," *The American Political Science Review,* 62 (June 1968): 455. It is impossible using Merelman's model to imagine any situation, even a suppressive one, as not being somewhat pluralistic: both conqueror and conquered, victimizer and victim, share in power. In contrast, the model offered by Dahl and Polsby defines power as the ability to prevail in a given issue conflict.

31. Polsby, *op. cit.,* p. 118.

32. See Edelman, *op. cit.,* chapter 2 and *passim*; and Michael Lipsky, "Protest as a Political Resource," *American Political Science Review,* 62 (December 1968): 1148 and 1155.

33. Lipsky, *op. cit.,* pp. 1156–1157.

34. Here I am not referring to that category of nondecisions which Bachrach and Baratz see as encapsuled in the norms and beliefs of the sociopolitical culture and which are less frequently or less obviously the objects of deliberate manipulation. But even such "unconscious," "implicit" belief systems are not inaccessible to analysis. See Sutton *et al., op. cit.* and Edelman *op. cit.* Few political scientists have begun to think of belief-

systems as resources of power comparable to the other resources commonly identified in decision conflicts.

35. Harold Lasswell, *Psychopathology and Politics*, (Chicago: University of Chicago Press, 1930): pp. 196–197; also the critical comments in Kariel, *op. cit.*, p. 117f, and Bachrach, *op. cit.*, pp. 66–67.

36. Compare to E. E. Schattschneider's remark: "People are not likely to start a fight if they are certain that they are going to be severely penalized for their efforts. In this situation repression may assume the guise of a false unanimity." *The Semi-Sovereign People* (New York: Holt, Rinehart and Winston, 1960), p. 8.

37. Painstaking field work may no longer be necessary if one simply wishes to establish the fact that lower-class grievances exist. Expressions of ills have become so explosive and riotous as to have won even the glass-eyed attention of the mass media. In the summer of 1967 there were 75 major outbreaks of disorder and in the spring of 1968 over 100 cities suffered some kind of riot and disorder.

38. Nonparticipation can also be ascribed in part to conditions which are hardly exclusive to the poor. Thus it may not be clearly within the interest of any individual members of large groups to make the kinds of personal expenditures needed to win goals beneficial to the entire group unless there are more particularized rewards or coercions which act as personal incentives. To some extent this is a problem confronting all collective action. See Mancur Olsen, Jr., *The Logic of Collective Action* (Cambridge: Harvard University Press, 1963). One might still observe that economically deprived groups are unusually wanting in the resources which allow for particularized incentives and hence they suffer unusually severe difficulties of organization and leadership.

39. Kenneth Clark, *Dark Ghetto* (New York: Harper and Row, 1965), p. 156.

40. Contrary to an accepted notion, the great majority of the poor families of Newark, New York, New Haven, Chicago, Washington, D.C., and Watts—to mention a few of the places that have been studied—are stable, self-respecting and hard-working, headed by fathers, or in the absence of a male, by working mothers who care deeply and labor hard for their children, but they face substandard housing, inhumane hospitals and schools, poor work conditions, low pay, high rents, overpriced stores, etc. They find themselves trapped not by a "matriarchal slave-family cultural heritage" but by the socioeconomic system. See Studs Terkel, *Division Street: America* (New York: Pantheon, 1967); Paul Jacobs, *Prelude to Riot* (New York: Vintage, 1966); Charles Willie, "Two Men and Their Families," in Irwin Deutscher and Elizabeth Thomson eds., *Among the People*, (New York: Basic Books, 1968), pp. 53–66; and Clark, *op. cit.*

41. Many of the black poor of Newark fit Robert Lane's description of the alienation syndrome: "I am the object, not the subject of political life. . . . The government is not run in my interest; they do not care about me; in this sense it is not my government. . . ." *Political Ideology* (New York: Free Press, 1962), p. 162.

42. A similar conclusion is drawn by Terkel, *op. cit.*, after extensive interviews with whites and blacks in Chicago. See also the findings on black attitudes concerning the 1964 riots and the comparison to white

responses to J. R. Feagin and P. B. Sheatsley, "Ghetto Resident Appraisals of a Riot," *Public Opinion Quarterly*, 32 (Fall/1968): 352–362; and the "Kerner Report" on the 1967 riots: *Report of the National Advisory Commission on Civil Disorders* (New York: Bantam, 1968), Chapter 5 and *passim*.

43. Thus neither Dahl nor Polsby has much to say about the reactions of slum dwellers displaced by the New Haven urban renewal program. Polsby observes: "Who wanted urban redevelopment? By 1957, practically everyone who had anything to say in public strongly favored this program." *Op. cit.*, p. 71. Dahl makes a passing reference to those who did not have "anything to say in public": "several hundred slum dwellers without much political influence" and a handful of small business men. Nothing more is heard about those who suffered from urban redevelopment. *Who Governs?*, p. 244. (See comments by Gitlin, *op. cit.*, pp. 141–142). Polsby (*op. cit.*, pp. 96–97) further assures us that in regard to goals which are "in some way explicitly pursued by people in the community, the method of study in New Haven has a reasonable chance of capturing them." Whether that claim is true or not, his method of study will tell us nothing about those goals desired by large segments of the population but not "explicitly pursued" or which, if pursued, fail to achieve political visibility because of the organizational weakness of the deprived group or the unresponsiveness of community leaders. Similarly, Harold Lasswell's contention that "it is impossible to locate the few without considering the many" is highly questionable. Lasswell's own work repeatedly demonstrates that a student of power can focus on the activities of the few without finding it imperative to consider the well-being of the many. See his *Politics; Who Gets What, When, How* (New York: Meridian Books, 1958), p. 309 and comments by Bachrach, *op. cit.*, p. 66.

44. McCoy in the introduction to McCoy and Playford, *op. cit.*, p. 5.

45. Dahl, *Who Governs?*, p. 85; italics in the original.

46. In fairness to Dahl it should be said that his view of "potential power" is not as simple as that held by other students. In *Who Governs?* (p. 275), he notes that there are important "objective differences" among constituents which limit their potential power: ". . . being poor or rich, well-educated or uneducated, a professional man or an unskilled laborer, living in a slum area or a middle-class neighborhood—these are differences in objective situations of a most persistent and general sort that are likely to show up in a variety of different ways over a long period of time." It is our loss that Dahl did not see fit to develop these observations.

47. *Ibid.*, p. 97.

48. See the analysis in James Q. Wilson, "The Strategy of Protest: Problems of Negro Civic Action," *Journal of Conflict Resolution*, 3 (September 1961): 291–303; and Lipsky *op. cit.*, pp. 1145–1146.

49. Newark is not the only city in which the party regulars manifest either indifference or antipathy toward the issues raised by reformers. Describing Negro politicians in Chicago, Banfield notes: "Like all politicians, they had to consider their political futures. Only one or two were 'race men.' The others had accommodated themselves to a situation in which whites held the upper hand." The man who dominated Negro political life for so many years, Congressman Dawson, is described as one who does small favors for constituents, "takes care" of his precinct work-

ers and remains "indifferent to issues and principles including those of special importance to the race." Banfield, *op. cit.*, pp. 41, 260. A year as participant-observer in New Haven politics (1967–1968) leads me to the same conclusions about the Negro ward leaders in that city; they say and do nothing that might earn the disapproval of Democratic Town Committee Chairman Barbieri, raise no issues of racial or economic content, and oppose those white reformers and black activists who do—as on the issue of the black boycott in the spring of 1968.

50. Truman, *op. cit.*, p. 513.

51. See Michael Walzer, "Civil Disobedience and Corporate Authority," in Philip Green and Sanford Levinson (eds.), *Power and the New Polity* (New York: Pantheon, forthcoming).

52. Thus Truman notes that the rules of the game are part of "the substance of prevailing values without which the political system could not exist." *op. cit.*, p. 348; and James D. Barber writes: "To a large degree, a successful democracy depends on agreement as to how the system is to be used, on the rules of the game." *Citizen Politics* (Chicago: Rand McNally, 1969), pp. 93–94.

53. Richard Hatcher, speech delivered to a gathering of the NAACP, reprinted in *The Old Mole*, October 5, 1968 (a newspaper published in Boston). Richard Goodwin's observations are pertinent: "Even the speeches of mayors and governors are filled with exculpatory claims that the problems are too big, that there is not enough power or enough money to cope with them, and our commentators sympathize, readily agreeing that this city or that state is really ungovernable." "Reflections: Sources of the Public Unhappiness," *New Yorker*, January 4, 1969, p. 41.

54. For an extended discussion of this and related questions, see my *Power and the Powerless* (New York: Holt, Rinehart & Winston, forthcoming).

5

NONISSUES IN CITY
POLITICS:
THE CASE OF
AIR POLLUTION • *Matthew A. Crenson*

We all believe that there is more to politics than meets the eye,
but in practice most political research has tended to deal with the
eye-catching phenomena of politics—the observable political
actions, events, issues, and decisions. This is certainly the case
with research that follows the "pluralist alternative" for the investigation of community politics. The pluralists' stated purpose
is to account for decision-making *events,*[1] and they seek to do so
through the analysis of the activity that surrounds "key political
issues."[2] For pluralist investigators, the political universe is the
universe of political action.

Only recently, it seems, have political analysts begun to acknowledge that there is something to be learned from political *in*action
—from *non*events, *non*issues, and *non*decisions. Since Peter Bachrach and Morton Baratz published their article on the "other"
face of power[3] half a dozen years ago, many have pointed out that
the things which a polity leaves undone may be just as important
in determining policy outcomes as the things that it does. And
some have suggested that political systems do not leave things
undone through accidental oversight. Nondecisions may be just
as much a product of the political process as decisions—and a
particularly important product at that.

Through its nondecisions, a political system restricts the range
of topics with which it will deal. It decides not to make decisions

about certain subjects, and in so doing it marks the limits of its political agenda. Nondecisions are therefore important in determining what politics will be about. It oversimplifies the case only slightly to say that the decision-making process is one by which the winners of the political game are determined; non-decision-making helps to determine what the game will be in the first place. And of course, the nature of the game probably has something to do with who wins it. In short, nondecisions may go far toward establishing the basic character of the polity.

They may also help to fix the basic character of much political research. Specifically, the political issues that generate data for pluralist studies of local politics are the ones that have managed to pass through the filtering processes of non-decision-making. The issues and decisions which rise to the surface of local politics are just a sampling which the local political system has drawn from a much larger population of potential issues and potential decisions, and the pluralists have placed themselves at the mercy of this political sampling process. If the sample is biased, then the same bias will be incorporated into pluralist research. The pluralist investigator and the polity that he is investigating both look at the world through the same lens, perhaps one with the very same blind spots and distortions. Matters which are ignored by the political system are ignored by the investigator as well. No attempt is made to account for the seemingly important decisions that are never made, or for the seemingly critical issues that never arise.

It has been suggested that things cannot be otherwise. Nelson Polsby has pointed out that the universe of political nonevents, nonissues, and nondecisions is infinite. For every issue that arises in local politics, there are countless alternative issues which do not arise. And there is no objective way of determining which of these neglected alternatives is politically significant to the community—which ones have been consigned to oblivion by the operation of the political system and which have been overlooked through a political accident or simply because they are unimportant. Until the community itself accords importance to a nonissue by converting it into an issue, the investigator must himself decide which nonissues are worthy of political analysis. His own standards of political importance are his only guides. And, as Polsby has pointed out, research which is guided by these standards runs a serious risk of bias.[4] For example, it is obviously inappropriate for an observer to assert that certain political issues ought to arise, and that when they do not, some hidden non-decision-maker must be responsible for suppressing them. This line of reasoning is almost certain to produce a bizarre view of community politics.

In a recently completed study, I have attempted to use an alternative line of analysis for the examination and explanation of nonissues and nondecisions—one that avoids the pitfalls which Polsby has described. Specifically, I have attempted to explain why many cities and towns have failed to make an issue of their air pollution. The results of that investigation reveal something about the political sources of political inaction and I think that they may also disclose some serious shortcomings in the pluralist view of community politics.

The Power of Non-decision-Making

The study was a comparative one of about fifty American cities ranging in population from 50,000 to 750,000. In a comparative investigation of nonissues, there is no need for an observer to impose his own standards of political importance—his own pet political issues—upon the communities that he is investigating. He need only recognize that standards of political importance vary from one city to another, producing local political agendas of varying composition. His job is to explain those variations in composition. For example, some towns make an issue of air pollution while others do not. It should be possible to identify those community characteristics that are associated with the failure to make an issue of dirty air, and in that way it should also be possible to explain why air pollution remains a nonissue. That is what I have tried to do.

The data for this investigation came from a survey conducted by the National Opinion Research Center late in 1966 and early in 1967. NORC field workers interviewed ten formal leaders in each of the fifty sample cities. The respondents were local mayors, Chamber of Commerce presidents, newspaper editors, political party chairmen, labor council presidents, and the chief executives of several other community agencies and organizations. These respondents supplied most of the necessary information about community political characteristics and about the "issueness" of air pollution in their respective towns.

Briefly, I attempted to determine whether a community had made an issue of air pollution by examining the reported activities of several of the local organizations whose chief executives were included in the local panels of community informants. Issueness was defined in terms of the position-taking activities of these organizations—whether or not they had taken sides on the matter of air pollution. Quite unexpectedly, the indicators of position-taking activity for the various organizations were found to form a Guttman Scale. In other words, there was a regular sequence of activity on the dirty air issue which tended to be repeated when-even the issue arose. First the local newspaper took a stand on dirty air, followed by the Chamber of Commerce, followed by the local labor council, followed by the two political parties. It was possible, then, to estimate the issueness of air pollution in a city by finding out how many of the steps in this sequence had been performed.

The next task was to find out what if any factors might *inhibit* the performance of these steps in the development of the issue. A tentative list of factors was completed after conducting detailed case-studies of air pollution politics in just two cities. This list of items subsequently served as a research agenda in the attempt to determine what it is that makes communities ignore their dirty air.

First on the list of factors was the influence of local industrial corporations. The costs of air pollution control often fall quite heavily upon manufacturing firms. It is not surprising, therefore, that when the dirty air issue does rise to the surface of local politics, industrial corporations are frequently found among the opponents of pollution abatement proposals. That much is evident from observable decision-making activity on the dirty air issue. But these activities do not reveal the part that industry plays in determining whether or not the pollution issue will arise in the first place.

Because the pollution issue threatens to impose costs on manufacturers, industrial influence might be expected to block the emergence of the dirty air debate. If it really is an obstruction to the emergence of the issue, then there should be a negative association between levels of industrial influence in the fifty sample cities and the issueness of air pollution in those cities.

The level of industrial influence was measured in much the same way that Floyd Hunter has attempted to gauge political influence generally—by using the "reputational" technique.[5] There were, however, several departures from Hunter's method, the most important of which was that industry's reputation for power was calculated for specific issue-areas rather than for decision-making in general. What I expected to find, therefore, was a negative association between the issueness of air pollution and industry's *reputation* for power *in the field of air pollution*. And I did find that relationship, but it was quite weak, suggesting that industry's reputation for power does not make any great difference for the life chances of the pollution issue. But a more careful look at the data tells a somewhat different story.

The prominence of the air pollution issue in a city will obviously have something to do with the actual severity of air pollution. In a low pollution city, the dirty air issue may fail to arise even though there is no industrial influence to block its path. Conversely, a heavily polluted city may produce an air pollution issue in spite of industrial influence. Before examining the impact of industrial power reputations upon the growth of the dirty air issue, it is clearly important to take account of actual pollution levels—to control for variations in the dirtiness of air. And in arranging the data, that is what I did.

Industry's reputation for power does operate as a modest deterrent to the development of the pollution issue, but the nature of its deterrent effect seems to depend upon the level of pollution in a city. In towns where the pollution rate is high, industrial influence is brought to bear on the dirty air issue only at a relatively *early* stage in the development of the issue. In low pollution cities, industry's reputation for power has its negative impact during a relatively *late* stage in the development of the issue. There are some intriguing explanations for these results, but they would only lead us astray. The important fact is that perceived industrial influence does tend to stunt the growth of the dirty air debate.

MATTHEW A. CRENSON 149

This finding is probably an obvious one to anyone who bothers to reflect on the political sources of inaction in the pollution field. But few investigators have thought it worthwhile to inquire about the political origins of political inaction. The evidence, then, provides a fairly obvious answer to a not-so-obvious question.

The question has been overlooked, in part, because of a widespread conviction that in American communities, the sources of political inaction are not themselves political. Partisans of the pluralist theory of local politics have argued that no political inhibitions prevent the citizens from converting their private discontents into political issues. "The independence, penetrability, and heterogeneity of the political stratum," writes Robert Dahl, "all but guarantee that any dissatisfied group will find spokesmen in the political stratum. . . ."[6] But the findings indicate that this impenetrability is not all that it has appeared to be. Political penetrability is compromised by the power of non-decision-making, whose operation can prevent some potential issues—like air pollution—from ever rising to political prominence. These nonissues, and the political power that made them nonissues, are hardly likely to figure in the pluralists' studies of "key political issues."

The restrictive operations of perceived industrial influence indicate that political inaction on the pollution issue is not a politically random phenomenon. There is an element of political consistency in the occurrence of non-decision-making. And if non-decision-making is not a politically random phenomenon, then the occurrence of decision-making cannot be politically random either. It follows that any investigation of community affairs which confines itself to the study of decision-making alone—to the examination of political actions, issues, and policies—will have founded its conclusions upon a politically biased sample of phenomena. The methodological canons of pluralism direct us to rely on just such a sample. Its bias is a serious one. Imagine, for example, an investigation of pollution politics whose attention is restricted to those instances in which the dirty air problem has developed into a "key political issue," to use the pluralists' term—occasions on which the matter of pollution has been a potent stimulus to decision-making activity. The survey findings indicate that these situations would tend to be ones in which industry's reputation for power is relatively puny. Where industrial corporations enjoy impressive reputations for power, air pollution tends not to become a key political issue. It follows that evidence gathered in the hypothetical study would provide an unsound basis for inferences about industry's role in the politics of pollution. The findings will tend to understate the level and importance of industrial influence in the field of pollution.

A similar bias may account for the pluralists' contention that local political systems are highly "penetrable." Investigators who, like the pluralists, confine their attentions to those political issues which have risen to the surface of local political systems are likely to exaggerate the openness or penetrability of local political systems. The political issues that they examine, after all, are precisely those which have succeeded in penetrating the boundaries of the polity, and the study of these successful penetrations alone will understandably lead to the conclusion that the boundaries of the political system are easily pierced. It is likely to be asserted, as the pluralists have done, that the political system in question is highly penetrable, and that it is vulnerable to almost any issue that citizens choose to thrust upon it.

But the survey findings suggest something quite different. They indicate that a community's political agenda may be hedged about by concentrations of political influence—like the influence of industrial corporations—which inhibit the introduction of new political issues. Industry's reputation for power renders the political system "impenetrable" with respect to at least one seemingly important issue.

Indirect Influence and Democracy

The reputation for power does not figure in pluralist portrayals of community polities, probably because the pluralists tend to regard power reputations as political phantoms. They have pointed out that the reputation for power stands at one remove from real power, which can be detected only by the direct observation of decision-making activists and their activities.[7] The pluralists' skepticism about power reputations would not necessarily be dispelled by statistical findings which show a relationship between power reputations and real political events—like the relationship between industry's reputation for power and neglect of the air pollution issue. Evidence of this kind does not establish conclusively that the reputation for power is an effective force in politics, capable of shaping political outcomes. It does not show that the reputation for power is real power.

It might be argued, for example, that industry's reputation for power is not really the factor that obstructs the emergence of the air pollution issue. The acts of power which have created that reputation are in fact the things that silence the dirty air debate. The negative association between industry's reputation for power and the issueness of air pollution is spurious—a mere by-product of actions that industry has taken to snuff out the dirty air issue. Industry's power reputation in the pollution field is just a reflection of the influence that industry has exercised through its observable actions in the matter of dirty air.

There is another possibility, however. Industry may enjoy what Robert Dahl has called "indirect influence." Advocates of pollution control may keep silent about the dirty air problem, not because industry has taken action to enforce that silence, but because they anticipate that their efforts on behalf of clean air may induce industry to exercise the power which they believe to be at its command. In other words, they are intimidated by industry's mere reputation for power, even if it has not actually been exercised in this particular case. Industry's influence in this case is of the indirect variety, because there is no direct interaction between the person being influenced and the influential to whom he responds. The political actor who is indirectly influenced anticipates the preferences of those whom he perceives to be powerful, and he acts in accordance with those preferences. He responds to the mere perception of power, not to the direct application of power through political action.

In order to find out whether industry's power of non-decision-making constitutes direct or indirect influence, it is necessary to know two things. First, one must find out whether industry's reputation for power in the pollution field is "justified by behavior" —whether it is a reflection of industrial action in the matter of dirty air. To that end, several of the survey respondents were asked whether they or any other officers of their organizations had ever talked with industrial executives about the air pollution problem. Conversation, after all, is one form of political action—perhaps the most prevalent form—and it is a possible medium for the exercise of direct influence. If industry's reputation for power in the pollution field is a reflection of industrial action, then we can expect to find a positive association between the occurrence of dirty air conversations with industrial executives and the "reputational" measure of industrial influence.

A second piece of statistical evidence is necessary if the "direct influence" argument is to be fully supported. It must be shown that the occurrence of dirty air discussions with industrial executives is *negatively* related to the likelihood that an organization will take a public position on air pollution. This result would signify that industry's actions are responsible for inhibiting the growth of the dirty air debate. Taken together with the evidence that industry's power reputation is a reflection of industrial action, this second link in the direct influence argument would establish that industry's power of non-decision-making does not reside in the mere *reputation* for power, but in the *acts* of power which lie behind that reputation. Mere reputation plays no effective role in determining the fortunes of the dirty air issue. The first piece of evidence would show that this reputation is only the shadow cast by actions, and the second piece of evidence would demonstrate that it is the actions, not the reputation, which enforce the neglect of the air pollution issue.

The findings appear to refute the direct influence argument on both counts. I first compiled measures of association between industry's reputation for power, on the one hand, and its participation in dirty air discussions with various local organizations, on the other. The findings indicate that industry's power reputation in the pollution field is not a reflection of industrial action in that area. In general, industry's participation in dirty air discussions does not enhance its reputation for power. In fact, there are several critical cases in which industrial participation seems to have just the opposite result.[8] It is negatively associated with industry's reputation for power. These findings seem to support the odd conclusion that in towns where industry keeps silent on the matter of dirty air, it tends to enjoy a more impressive reputation for power on pollution matters than in cities where it speaks up.

Similarly, additional findings upset the second prediction of the direct influence argument—that industrial action is what deters the organizational respondents from taking positions on the dirty air issue. If anything, these actions have just the opposite effect: in the case of every organization surveyed, talking to industrial executives about air pollution is positively associated with taking a stand on the issue.

In short, industry's power of non-decision-making in the pollution field seems to be a form of indirect rather than direct influence. It is industry's "unjustified" power reputation that inhibits the emergence of the pollution issue. This means that manufacturing corporations can influence the course of pollution politics even while they remain inactive on the pollution issue. The mere perception of industrial power in the dirty air field, though it be a mirage, is sufficient to discourage would-be promoters of the dirty air debate.

Some questions remain concerning the operation of industry's indirect influence in the pollution field. It is especially puzzling that industry's reputation for power is sometimes *negatively* associated with industrial action, suggesting that a manufacturer may earn a power reputation by political inaction, and not by active participation. In fact, the relationship between action and reputation is probably the reverse of this one: it is not political inaction that earns the reputation, but the reputation that earns the luxury of political inaction. Where industry's reputation for power is sufficiently impressive to obstruct the emergence of the dirty air issue, industry need not take action on the matter. But where industry's power reputation is not so impressive, it must take to the field as a political activist in order to defend its interests. That, very likely, is why a negative relationship sometimes exists between industry's power reputation and industrial action. Where such reputation exists, action is unnecessary.

All of this has certain rather obvious implications for the pluralist view of community politics. The findings suggest, in the first place, that there are some forms of power which do not reveal themselves in the political actions of the power holders. It follows that any political investigator whose attention is confined to observable political actions is likely to overlook these other forms of power and perhaps misrepresent the distribution of power within the political systems that he studies. It is important to take account, not only of the acts of power, but of power reputations as well.

Most representatives of the pluralist approach have staunchly maintained that the mere reputation for power does not constitute real power. And, in a sense, they are right. Such reputation becomes genuine power only when it is capable of producing real political results. But the survey indicates that power reputations do sometimes produce observable political effects. There is nothing necessarily unreal about the reputation for power. A man who affects policy outcomes through his reputation is no less influential than another who achieves equal results by his actions. The only difference between the two is that the active power holder uses direct influence while the reputational power holder enjoys indirect influence.

Some adherents of the pluralist persuasion have acknowledged the existence of indirect influence and even assigned important political functions to it. But paradoxically, indirect influence seems to have no place in the pluralists' empirical research. Pluralist political studies are concerned almost exclusively with the kinds of influence that may be exercised through direct participation in decision-making.[9] What indirect influence adds to this direct influence, according to Robert Dahl, is a measure of democratic control.

In any community, says Dahl, there will be a small minority of citizens who are much more highly involved in the town's political life than is the great bulk of the population. Members of this small "political stratum" naturally exercise much greater direct influence than do ordinary citizens. But these leading political activists do not constitute a cohesive elite. They are a highly fragmented group, and the various fragments compete with one another by vying for the support of the public at large. They must therefore "keep the real or imagined preferences of constituents constantly in mind in deciding what policies to adopt or reject."[10] Thus, though most community residents take no active part in policy decisions, their preferences are nevertheless taken into account when those decisions are made. The citizens enjoy indirect influence, and their possession of it helps to reduce the mismatch in power between the minority who are members of the political stratum and the majority who are not. Indirect influence is more democratically distributed than direct influence.[11]

Especially interesting for our purposes is Dahl's contention that indirect influence enhances the openness or penetrability of local political systems by helping to convert the inarticulate discontents of apolitical citizens into political issues themselves. This job is usually performed by members of the political stratum, who anticipate and respond to the presumed concerns of citizens by translating those worries, aggravations, and aspirations into items for the local political agenda. Indirect influence therefore increases the readiness of local polities to receive and nurture nascent political issues.[12]

What Dahl has neglected to point out is that indirect influence may also have exactly the opposite effect. Influence that is capable of stimulating action within the polity may also operate to prevent action, and though indirect influence may clear the path for some issues, it can raise a barrier for others. That possibility is illustrated by the impact of industry's indirect influence upon the growth of the dirty air issue.

The same illustration also suggests that indirect influence is not merely the mechanism by which the preferences of ordinary citizens are brought to bear upon the conduct of local politics. If indirect influence can work for ordinary citizens, there is no reason why it cannot also work for U.S. Steel, General Motors, bank presidents, or members of social register families. It may just as easily serve the interests of social or economic elites as the interests of the great mass of ordinary citizens. In fact, there is nothing inherently democratic about indirect influence, and no reason to presume that indirect influence is any more democratically distributed than direct influence. The argument that pluralism leads to democracy is founded upon an optimistic assertion about the democratic role of indirect influence, and the survey evidence casts doubt upon this central assertion of pluralist theory.

Indirect Influence and Pluralism

The distribution of political influence within one issue-area is seldom reproduced exactly within others. Though local industry may figure prominently in the pollution field, its power will not necessarily extend to matters of urban renewal or municipal bond referenda or social welfare programs. This variation in the distribution of power from one policy area to the next is a defining trait of a pluralistic political system, and the contention that community political systems tend to exhibit this trait is a defining proposition of the pluralistic persuasion. The pluralists hold that each issue-area within a local polity is likely to constitute an independent political sovereignty, governed by its own group of decision-makers, whose influence is often confined to that issue area. Power, as Nelson Polsby puts it, is tied to issues.[13]

But this pluralistic view concerning the distribution of power is founded upon the observation of political actions alone, and we have already seen that political action is not the only vehicle of political power. It may well be the case that local decision-makers confine their political actions to one or a few issue-areas, but this does not necessarily mean that their political influence is similarly confined. The *indirect* influence of political activists may extend well beyond the issue-areas in which they are observed to be active. Reputations for power established in one field of policy-making may have an important impact on other policy areas. For example, even when industry enjoys no reputation for power in the pollution field, it may affect the course of pollution politics through power reputations that it has established in other issue-areas. Potential supporters of a clean air campaign may refrain from taking action, not because they perceive industry to be powerful in the pollution field, but because they are apprehensive about dealing with industry in other fields where it *does* enjoy a reputation for power. Industry's power reputations in urban renewal or in political party nominations or in matters of municipal taxation may therefore become factors to be reckoned with in the dirty air field. For influence which industry has established in other areas may be transferable to the pollution issue.

To the extent that power reputations are transferable in this way from one issue-area to another, the apparent pluralism of local politics would be diminished. The independence of one policy-making region from another would be reduced, as would the political significance of variations, from one policy area to the next, in the distribution of direct influence.

The survey evidence indicates that, to some extent, transfers of influence from one issue-area to another actually do occur. Industrial power reputations in urban renewal, municipal bond referenda, mayoral elections, and school board appointments were all gauged in exactly the same way that industry's reputation for power in the pollution field was measured. Several of these other measures of perceived industrial influence turned out to be negatively associated with the emergence of the air pollution issue, and these associations were independent of the one observed earlier between industry's power reputation in the dirty air field and the issueness of air pollution. In other words, perceived industrial influence in urban renewal or in municipal bond referenda subtract something from the life chances of the dirty air issue—something more than is subtracted by industry's power reputation in the pollution field alone.

I further found that industrial power reputation in municipal bond referenda and in urban renewal do have a noteworthy negative impact upon the fortunes of the air pollution issue, and this inhibiting effect tends to be most pronounced in cities where air pollution is heavy—perhaps because it is there that the pollution issue threatens to impose the heaviest costs on industry. From other findings, it is also apparent that industrial reputations for power in school board appointments and in mayoral elections have relatively little influence upon the life chances of the dirty air issue. To put it more abstractly, an industrial power reputation seems more readily transferable to pollution politics when it arises in a policy-area that involves the distribution of material resources than in one that involves the selection of governmental personnel.

The fact that power reputations are sometimes transferable from one policy region to another does not refute the pluralist contention that community power tends to be fragmented among issue-areas. It does suggest that the fragments may be somewhat larger than most pluralist research would lead us to believe. A single set of power holders may enjoy indirect influence across a wide range of issues and issue-areas.

Pluralism and the Local Ecology of Issues

The pluralists appear to have overestimated the disjointedness of community political systems. It is not simply that they have overlooked the transferability of power reputations from one issue-area to the next; they have also failed to take account of the extent to which the issues themselves may influence one another. Some of the survey informants, for example, made the plausible-sounding argument that a town can deal with only so many political concerns at one time, and that political issues must therefore compete with one another for a community's attention. They do not rise and subside independently. When one issue gains in prominence, others must lose. The life chances of one issue are bound up with the life chances of others.

This view is sharply inconsistent with the essential themes of pluralist theory—particularly with the notions of "penetrability" and "slack resources." Pluralists would probably argue, for instance, that if a city's political activists are so busy with some issues that they lack the time and energy to deal with others, then additional activists may arise to cope with the neglected issues. A pluralistic political system is supposed to be open to infusions of extra political manpower, and this penetrability, together with the availability of additional political activists, reduces the likelihood that issues will have to compete with one another for attention. In short, the theoretical presuppositions of pluralism do not permit the pluralists to make much of the idea that political issues must vie with one another for positions on local political agendas.[14] In the pluralist view, different issues remain largely independent of one another.

If the pluralist view is an accurate one, then we should find little or no association between the prominence of one issue and the prominence of others. If there is competition among issues, on the other hand, then we should find that the prominence of one issue is negatively associated with the prominence of others. In fact, we find some evidence to support the pluralist view, some to support the "competitive" view, and some that supports neither.

The evidence comes, once again, from interviews with formal community leaders. Eight respondents in each of the fifty sample cities were asked, in an open-ended question at the very beginning of the interview, to name the most important problems that their town had faced since 1960. The answers to these questions were used to construct measures of the prominence of about twenty different kinds of issues (including the air pollution issue) in each of the fifty sample cities.

The intercorrelations among these measures show, among other things, that there are some political issues whose presence within a polity tends to drive away the air pollution issue. The most important of these "inhospitable" issues is business and industrial development. Even when the actual level of local air pollution is held constant, there remains a noteworthy negative association between the salience of the dirty air issue and the salience of business and industrial development ($r = -.37$). The prominence of one issue is connected with the subordination of the other, and the existence of this connection calls into question the pluralist view that different political issues tend not to be dependent on one another. But the relationship is precisely the sort that might be expected if different issues had to compete with one another for attention.

Competition among issues, however, does not appear to be widespread. There are several political agenda items (unemployment, central business district renewal, and public education, for example) whose prominence is unrelated to the prominence of the air pollution issue. Rivalry among issues is not a general phenomenon, but occurs only within certain pairs of issues, and it should not be difficult to understand why the dirty air and economic development issues should constitute one of those competitive pairs. They represent two civic projects which are likely to impose sharply contradictory demands upon a city. Pollution control can be expected to require an increase in the operating costs of local industrial corporations. But efforts at business and industrial development are likely to call for a reduction of those costs so as to make the community a more attractive site for manufacturing firms. A polity that has occupied itself with the task of economic development will therefore tend to be "impenetrable" where the air pollution issue is concerned. A city does not ignore its dirty air simply because it is busy with other things, but because its other concerns are incompatible with the pursuit of clean air.

Only certain kinds of political issues seem to compete with the dirty air problem for the attention of a community; other issues are neither competitors nor allies; and still others exhibit a special affinity for the air pollution issue. Cities that take up the pollution problem, for example, are also quite likely to be concerned about the matter of government organization for metropolitan areas ($r = +.42$), and the association between these two topics seems to be quite reasonable. Atmospheric contamination is seldom a problem that begins and ends within the jurisdiction of a single municipality. It tends to be a regional or a metropolitan area problem, and its solution may require a regional or metropolitan area form of government. Concern about clean air may therefore generate demand for clean air. Having taken up the cause of metropolitan organization, civic activists may search out those problems for which metro-government seems to offer an appropriate solution. Dirty air is one of those congenial problems.

The existence of this affinity between issues is anticipated by neither the "competitive" view, which holds that all issues tend to vie with one another for attention, nor by the pluralist view, which holds that different issues tend to be independent of one another. It appears that there is a need for some third view of the relationships that exist among political agenda items. Only the barest outlines of such an alternative can be presented here.

A community's political agenda does not constitute a random sample of possible political concerns. Though there may be considerable diversity in the collection of issues and issue-areas that a community generates, that collection will nevertheless exhibit some bias, or perhaps a set of biases under which some kinds of issues prosper and other succumb. The pluralism of the political agenda is slanted and inhibited. Once a town has addressed itself to the economic development issue, for example, it reduces the probability that it will subsequently deal with the problem of dirty air. It introduces a bias into the substance of its political deliberations, and restricts the enrichment of its political agenda. It should be noted that this bias is a relatively comprehensive one; it tends to exclude several subjects in addition to the air pollution issue.

There is no clear evidence of the processes through which these biases operate, but some plausible possibilities do come to mind. For example, the mere fact that a community is engaged in efforts to attract heavy industry may discourage would-be political activists from making an issue of dirty air. Anticipating conflict or indifference, the advocates of pollution control may decide to remain politically negative.

The implictaion here is that the kinds of issues which arise within a community may have something to do with the kinds of people who become civic activists and the kinds who do not. The character of a town's civic activists will have something to do in turn with the subsequent composition of the community's political agenda. Political issues may therefore transmit bias to a local political agenda by affecting the character of local political manpower. Issues produce activitists, and the activists subsequently produce other issues.

Conclusions: Does Pluralism Fail Democracy?

It would misrepresent the findings of the present study to refer to them all as conclusions, because they are not really conclusive. The investigation provides some highly probable but not definitive explanations for the fact that some towns have ignored their dirty air. Even if these explanations were absolutely certain, they would not account fully for local neglect of the air pollution issue. Taken together, they do not explain all of the inter-city variation in the prominence of the dirty air issue. Finally, even if it had been possible to offer an exhaustive explanation for the neglect of the air pollution problem, it would certainly not account for political neglect in general. The dirty air issue is not representative of all community political issues. It may be easier to overlook than other matters of public concern, and the factors that promote neglect in the pollution field are undoubtedly different from the factors that consign other policy areas to political oblivion. Granting all of these shortcomings, the findings still have some important general implications for the pluralist view of community politics.

The findings stated in their most elementary form are these: First, community political power may consist of something other than the ability to influence the resolution of political issues. There is also the ability to prevent some topics from ever becoming issues, and to obstruct the growth of emergent issues. Second, this power to enforce political inaction need not be exercised in order to be effective. The mere reputation for power, unsupported by acts of power, is sufficient to restrict the scope of community decision-making. People and groups who do not actively participate in ·a community's political deliberations may nevertheless influence the content of these discussions. Likewise, the "victims" of political power may remain politically invisible. Would-be promoters of the air pollution issue, for example, may never enter the field of political action because that field has already been occupied by promoters of the business and industrial development issue. The operation of political power, therefore, is often not revealed in observable political action and participation. Nor do community political decisions reveal the full range of local policy-making. One must also consider the policy that is made through nondecisions. To put it simply, there is more to politics than meets the eye.

What does meet the eye is the disjointedness of community affairs. Studies of local political activity undertaken by political scientists have disclosed that community decision-making is a highly fragmented process. In fact, it is not a single process at all, but an array of relatively independent processes, each set in motion by a different political issue or set of issues. Different kinds of issues tend to activate different groups of political decision-makers, different kinds of political alignments, and different styles of policy-making. In effect, each issue brings into being its own species of political order and the result is a high degree of disorder.

But the survey findings indicate that the emergence of the issues themselves may be politically regulated or coordinated, and while this does not change the facts of observable political activity, it does alter the impression of disjointedness that those facts convey. The seemingly uncoordinated process of decision-making is in fact channelled and restricted by the process of non-decision-making. Concentrations of political influence can obstruct the emergence of many political issues and so prevent them from stimulating observable political activity. In other instances, the viability of a political issue may be seriously damaged by the issues which have preceded it as subjects of community concern. There are, in short, politically imposed limitations upon the scope of decision-making. The visible political activities of a community are more ordered and inhibited than an inspection of the activities alone would reveal.

None of this endangers the essential empirical results of pluralist research, only the pluralists' interpretation of those results. The discovery of a power to enforce inaction does not invalidate the pluralist finding that local political activists tend to specialize in the affairs of one of a few issue-areas. Nor does it necessarily imply that the American community tends to be governed by a hidden, cohesive elite. Members of the local political stratum may be unanimous in their avoidance of certain political issues, but this does not mean that they are all acting at the direction of a singly political control center or that the neglect of every proscripted issue can be attributed to the same small clique of "non-decision-makers." The perceived influence of local industry, for example, tends to obstruct the career of the air pollution issue, but it may be the power reputation of the local labor council that blocks the emergence of a right-to-work debate or the power reputation of city police administrators that enforces silence on the matter of a civilian review board. The power to enforce inaction may be almost as fragmented as the power to command action. It might be argued, therefore, that the process of non-decision-making simply adds another dimension to political pluralism.

There is no logical flaw in this argument, but it misses the point. The fragmentation of political power is, true enough, the distinguishing trait of a pluralistic political system. But fragmentation is a characteristic whose political significance depends on the contention that it has momentous consequences for the nature of the polity, and the occurrence of non-decision-making calls those consequences into question.

Pluralism, the argument goes, helps to assure that popular sentiment will be brought to bear on a community's decision-makers. Where there is pluralism, there is likely to be competition among political leaders. And, where leaders must compete with one another, they will actively seek the support of constituents. In order to get that support and hold it, leaders will keep popular preferences in mind when they are making policy decisions. The pluralistic organization of the political elite therefore helps to assure that the great bulk of the population will enjoy a substantial amount of indirect influence over public decisions, even though the great bulk of the population seldom participates directly in the making of *any* public decision.

Pluralism, then, acquires much of its importance from its presumed relationship with democracy. But much of the evidence presented here suggests that this relationship may be a tenuous one. First, there is the matter of competition among elites and its contribution to the democratic responsibility of local leaders. Political competition is undeniably important for the maintenance of popular control over political elites, but much depends on just what the competition is about. If popular sovereignty is contingent upon leadership competition, then it will not extend to those matters on which leaders choose not to compete. In other words, the limited democracy that is apparent in the decision-making activities of a pluralistic political system may be limited still further by the occurrence of non-decision-making, which places some potential political issues beyond the reach of both leadership competition and popular sovereignty. Visible political competition in *some* policy areas does not necessarily signify that a community's leadership is *generally* vulnerable to popular sentiment.

A second dubious step in pluralist theory is the assignment of an important democratizing role to indirect influence. The pluralists have acknowledged that direct influence over the formation of public policy is confined to a relatively small group of active participants in local decision-making. But they assert that *indirect* influence is distributed far beyond this small circle of active participants to the politically inactive citizenry. In effect, the pluralists have maintained that the public at large enjoys a reputation for power which is far out of proportion to its observable acts of power. Community leaders respond to this "unjustified" power reputation by incorporating the public's wishes into their policy decisions. By virtue of the competition that exists among political leaders, indirect influence is more democratically distributed than direct influence.

The effect of this argument is to soften the apparent inconsistency between the principle of majority rule and the fact of minority participation in policy-making. But it introduces a disturbing paradox into the pluralist approach to local politics. On the one hand, pluralists urge us to attribute no more power to reputed political elites than we can actually see them exercise. On the other, they maintain that the power of nonelites is really much greater than we can actually see them exercise.

Beyond this methodological inconsistency there lies a more serious problem. How do we know that, in pluralistic polities, indirect influence is more democratically distributed than direct influence? Partisans of the pluralist alternative have never bothered to gather the evidence to support this claim. In order to do so, they would have to depart from pluralist research techniques. It would be necessary to find out something about *reputations* for power, and not just acts of power. In other words, the pluralists would have to make use of a mode of investigation which they have explicitly rejected.

More important still, investigations which *have* employed the reputational technique tend to detract from the plausibility of the pluralist contention. They suggest that reputations for influence may be *less* democratically distributed than actively exercised influence. This finding does not necessarily refute the pluralist claim. It would still be necessary to find out whether these oligarchically distributed power reputations actually affect the making of policy. The survey findings indicate that they do. They show that the perceived influence of political and economic elites can have an important effect upon the level of political activity in the field of air pollution.

There is good reason to doubt that the competition engendered by pluralism really inflates the indirect influence that the ruled have over their rulers. It is just as reasonable, indeed probably more so, to maintain that indirect influence is no more democratically distributed than direct influence. And, as the pluralists themselves have pointed out, direct influence tends to be concentrated in the hands of a minority. Local political systems are seldom dominated by monolithic elites, but they are elitist nevertheless.

Pluralism does not necessarily lead to popular sovereignty. Nor, as we have seen, does it guarantee the openness of political systems. We may celebrate the diversity of the decision-making groups that comprise a town's political stratum, but it should be remembered that this visible diversity tells us nothing about the issues and the groups which have been shut out of a town's political life.

And, for that reason, there may be something fatuous in the celebration. The only sure inference that can be drawn from the visible diversity of a political system is that it is visibly diverse. It need be no more open and tolerant than the private club that proudly admits members of all religious creeds, but excludes Negroes, women, and people with unorthodox political opinions. Diversity need imply nothing more than diversity, and while that may count for something in itself, it does not constitute political democracy.

NOTES

1. Nelson Polsby, *Community Power and Political Theory* (New Haven: Yale University Press, 1963), p. 69.

2. Robert Dahl, "A Critique of the Ruling Elite Model," *American Political Science Review,* 53 (1958): 463–469.

3. Peter Bachrach and Morton Baratz, "The Two Faces of Power," *American Political Science Review,* 56 (1962): 947–952.

4. Polsby, *op. cit.,* 97.

5. See Floyd Hunter, *Community Power Structure* (Garden City, N. Y.: Anchor Books, 1963), pp. 255–263.

6. Robert Dahl, *Who Governs?* (New Haven: Yale University Press, 1961), p. 93.

7. Polsby, *op. cit.,* pp. 50–51.

8. Data were not collected on dirty air conversations between industrial executives and political party officials.

9. See, for example, the description of Dahl's research techniques in *Who Governs?,* pp. 330–331.

10. *Ibid.,* p. 92.

11. *Ibid.,* p. 164.

12. *Ibid.,* pp. 90–92.

13. Polsby, *op. cit.,* p. 115.

14. See Dahl, *Who Governs?,* pp. 191, 271–275.

III

POWER "HERE"
AND
POWER "THERE"

I N no field of political science has the dominant ideology run more rampant than in the study of international politics and foreign policy. It is only recently with the impetus of the antiwar movement that there has emerged a renewed critique of America's counterrevolutionary reflex and one of its major allies, cold war scholarship in the social sciences. The following essays by Edward Friedman, James Petras, and James Weeks are attempts to extend this critique and open new areas for the analysis of American foreign policy. Friedman rejects simplistic notions of imperialism as rationales for America's Asian policy and demonstrates how the Pacific rim strategy has been both a partially rational extension of U.S. power politics in Asia and a partially irrational extension of communist containment. Latin America is the subject of James Petras's essay. In this area, perhaps more than any other, is the analysis of American imperialism essential to an understanding of U.S. policies. Petras expands this analysis, especially in regard to U.S. business interests in Latin America. James Weeks has written a detailed analysis of COMSAT in which he demonstrates the extent of U.S. hegemony abroad.

6

AMERICAN POWER
IN ASIA:
RATIONALIZING THE
IRRATIONAL • *Edward Friedman*

What perspective permits one to comprehend critically American foreign policy in East and Southeast Asia? If it were true that that region of Asia provided markets, resources, and profits necessary for a continuation and consolidation of the power of ruling groups in the United States, then nothing less than an explicit accounting of these real interests and ties might be required. In addition, nothing less than a fundamental change in both power base and social structure in the United States might be needed to change such an integral and imperialist foreign policy. It is the assumption of this essay, however, that vital interests of U.S. ruling groups are so little involved in continental Asia—in contrast perhaps to Canada, Europe, or Latin America—that nothing more than a conservative standpoint is required to comprehend and criticize American policy there. After all, the success of the Chinese revolution may have produced McCarthyite attacks on scholars and Foreign Service officers, but Standard Oil and the like were not shaken by the loss. In fact, indications are that American business would have preferred recognition of and trade with the new China.

The most important social-historical change after World War II was the success of the Chinese revolution. An attempt to understand the nature of international conflict in postwar Asia can fruitfully begin by considering the minimal impact of the Chinese revolution on American interests and policy in Asia. The President of the United States did not want self-proclaimed Communists to succeed in China or elsewhere in Asia. In the bipolar conflict envisioned by American leaders, such Communist successes strengthened the forces of totalitarianism and weakened the forces of freedom. Such successes reduced the areas open to the progressive, liberating, and mutually beneficial influence of American commerce, capital, and culture. The wish to prevent such successes, however, did not automatically create the wherewithal to make the wish father to reality. Preferences are not self-implementing, successful policies.

The Chinese revolutionaries won despite billions in aid, advisers, and equipment to their armed opponents. The United States did not follow up with a massive intervention of American combat troops. In fact, the Truman administration was having a hard enough time persuading powerful fiscal conservatives to finance a military force in Europe to contain possible Moscow-based aggression. Lesser concerns in a turbulent, changing Asia would have to wait till the dust settled.

Secretary of State Acheson, with his usual lucid brilliance, made explicit in January 1950 that America's vital interests to its west would be protected by an island chain tending south from Alaska and the Aleutians, through Japan and the Ryukyus, down out and back by way of the Philippines. This Pacific rim strategy would make the Pacific a secure American lake, a buffer in front of which were semiallies that were semipawns to America's ultimate defense. By 1970 such a strategy, which defines military security in terms of defense against potential U-boats and island hopping marines, seems a bit outdated by technological developments. Indeed long distance bombers, atomic weapons, and resurgent nationalism may have outmoded it two decades ago. It was in some significant part on the basis of this Pacific rim definition of America's vital interests that men such as Walter Lippmann argued against large scale involvement in Vietnam as an overly large risk with little of worth at stake.

Although the Pacific rim strategy was useful in the 1940's to rationalize the expansion of American military, political, and economic power to Japan, the Ryukyus, and the Philippines, it does not justify today the American military commitments to Korea or

Vietnam in particular or continental Asia in general. Conse-quently, the exponents of the expansion of America into con-tinental Asia have almost imperceptibly changed the meanings of the Pacific rim strategy till it has emerged into a new notion that America in Asia has long had and continues to have a vital interest in "preventing one-nation dominance of Asia," as Kenneth Young, one-time negotiator with China, Ambassador to Thailand, and President of the Asia Foundation, put it.

The view is not merely Mr. Young's. It has been maintained and propounded by a number of men connected formally with foreign policy decision-making from academic advisers to high level diplomats. Perhaps the fullest statement of the argument is Bernard Gordon's *Toward Disengagement.*[1] He argues in a book written during time off from the Army's Research Analysis Corporation that "the United States was compelled to undertake war" against Japan in 1941 to prevent Japan from achieving dominance of East Asia.[2] Gordon undertakes an historical exercise to show that if America in the 1960's was trying to prevent the spread of Chinese influence to Southeast Asia and was willing to fight in Vietnam for that major goal, such an effort is consonant with half a century of American policy in Asia. China has merely replaced Japan as the power to be balanced. Unfortunately, Gordon relies on a selec-tion of works published in the 1930's and 1940's to establish the facts of that time. He ignores the research of the 1960's which has had available to it the archives of the 1930's and the 1940's. The research of Akira Iriye and others seems to have established, con-trary to the views of Gordon, Charles Wolf (RAND), Morton Halperin (Pentagon), Fred Greene (Council on Foreign Rela-tions), et al., that America did not go to war with Japan to pre-vent Japanese dominance of East Asia but rather that, as the head of the Harvard East Asian Center, John Fairbank, told the Ameri-can Historical Association in 1970, until 1941 "the American national interest had never been felt to be vitally in question nor fully committed to the East Asian scene." Invasion of Singapore and perhaps even the Philippines could have passed without an American declaration of war. It was, after all, Japan in alliance with Germany which attacked America. And then Washington chose to respond with a major effort in Europe. Prewar and post-war American political leaders decided that, based on limited resources, America would act on prior European interests. The Pacific rim strategy, while actually rationalizing a new American expansion into Asia, was experienced as a defense line, a holding position while the major struggle went on in Europe.

American policy began to change fundamentally with the Korean War. Gordon has hardly a word to say about the Korean War of 1950–1953. A. Doak Barnett, now of the Brookings Institution and formerly of the Political Science Department and the China Center at Columbia University, called that war, in a book written for the Council on Foreign Relations, "a major turning point."[3] Barnett is right. I will continue to use Barnett's account of pre-1961 years because it is far and away the most lucid and comprehensive argument for America's cold war against China in the 1950's.) The war, America's swift military intervention in Korea, and China's belated response to the American advance, made real for fiscal conservatives "the military dimension of the Communist threat."[4] The National Security Council would get its defense funds—for Europe. Comparatively, little more than the crumbs went into expanded "efforts to build up an anti-Communist defense system in the Far East."[5] Even in America's first major war on the continent of Asia, Europe came first. A growing tendency today to explain America's war in Korea as a defense of Japan and the East Asian balance has no basis in fact. In fact, General MacArthur worried that depleting Japan of American troops by sending them to Korea would pave the way for a Russian occupation from the north.

America's post-Korean war policies in Asia can best be understood in a framework of American domestic politics and the power realities of postwar Asia. Already in 1948 the Truman administration had to justify its new policy of using Japan as a base in opposition to Russian Communist imperialism as a means of saving the taxpayer's money. This does not mean that the fiscal rationale was all fig leaf. The conservatives are strongly rooted in the American power structure. Their demands must continually be met by the liberals if the liberals are to pursue their own aims. But once the conservatives win, it becomes the all-American way. In order to quiet opposition to his expensive military policies, Truman on June 27, 1950 met the demands of the conservative, pro-Chiang Kai-shek, China lobby and announced that the American Seventh Fleet would prevent Chinese soldiers from moving on to Formosa, uniting China, and ending the Chinese civil war. For twenty years no American president has been able to back off significantly from this American intervention in China's civil war despite its irrelevance to any significant strategy or security policy of the United States. When John Kennedy in his presidential campaign suggested an end to the provocative military occupation of China's tiny, neighboring offshore islands, the conservatives condemned his alleged sellout of Chiang Kai-shek and forced Kennedy to abandon his proposal. It is largely because liberals have had a prior European orientation that they have so readily given in to the demands of conservatives on Asian matters.

But there is more in America's domestic politics. The experience of Munich and not standing up to Nazi Germany taught the subsequent generation of leaders that aggression must be stopped at the start because aggression feeds on aggression. From Truman to Nixon, limited American wars are experienced as means to prevent larger world wars. As former Ambassador Reischauer put it, "we have a containment policy against aggression throughout the world."[6] After the "loss" of China, the coup in Czechoslovakia, the Russian military occupation of East Europe, Manchuria, and north Korea, an American administration would feel it had to stand up to Communist aggression or become vulnerable in conscience and politics. Korea—or Vietnam—could not, whatever the facts, be experienced as a local, civil war.

Once America intervened in Asia, it brought to bear the power to determine decisively Asian events. The European powers had been weakened by World War II. Japan's takeover of much of East and Southeast Asia had destroyed Europe's legitimate power among Asia's colonial elites. In the wake of the retreat of European colonialism, new nationalist forces seemed to emerge throughout the region. The Chinese leaders hoped these Asian nationalists would join with China on the basis of a common desire to prevent a renewal of foreign incursions in Asia and to promote independent and flourishing economies. American leaders worried that such allegedly racist (antiforeign means antiwhite) and naive (cooperation with Communism means openness to subversion as in Czechoslovakia in 1948) linkages would win Asia for the expanding Communist bloc. China's hopes would not be fulfilled. American fears would prove unfounded.

The nationalist Asian leaders found, by and large, that their own interest lay in development which did not overly disturb the existing cultural and economic institutions. That was the base of support of these leaders. Despite contradictions within these dominant structures, the elites saw little future in the kind of fundamental confrontation with the old order undertaken by the revolution in China. But development that did not overly disturb the status quo required capital from sources other than the established forces. China did not have excess capital to offer. America did. China could try this way or that way to meet the demands of other Asian leaders on policy toward immigrant Chinese living for generations in neighboring lands. China could try to reassure these leaders by making concessions on disputed borders. It all made little difference. China was weak and poor. It had little to offer that these leaders wanted. And the few leaders friendly toward China, neutralism, anticolonialism, and fundamental social reform seldom lasted long.

Even in the mid-1950's Washington readily outbid and undercut Peking. A military coup in Thailand turned that country away from a neutralism which China had welcomed, turned it into the American camp. The tiny Thai trade with China ended. Aid from America grew tremendously. In Laos the coup had to be pushed a bit harder by the CIA. It won temporarily and upset a neutral government. The new government subsisted on American largesse. In Indonesia the CIA-sponsored coup based in Formosa and the Philippines failed. With America as a political opponent, Sukarno welcomed Chinese overtures and drew closer to the Chinese on their joint need to survive a hostile and active American threat. The Tanzanian experience more recently repeats these developments. When political developments in Tanzania were opposed by the United States, the World Bank, British, and German financiers swiftly cut back on financial help. China then had an opportunity to strengthen political ties with Tanzania through economic aid.

In general, China's Asian friends arose from political necessity. China does not have the trade, ships, capital, or industry to significantly underwrite major foreign economies as America can. So India became a friend of China in the 1950's when New Delhi needed an ally against a Pakistan backed by the United States. Similarly, Pakistan turned to China in the 1960's when a hostile

India allied with the U.S.A. and U.S.S.R. needed a bit of balancing. Nepal uses China as a counterweight to expand its independence of India. And Cambodia can use China as a counterweight to maintain its territorial integrity and national sovereignty against American-backed Thailand and South Vietnam. And, of course, in North Korea and North Vietnam a greater and lesser commitment of Chinese military power has helped these socialist governments maintain their independence against expansive American military might. In short, around her immediate periphery China can help governments made popular by opposition to a palpable foreign threat maintain a greater semblance of self-rule. She can, however, do little else.

In the middle and late 1950's American expenditures against China were relatively small. Nonetheless the threat seemed large to China as missiles carrying nuclear weapons were set up in Korea, the Ryukyus, and Formosa. The massive retaliation policy of the Dulles-Radford era was premised on this philosophy of maximum explosive power for the smallest possible expenditure. In the Eisenhower years fiscal conservatives like the Secretary of the Treasury, Chairman of the House Armed Services Committee, and other major figures kept increases in military spending at a steady, low level. Dulles's diplomatic tours and numerous treaties did not raise the power potential of America in Asia. Motion in a relative vacuum stirs up only a minimum of friction. The requests of Rockefeller-Kennedy-style liberals for huge spending increments to significantly increase America's military capability for everything from missiles to transport were brushed aside. Still, in the vulnerable, unstable border areas of Asia the CIA could do much mischief on the cheap. Arms were flown to rebellious tribesmen fighting against the Chinese in Tibet. Chiang Kai-shek's troops, who had retreated into Burma and then Thailand, were kept supplied and continued their feints toward southwest China. Valley forces of the Laotian elite were fully aided in their civil war against neutralist and popular hill forces in Laos. Attempts at insurrection continued in Cambodia.

The intellectual justifications for these policies contained a large built-in element of overkill. Liberals moved by the alleged lesson of Munich and by fear of seeming soft on Communism (only a hard line against Communism abroad permitted advocacy of pseudosocialist measures at home against the "pinko" charges of entrenched conservatism) had rationalized—this word is not intended to question the sincerity of the advocacy but only to point up its lack of priority—American interests in Asia such that Eisenhower's activities there hardly seemed sufficient. First, men such as Walt Rostow believed that in 1948 a "new policy" was adopted by "the world Communist movement" which launched insurrections in Asia.[7] Although there is precious little evidence of such a policy, let alone such a movement,[8] this theory justifies large American intervention in Asia as a defensive reaction to a major foreign threat. Second, the success of the Chinese revolution and Chinese aid to the war against France in Vietnam seemed to indicate that China would be aiding insurrections in Asia. China, then, would have to be stopped. Third, the war in Korea was cited as proof that Communism was entering a new aggressive stage. Soon Chinese intervention in Korea made it seem that China was a major aggressive threat in the new expansionist policy. No evidence was needed to assert that "the Chinese Communists were called up by the Russians to intervene militarily in Korea."[9] Evidence that fit into these theories, such as rebellious Chinese migrants in the Malay peninsula, was accepted without question. Few people could gain a hearing for the unpopular notion that Korea was a civil war in which Moscow's champion jousted with America's champion; that Peking intervened defensively against an out-of-control American army headed for China's borders; that Peking was trying to keep overseas Chinese out of the domestic politics of their respective countries so that Peking could establish good state-to-state relations; that Peking would not support revolutionaries (the White Flags) when the local government pursued a policy of genuine neutrality as did Burma. China's working for independent buffers on her Asian borders at Geneva in 1954 and elsewhere was seldom contrasted with Russia's desire for imperial hegemony around her borders. Instead, a technologically deterministic view grew in which China was seen as "a 'have-not' nation" "in a relatively early stage of development" which consequently tended to be more "unsatisfied" and more willing to take "risks" than the U.S.S.R. Therefore America should "encourage the Russians to exert a restraining influence on the Chinese."[10]

Actually in Berlin, Cuba, and the Middle East, Moscow each time risked more than China ever did in all its foreign policy. The result of these confrontations between America and Russia was a stalemate. Neither side could defeat the other. It was preferable to probe, prod, and then join to negotiate settlements where major interests were at stake. Mutual respect based on mutual fear created cooperation premised on conflict. The large element of conflict made both sides acutely conscious of the tenuous nature of the cooperation. The significant resultant cooperation made China acutely conscious that it was now to be pressured on issues ranging from India's territorial claims and the civil war in Laos to nuclear weapons policy and the status of Formosa by America *cum* Russia.

Detente with Russia permitted Kennedy and then Johnson to concentrate more time and energy on Asian matters. Great jumps in military spending provided the wherewithal to expand America's power in Asia and implement policies closer to the long standing rationales which saw Southeast Asia as a major battleground to be saved from China and preserved for Japan (or India, or America). Kennedy had to reject large-scale American military involvement in Laos in 1961 because he lacked the hardware to carry through a major conventional intervention. By 1965, operating on new resources which permitted spending for two and one-half wars, one in Asia, Johnson had the wherewithal to send hundreds of thousands of American soldiers to Vietnam.

Throughout the 1960's, China's conventional military forces weakened and her potential for intervention to her south, miniscule to begin with, diminished further. China's nuclear capacity, however, increased. Given the already terrifying vision of a Chinese threat in the minds of many American policy-makers, a number of top level people began to push for a showdown with China sooner rather than later. In 1962 such people in league with right-wing leaders in Formosa, Laos, Thailand, and northern India presented China with the threat of a multi-pronged offensive. Kennedy, however, momentarily restrained these pressures from within the American bureaucracies and its foreign friends. Kennedy reassured China on an offensive from the Formosa area and checked Chiang Kai-shek. Averell Harriman booted the CIA chief out of Laos; America gave new assurances to Thailand; and a neutral Laos was negotiated with China and Russia. The American government helped talk the Indian government out of bomber strikes against China.

Kennedy still went on to weigh seriously the possibility of a strike against China's fast progressing nuclear development. Such a strike still seemed too dangerous to Dean Rusk in 1964. It raised the specter of Russia coming to China's aid. The liberals, however, had the resources now to press a new forward strategy all along China's periphery. American pressure, at a time of economic and political crisis in South Korea, forced a settlement between Korea and Japan. Russia protested hardly at all. Russia, too, moved toward friendlier relations with Japan. For the first time since 1905 Russia emerged as a major Asian power. China found its north increasingly vulnerable to hostile powers potentially working in concert just as America escalated the wars in Laos and Vietnam.

Although it is difficult to see how China needed to be further contained or balanced, new rationales were added to the old to help justify the new American expansion. Some saw an international civil war in progress. If the revolutionaries could be turned back now in Laos and Vietnam, peace would reign for generations. Some saw a militant Asian communism with headquarters in Peking. The response to such militancy in Asia by America would win victory for more peaceful and evolutionary Russian types and thus again assure an Augustan era of peace. Some saw the war as assuring that a vital area would be integrated into the economies of the free world, thus permitting a greater likelihood of evolutionary development that would obviate the need for revolutions. The rationales were many (e.g., communists were romantics or luddites who did not understand modernization; Asian militarists were pragmatists who understood modernization). The reality was singular. America had the power to expand in Asia. China lacked the power to do much about it.

There was great ideological overlap between conservatives and liberals in the American bureaucracies. But the initiative lay with the right wing. They proposed forward policies. The liberals met them part way. The liberals saw themselves as moderates, even doves, not because their policies were not militaristic but because they were less aggressive than the right. After all, a forward containment of China was mild compared to bombing China im-

mediately. The tragedy which was to play itself out in Vietnam
had already been staged in the main in Korea.

The military on the scene helped create the extensive commitment. While flying to Korea, General MacArthur, without
orders, dispatched B-29s to bomb North Korea. While flying out
of Vietnam, Admiral Sharp, without orders, dispatched an aircraft carrier to the Gulf of Tonkin and helped create the Tonkin
Gulf incident. Is there a folklore in the military of how to get
away with military initiatives without being checked by the
president?

Once the initial large-scale commitment is made and new de-
fenses contract expectations grow, it is difficult to readily de-escalate
because softness on communism and disregard for the cause of the
martyred dead will have bad political and economic repercussions.
The President feels that to back off will make him vulnerable to
charges which may help win the next election for the opposition.
The military on the scene find career and conscience united as
they too press for a "win" policy against the alleged source of
aggression. Working at one with the local right-wing despot (Rhee,
Diem, et al.), they can in significant measure control the information sent to Washington and the interpretation of orders coming
from there. Thus, extreme right-wing forces on the scene often
structure both the making and implementing of decisions. In addition, these men will have powerful friends and spokesmen in the
press, the Congress, and the Executive. The President's choices are
narrowed. His ability to control the war is constrained. What
finally offers the President an opportunity to act on the basis of
limited objectives is defeat of the American army in the field and
of its local allies by the enemy. Thus it was successful Chinese
intervention in Korea and the threat of such in Vietnam, and
eventually the Tet offensive, which permitted the President to
remove MacArthur, Van Fleet, Westmoreland, and not give in
totally to the aggressive military designs of Rhee or Ky. The
enemy's brave dead, by raising the cost of the war, decrease the
likelihood of a cheap American victory, and make it necessary to
call on further sources of American power, thus increasing the
possibility of checking the expansive American power from within
the American political system.

The works of political science on such matters are seldom of much use. They tend to assume first and foremost a real enemy out there and real American foreign policy initiatives contrived by the President to deal with that enemy. They seldom study the possibility that the initiative lies within America's explosive political dynamics. The actual politics of the struggle as, say, the Air Force necessarily arguing for planes and bombs as a solution and the local ally pressing for ever more American money and support are strangely muted in the overall story. Because political scientists tend to minimize the political (not merely bureaucratic) guts of American foreign policy decision-making, their writings do not make for much of a science. Because they are so much a part of the ideology that makes for the expansive commitments, political scientists spend more effort rationalizing American policy than critically trying to comprehend its sources.

This is not to say there is no truth in the rationalizations. There is some truth, but not the established one, in the idea that America in the 1950's and 1960's was treating China a bit as it had the Soviet Union in the 1940's and 1950's. Given what we now know about Russian policies in those years, one can wonder whether similar American actions foster or hamper conciliation. As Brigadier General, U.S. Marine Corps, retired, Samuel Griffith told Senator Fulbright on March 18, 1966,

We are doing the same thing now in respect to the Chinese that we did with respect to the Soviets in 1949, 1950 and 1951. I remember in those years it was fashionable to give the Soviets all sorts of capabilities which they couldn't conceivably have practiced. We were giving them the capability to overrun Iran and the capability to intervene in Turkey. We were over-reacting. We are doing the same thing now, I think, Senator, in respect to the Chinese.[11]

And if one is interested in analogues and symmetries between postwar Europe and Asia, then perhaps one must seriously consider the view of Gregory Clark, formerly a specialist in Chinese affairs for Australia's Department of External Affairs. Clark sees America's role in Asia in the 1960's as similar to that of Russia's in East Europe. As the Russians, whatever progress they brought, suppressed European nationalisms and liberalization in the interest of finding men who are primarily safe and subservient, so the United States opposes popular leaders of nationalism and social reform in Asia. Men such as Lee Kuan Yew as late as 1959, Sou-

vana Phouma as late as 1962, Sihanouk as late as 1967, and
Ho Chi Minh till his death in 1969 survived despite western opposition. Independence and liberation in both areas mean first and
foremost a removal of the hegemonic dominance of the particular
superpower. China has had little to do with precluding or promoting these popular nationalist movements in Asia, even in
Vietnam.

It is clear now that the Vietnamese did not need to be encouraged by the Chinese, that Hanoi rejected Lin Piao's advice, that
Peking refused to cooperate fully in a joint Asian-Russian Communist effort on behalf of Hanoi and the NLF. For Mao, China's
internal revolutionary development came first. That meant positive
economic ties with big capitalists in Japan, Australia, Canada,
France, Britain, and Germany to assure China of the industrial
goods she needed. It made concessions to Russia impossible since
it was the Russian specter that haunted Mao domestically. Indeed
it made the growing Russian threat from the north appear at least
as, if not more, worrisome than the American threat from the
south.

But the significant lack of congruence between the facts and the
various rationales for American anti-Chinese escalation in Southeast Asia is largely besides the point. All the men of influence in
the administration called for increased intervention. There was no
fundamental dissent. The power resources were there; America
acted. Some said bomb Hanoi. Others feared that bombing Saigon
would prove more useful. But who argued for letting the solution
of Vietnamese arms and interests stand?

Our political scientists and political intellectuals will invent new
rationales for present policies and future interventions. We need
not overly concern ourselves with these arguments here. What
matters for the powers that be in America is far less reason than
power. And economic and political power is undermined by the
massive waste of America's war in Vietnam and the monumental
struggle of the National Liberation Front. This occurs at a time
when new, large expenditures are needed to deal with or buy off
pressing problems and interests at home. America is back in the
1950's in Asia. It cannot do all its ideology justifies.

Why as 1970 began was President Nixon suddenly open to
better relations with China? (Which is not to say he has changed

on Vietnam, Laos, or Thailand.) Certainly no one suggested that Mao Tse-tung and his so-called romantic revolutionaries were out of power. The falseness of the prior anti-Chinese rationales as genuine explanations of American actions is made manifest by the American policy change. One might hope, if one were the hoping type, that such exposure might lead various political scientists and political intellectuals to wonder what interests they actually were serving.

This essay has not had much to say about economic interests or imperialism. I could be persuaded of a large measure of validity with regard to such economic arguments where America's Asian insular interests—Japan, Formosa, the Philippines, Australia— were concerned. To be sure, such interests have been involved in continental Asia, too. Nonetheless, America's commitments in continental Asia grew because of the actions not of these economic interests but of bureaucrats in the CIA and the military in conjunction with foreign tyrants. It is probably true that these military, para-military, and civilian officials, imbued with a very capitalistic ideology and a bit worried about the semisocialist nature of their government perquisites, were probably more Rockefeller-ist than Rockefeller and invented rationales to woo such economic interests to their actions. Nonetheless their actions did not even serve enlightened American imperialism. Serious inflation, a huge gold drain, a balance of payments crisis, a decrease in the competitive standing of American business abroad all stem in large measure from their actions. Thus American expansion into continental Asia has almost singularly served the parochial and petty career interests of bureaucrats abroad and of foreign despots.

It is even doubtful if American expansion into Asia has served, except by inadvertence, the cause of national independence there. American economic, military, and cultural penetration frequently suffocates local nationalisms. As we have seen, a number of these countries had to turn to China to protect and promote their independence. Without suggesting that the Chinese are invariably on the side of maximizing the independence of Southeast Asian countries—the popular government of Singapore, for one, would doubt it—such independence outside the context of great power conflict seems a worthwhile goal. As the U.S.A. continues to have conflicts with the U.S.S.R. in the Middle East and elsewhere, as the Soviet

Pacific fleet grows, as Japan seems destined to become the dominant economic power in Asia, as China is preoccupied with domestic development and a threat from the north, all sorts of new possibilities seem to have opened up.

If one wanted, it should be possible to negotiate a large-scale neutralization in Southeast Asia. Vietnam could be united and removed from international, great power military conflict. Korea could be made a united, neutral buffer. But would Japan permit? Such policies, which could foster independence, peace, and a commitment of resources to social progress, are possible. But if one looks into the works of political scientists concerned with this area for some general theory about how to achieve such goals, one will largely look in vain. Political science is not interested. Political science by its own choice of subject matter and values to be served defines this disinterest. To list the senior men at the major prestigious universities in political science concerned with development in East and Southeast Asia is, with too few exceptions, to define the parameters of the irrelevant rationales of the American war in Vietnam.

NOTES

1. Bernard Gordon, *Toward Disengagement* (Englewood Cliffs, N. J.: Prentice-Hall, 1969).

2. *Ibid.,* p. 13.

3. A. Doak Barnett, *Communist China and Asia* (New York: Vintage, 1961), p. 92.

4. *Ibid.,* p. 93.

5. *Ibid.*

6. Edwin Reischauer, *Beyond Vietnam* (New York: Vintage, 1967), p. 164.

7. Walt Rostow, quoted in Barnett, *op. cit.,* pp. 90, 152.

8. Cf. John Gittings, "The Great Asian Conspiracy," in E. Friedman and M. Selden, *America's Asia* (New York: Pantheon, forthcoming).

9. Barnett, *op. cit.,* p. 288.

10. *Ibid.,* p. 383.

11. U.S., Congress, Senate, Committee on Foreign Relations, 89th Cong., 2d sess., March 18, 1966.

7

PATTERNS OF INTERVENTION: U.S. FOREIGN POLICY AND BUSINESS IN LATIN AMERICA • *James Petras*

This essay will analyze the changing patterns of U.S. intervention in Latin America and present a case study of one such pattern: indirect rule by U.S. business. Intervention can be defined as the deliberate use by one nation of military, political, or economic force to secure the action it desires in the target nation.

Policies of one nation which affect another by virtue of the complexity of interdependent relations are not included. Dependent nations, of course, are by nature more vulnerable to external changes (whether they are inadvertent or not) than more autonomous nations. The vulnerability of the Latin American nations based on their external dependence makes them more susceptible to intervention by the United States. An important factor which makes Latin American nations susceptible to North American intervention is the existence of linkage groups (American investors, Latin military officials trained in the United States, etc.) which reside or carry on business in Latin America but owe allegiance to or depend on the United States for support.

U.S. intervention has taken many forms. It may take, as in Vietnam, the form of a movement of massive military forces to an-

Portions of this essay are reprinted from James Petras "United States Business and American Foreign Policy in Latin America," *New Politics*, 4, No. 4 (1967) with the permission of *New Politics*.

other country, thereby establishing a client-state likely to accept Washington's international policies. U.S. intervention may also take the form of a threat to withhold loans or credits, or the manipulation of import quotas of one-crop-exporting countries in order to change a policy of a government on a specific issue, or promote U.S. investor interests.[1]

While it is only since World War II that U.S. foreign policy-makers actively pursued a policy of manipulating governments in Asia and Africa to fit with their global views, this is not the case with Latin America. For at least half a century Latin America has been recognized as largely in the United States' "sphere of influence."[2] This has meant that in matters of trade, economic development, and foreign relations U.S. policy-makers have played a predominant role. Beginning as early as the middle of the nineteenth century, the U.S. government has actively promoted an interventionist policy with a variety of policy goals. In the Mexican province of Texas and later throughout ·the southwest and far west, U.S. colonists settled and soon became the advance guard of annexationist movements. Before the turn of the century, armed U.S. military forces occupied Cuba and Puerto Rico and threatened to become involved elsewhere.

In the twentieth century, however, a substantial shift in U.S. policy occurred—control over the economy and the establishment of legal restrictions on the sovereignty of a Latin nation (rather than outright annexation) were considered adequate adjustments from the point of view of U.S. policy-makers. Annexation was replaced by indirect rule—the establishment of semicolonies. Military interventionist policy was largely directed to the countries bordering the Caribbean: Mexico, Nicaragua, Colombia, the artificial creation of Panama for purposes of the canal, Dominican Republic, Haiti, etc. The necessity of repeated military interventions indicated the precarious nature of the regimes installed by previous interventions—their lack of firm popular support—and the lack of expertise of U.S. policy-makers in creating efficient administrative machinery to effectively control and repress popular movements.

Beginning in the early 1930's this situation began to change. The Somoza, Trujillo, and to a lesser extent Batista regimes—outgrowths of U.S. military or diplomatic intervention—were able to capitalize on the assistance of U.S. advisory missions and created effective mechanisms for control; dictatorial rule over their populations in one case lasted thirty years and in the other continues to this day.

Beginning in the 1930's a new pattern of intervention began to appear, to a certain degree based on the success of the previous types. In the nineteenth century through successful territorial annexationist intervention the United States came into possession of large areas of Mexican territory. The social and economic cost of annexation was relatively cheap. The benefits were high: the annexed territory provided excellent mineral resources (gold and oil), cattle and farm land, etc.—more than sufficient in terms of the availability of entrepreneurs able to exploit the new conquest. The military interventions were also successful—only partially so in the case of the Mexican revolution—in establishing governments whose policies allowed U.S. investors liberal terms and who followed U.S. policy in the international arena. By the 1930's when favorable boundaries and governments were established, the policy of intervention was modified toward stabilizing the status quo (existing regimes) and consolidating gains (excluding external competition). The Good Neighbor Policy befriended governments in the Caribbean which were largely creatures of U.S. policy, whose economies were shaped to U.S. needs, and whose governments were preoccupied with staying in power.

The worldwide crises during the 1930's also deeply affected the interventionist capacity of the United States. The ability of the U.S. government to intervene has not been always and everywhere the same. Despite the fact that Washington strongly opposed the Mexican government's expropriation of North American oil interests, the strong popular backing of the Cardenas government, the United States' overriding preoccupation with the impending global confrontations in Europe and Asia, and the existence of an organized opposition to military intervention within the United States made an interventionist policy unfeasible. On the other hand, in the case of Cuba, during the social revolution of 1933, the United States through its nonrecognition of the reformist Grau government and support for Batista managed to preserve the status quo and U.S. economic and political hegemony. Manipulation of political-economic and diplomatic measures and the threat, rather than the actual use, of overt military force to maintain hegemony, became the policy which the U.S. government followed in the period during and immediately after World War II. The overwhelming economic and military power of the United States forestalled any major crises. Latin governments anticipating U.S. reactions failed in most cases to vigorously pursue nationalist policies. In summary, up till the early 1950's the pattern of U.S. interventionist policy can be understood as the result of cumulative favorable outcomes in which successful military intervention and annexation prepared the groundwork for more flexible strategies: politico-economic mechanisms of control and the manipulation of elites.

After the 1954 U.S.-directed military coup in Guatemala, the United States began to rely on a multiplicity of policy instruments in intervening. Beginning with diplomatic and economic pressures—a resolution at the Tenth Inter-American Conference at Caracas in 1954,[3] the cutting off of economic assistance, etc.—U.S. officials proceeded to organize a military force composed largely of Guatemalans to realize U.S. policy ends. The policy of indirect military intervention was a modification of the earlier approach of direct U.S. military occupation and U.S. economic and diplomatic pressure. Indirect military intervention was successful in realizing U.S. political and economic goals, defending U.S. investors' property holdings, and installing a government which supported U.S. international policy. The U.S. government's organization and direction of the Cuban exile invasion of 1961 was a policy similar to that which engineered the 1954 Guatemala coup—indirect military intervention to restore U.S. property interests and a government willing to follow U.S. international policy. The success of this type of intervention in one country encouraged the U.S. government to attempt to alter another government by similar means. But the Cuban government's ability to defeat the invaders challenged the conception that U.S. policy-makers had of the adequate basis for successful intervention.

While U.S. policy-makers continued to operate through indigenous elites to maintain a favorable politico-economic status quo in other Latin countries, they realized that certain innovations in interventionist strategy were in order. On the general ideological level, President Johnson presented the doctrine that civil wars were now international. This was a post hoc rationalization for unilateral U.S. intervention in the Dominican Republic and laid the basis for possible future unilateral U.S. military intervention in other areas of Latin America. The impotence of Latin and North American political opposition to the brutal U.S. occupation of the Dominican Republic accelerated the process of institutionalizing U.S. hegemony in the hemisphere.

More recently further innovations in U.S. interventionist approaches have been suggested. There is, for example, the growing importance that U.S. policy-makers are giving to the idea of a continental police force, capable of intervening in any country where the status quo is endangered—euphemistically called an Inter-American Peace Force.

A key event which appears to have greatly influenced U.S. policy toward a more aggressive militaristic type of intervention occurred during the presidency of John F. Kennedy. The U.S. military blockade of Cuba, backed up by the explicit threat of nuclear warfare on a global scale, was successful intervention (at least in the short run): it allowed the United States to intervene in Cuban political life to the extent of vetoing the type of military resources which the Cubans were allowed to acquire from the Russians for defense purposes. More significant in the larger perspective, this successful intervention through a show of massive military effort and the ability to cause the U.S.S.R. to withdraw its support encouraged U.S. policy-makers to follow this approach in future instances where situations were to be defined as critical.

The direct military intervention in the Dominican Republic followed the failure of the client military junta and its subsequent defenders to stem the popular revolution even with U.S. military aid (indirect military intervention). Across the globe in Vietnam a similar pattern could be observed: the gradual shift from indirect military intervention (aiding a client government) to direct military intervention on a massive scale. An intervention multiplier had set in. Successful intervention of one type in one area was replicated elsewhere.

While we can observe a pattern in the sequence regarding type of intervention, this should not be interpreted in an overly schematic way. There is a continuity of types of intervention from one period to another, and in some cases the types of intervention alternate depending on the particular political developments. Nevertheless we can view several types of interventionist policies operating at different periods and in different political contexts.

If we were to range the types of U.S. intervention on a spectrum of "overtness" we might describe the following cases in the last fifteen years in this fashion:

TABLE 7-1

TYPE OF INTERVENTION	COUNTRY
Direct military intervention	Cuba 1962 Dominican Republic 1965
Indirect military intervention	Guatemala 1954 Cuban invasion 1961
Direct economic intervention	Cuba 1960 Dominican Republic 1961
Economic manipulation (loans, credits, debt payments, grants, utilized as policy instruments)	Throughout Latin America
Political and diplomatic manipulation (training and indoctrination of military personnel, recognition of governments, etc.)	Throughout Latin America

In evaluating the consequences of intervention, we must distinguish between the "benefits" as perceived by U.S. policy-makers and economic interests and the benefits accruing to the nations themselves. More often than not U.S. policy-makers merely utilize the democratic liturgy as rationalizations for interventionist policies which provide few if any benefits for the intervened nation. A major preoccupation of U.S. policy-makers who rely on interventionist techniques is insuring that Latin governments support U.S. policies in the Cold War and maintain favorable economic conditions for U.S. commercial and investment groups. In calculating benefits resulting from U.S. interventionist policies, it is misleading to lump together the several components—the real interests and ideological rationalizations. If we evaluate the four cases

of military intervention (direct and indirect) utilizing the above
realistic criteria, we will find the following:

TABLE 7–2

Guatemala (1954):	*Low Cost* (economically and in terms of social costs—dead soldiers) *High Benefit:* Overthrow of reform government; restoration of land to United Fruit; government that clearly supports U.S. policies to the extent of lending itself as a training base for attacks on Cuba, etc.
Cuban blockade (1962):	*High Cost:* Global mobilization in preparation for nuclear confrontation. *High Benefit:* Withdrawal of missiles: isolation of Cuba from rest of hemisphere and successful reassertion of hegemony in Western hemisphere; successful use of massive military force to change defense policy of Soviet ally forcing Russian retreat from commitments.
Cuban invasion (1961):	*High Cost:* U.S. prestige placed in support of invaders; U.S. politically identified with invaders. *No Benefits:* Loss of prestige; loss of political support in Latin America and within Cuba; strengthened revolutionary left in Latin America; eliminated possibility of recovery of one billion dollars in U.S. investment in Cuba.
Invasion of Dominican Republic (1965):	*Low Cost:* Relatively inexpensive economically and in terms of troops lost; verbal opposition by Christian Democrats and liberals in North and South America. *High Benefits:* Eliminated from power nationalist reform group which based on armed populace might have followed a more independent foreign policy and a more restrictive domestic policy vis-à-vis U.S. investors; elected pro-U.S. business and pro-U.S. foreign policy president; disarmed populace and restored old military apparatus.

In three out of the four cases intervention has been a successful tool in securing U.S. policy, restoring a favorable political environment for business interests, and in creating conformity with U.S. international policies.

However, from the point of view of the great majority of the population residing in the intervened countries, there is a somewhat different balance sheet. In Guatemala substantial areas of land that were distributed to peasants were returned to U.S. investors; trade unions were dissolved; little has been done in the way of education, health, and welfare. Politically, Guatemala has been ruled by military dictators or militarily controlled civilian governments with the able assistance of right-wing terrorist vigilantes who have accounted for upward of three thousand deaths the past two years.[4] In the Dominican Republic several thousand civilians were killed, and the old economic and military elites were returned to power in the course of dissolving the popular militias and physically eliminating selected constitutionalist rivals. Elections are under military tutelage resulting in the entrenchment of the supporters of President Balaguer, ex-president under the Trujillo dictatorship. Massive unemployment, large landholdings, and low levels of literacy continue.[5]

As these illustrations suggest, for the *intervened* nation the consequences of indirect or direct military intervention against leftist reform regimes are largely negative both in terms of socioeconomic development and political freedom. The pattern that emerges from past U.S. intervention in Latin America is one in which high benefits to the United States coincide with largely negative consequences for the intervened nation. The history of *past* direct and indirect intervention (pre-World War II) suggests a similar pattern. Largely confined to the Caribbean countries, the result has been dismal from the point of view of the intervened nations. U.S. intervention has probably contributed to the low score which most of these countries in Latin American achieve on scales of social, economic, and political development.

In terms of measuring benefits that accrue to U.S. policy-makers and economic interests, it should be noted that short-term payoffs may result in serious losses in the next generation. For example, the successful intervention in Cuba in the mid-thirties resulted in temporarily stabilizing a status quo favorable to the United States.

However, it may have created conditions for a more radical social revolution in the 1950's by postponing many of the social reforms that popular forces were demanding. The same may now be happening in the Dominican Republic and in Guatemala.

U.S. interventionist policies are related to different types of relationships between the intervening and intervened nations. In a somewhat schematic categorization we can classify these relationships in the following way:

TABLE 7–3

TYPE OF INTERVENTION	STATUS OF INTERVENED STATES
Direct and indirect military intervention.	*Colonial and annexed territory:* (Puerto Rico, the southwest states incorporated in the U.S.—Texas, etc.) *Semicolonial or indirect rule:* (Cuba 1900–1958, Guatemala 1954–present, Haiti 1900–1933, etc.)
Direct economic intervention and routine economic and political manipulation and pressure.	*Client-states:* Venezuela, Colombia, Brazil (1964 to present), Costa Rica, Haiti, Ecuador, Paraguay, Bolivia (1964 to present), Panama, Mexico (till 1910). *Dependency:* Chile, Mexico, Argentina (1945–55), Uruguay, Brazil (1950–1964).

A number of observations are in order: the Caribbean area is still subject to direct and indirect U.S. military intervention. As a consequence, with the exception of Cuba and Mexico, these countries are countries that remain under direct or indirect U.S. rule, the remainder being largely among the client states. The countries subject to indirect rule are those in which the selection of key governmental officials was accomplished in the physical presence of the United States. The client-states, on the other hand, nominally select their own officials, but these officials are filtered through social and political selection processes to ensure their acceptability to the United States. In government they largely direct their economies to serve U.S. economic needs—guaranteeing U.S. investments, maintaining one-product export economies, and consistently voting with the United States in international policy matters.

The ability of the United States to intervene to effect policies favorable to U.S. economic interests through routine channels is illustrated by the resolution of the conflict between the Boston Panama Company and the government of Panama.[6] The Boston Panama Company owned 500,000 acres of land (an area one-half the size of Rhode Island) and only utilized 5,000. Applying a tax law on uncultivated land, the Panamanian government eventually asked for a two million dollar payment. The Boston Panama Company refused to pay the sum and conferred with U.S. government officials on ways to avoid complying with the enforcement of the law. Communications from the U.S. corporation were sent to the Department of Commerce's International Bureau and to Senator Long informing them of the corporation's economic interests, the relationship between the policy outcome in their case and the rest of the investment community in Latin America, and between U.S. development policy for Latin America and private investors. Senator Long and someone named Behrman of Commerce sent letters to the State Department. Political pressure was exerted on the Panamanian government through the device of threatening to cut off loans (the Hickenlooper amendment to the Foreign Aid Bill of 1962). In a matter of weeks the Panamanian government acceded to the demands of the corporation. In the process it was revealed that the President of Panama, Mr. Chiari, was on the board of directors of a processing plant operated by the Boston Panama Company. U.S. intervention through economic pressure and cooptation of members of the political elite is far more common and important in shaping Latin America policies to U.S. needs than military intervention. More will be said on this shortly.

The political pressures exerted through official bureaucratic and diplomatic channels in the Boston Panama case were preceded by similar activities involving the International Telephone and Telegraph Company in Brazil. In fact the Boston Panama executives leaned heavily on the procedures utilized by ITT in obtaining a favorable outcome vis-à-vis the Brazilian government. As in Panama, the Brazilian government sought to improve the use of economic resources—in this case the communication system which under ITT had failed to meet the increasing needs of Brazil's fast growing cities. Brazil attempted to nationalize the property of ITT and offered a monetary compensation. Refusing the sum offered, ITT turned to the State Department which utilizing the threat of the Hickenlooper amendment was able to arrange a favorable settlement for ITT.[7] Both the Brazilian and Panamanian governments were in extremely vulnerable financial situations and were dependent on U.S. financial assistance.

Through its numerous close ties with high military officials in Latin America—training schools, exchange visits, military assistance, etc.—the United States can indirectly veto potential presidential candidates who might be perceived as threats to what U.S. policy-makers consider critical interests. The parameters set for policy and personnel help the United States to intervene without appearing to intervene—it is routine activity conducted through established institutions by public officials or the self-selected, whatever the tradition may be in each particular Latin country. The interlocking of public and private interests does not involve any secret conspiracy by an evil cabal. The frame of reference is generally known by the political actors and is accepted as a matter of fact.

The dependent nations in Latin America are largely the more developed nations, which generally select their own public officials and contain a sizable domestic middle class. Apart from that, however, they are heavily dependent on U.S. corporations or government for foreign exchange earnings, loans and credits, imports, markets for exports, military alliances, and training of officers.

The recent agreement between U.S. copper corporations and the Chilean government is a case in point. In the course of a discussion with one of President Frei's top economic advisors, I asked why Chile had not made an effort to nationalize the highly profitable mines instead of granting tax cuts and buying into one of the least profitable mines. The Chilean official answered that he thought that nationalization would be a good idea *but* that it could not be done because of the Chilean government's several hundred million dollar debt to the United States. If we nationalize, he continued, your government will demand immediate payment, and if it is not forthcoming, we may have your navy and marines in

Valparaiso as in Santo Domingo. The sequence of events which this Latin official described fits in well with our discussion of the routine type of politico-economic intervention with one modification—manipulation and nonmilitary intervention appear to be backed up by the implicit or explicit threat of a more direct sort of intervention. In this case and in the multitude of day-to-day actions and policy choices which confront Latin officials, no one person or group presence is physically visible peering over their shoulders. Rather, the imperial presence is incorporated into the political culture of a client-state like Panama or a dependent one like Chile. Politicians are socialized to accept certain alternatives as the rules of the game, rules which do not, of course, make it any the less a form of intervention.

Among the client-states and the dependencies the pattern has been for the United States to rely almost exclusively on nonmilitary techniques in influencing and shaping the policies and makeup of regimes. It should be added, however, that this abstinence may be the result of the success so far achieved by these limited means. Should these limited measures prove insufficient, the United States probably would turn to unilateral military type of intervention. We have the testimony of the late President Kennedy who asserted right after the failure of the U.S.-approved invasion of 1961:

Let the record show that our restraint is not inexhaustible. Should it ever appear that the inter-American doctrine of noninterference merely conceals or expresses a policy of nonaction—if the nations of this hemisphere should fail to meet their commitments against outside Communist penetration, then I want it clearly understood that this government will not hesitate in meeting its primary obligations which are to the security of our nation.[8]

Beginning with the 1930's, U.S. intervention increasingly took the form of *routine economic-political-diplomatic pressures,* occasionally at the behest of U.S. corporations, largely in line with the overall strategic policies adopted by U.S. officials to defend U.S. political-economic hegemony in the hemisphere.

"Routine" implies the use of established institutions and patterns of interaction. This approach to shaping Latin American policies and institutions contrasts with the sharp discontinuities and more dramatic and abrasive policies involved in direct military intervention. F.D.R. and subsequent U.S. chief executives mainly relied on intervention through bureaucratic channels even when, in the cases of Eisenhower, Kennedy, and Johnson, they reverted on occasion to direct and indirect military intervention. U.S. officials have a variety of levers that serve to change Latin American policies, influence the choice of elected officials, and establish the boundaries within which political leaders can act. One obvious and important lever for intervention are the loans that the United States can offer to finance countries which are already heavily in debt to the United States, which have trade deficits, and which are in constant search for means of refinancing past debts. Through its influence in the international financial agencies, the United States can add further weight to its request for readjustment in the policies of a given Latin nation.

In this sense, to speak of routine intervention is to speak of the interests of the American business community, a form of intervention which should be presented in more detail.

The Intervention of American Capitalism in Latin America

Latin America has been and is now considered an important area for profit-making by U.S. corporations. Total U.S. assets and investments in Latin America amounted to eighteen billion two hundred and seven million dollars in 1965.[9] This represented approximately 17 per cent of all U.S. assets and investments abroad. The great bulk of these investments and assets, 14.4 billion, or 79 per cent, was accounted for by private investment.[10] As large and significant as the U.S. investment is in Latin America, much more important from the point of view of U.S. businessmen and policy-makers, is the annual *earnings* derived from their investments. Utopian liberals have on occasions argued that the U.S. government should finance the nationalization of U.S. enterprises, in the interests of both areas, by providing the capital for adequate compensation to U.S. investors. U.S. corporate executives have rejected the idea and so have U.S. policy-makers. The reason is obvious: the high earnings that accrue to the investors more than make up for their initial investment in a brief period of time. The U.S. government also prefers to have easy access and low prices on strategic materials: for example, the U.S. government saved (and Chile lost) 500 million dollars in the purchase of copper during World War II because of a price-fixing agreement. Between 1924–1951, one copper corporation, Braden, shipped over 324 million dollars from Chile to help develop the United States on an initial investment of 2.3 million.[11]

Between 1960 and 1965, income on U.S. investments in Latin America totaled 6.4 billion dollars. Of this amount direct investments accounted for 73 per cent of the income.[12] U.S. income from Latin America has risen considerably during this period. In 1960, U.S. income on investments in Latin America totaled 858 million. In 1965, it was 1.25 billion, a 45 per cent rise in five years.[13] U.S. corporate capitalism's earnings are derived from a variety of economic sectors which it controls. For the years 1964 and 1965, direct investment earnings in smelting and mining accounted for 404 million; petroleum, 679 million; manufacturing, 875 million; and a variety of other activities, 409 million.[14]

In those countries like Brazil, Argentina, and Mexico, which have developed to a certain degree independently of the United States, U.S. investors are oriented toward capturing the existing market for manufactured goods (chemicals and transportation equipment). In the more underdeveloped countries, U.S. investment is oriented toward mining, petroleum, and raw materials. In neither case does U.S. investment create new dynamic enterprises that might compete with enterprises in the mother country.

Business Latin America cites current events in the auto industry to provide evidence of this trend:

. . . Ford Motor Co. revealed last week that it is negotiating with Kaiser Industries to purchase the latter's interest in Willys Overland do Brasil. Ford is believed to have similar designs on Kaiser's holdings in Industrias Kaiser Argentina. IKA in turn acquired the automotive division of Siam di Tella two years ago. Volkswagen bought out Brazil's Vemag and has reportedly made a bid to acquire Automotriz Santa Fe in Argentina. . . .

Ford, which now has about 14 percent of the Brazilian commercial vehicle market and has just entered the passenger car field by introducing its relatively high-priced Galaxie, would immediately obtain a strong position (about 33 percent of total sales) in the auto market if it succeeds in buying into Willys. IKA holds a similar attraction in Argentina, where such an acquisition would expand Ford's range to middle and lower-price cars.[15]

The article notes that:

In the main, these actions represent attempts to enlarge the companies' shares of the market and to consolidate resources, particular production facilities.[16]

In 1965, to take a "typical year," U.S. earnings on direct investment in Latin America amounted to 1.170 billion dollars. Of this repatriated profits amounted to 888 million.[17]

In addition, for the same two years, 1964 and 1965, direct investment receipts of royalties and fees amounted to 319 million dollars.[18] If we include such items as undistributed subsidiary earnings, we can add another half-billion dollars to the U.S. take.[19] Most of these earnings are returned to the United States at the expense of Latin American development, perpetuating backwardness and stagnation, depleting resources and perpetuating concentration of wealth and great inequalities. We might consider this Latin America's "aid" to U.S. corporate development. In addition, a substantial proportion of funds used by U.S. capitalism to extract their profits originates in Latin America. In 1965, foreign funds borrowed by U.S. corporations through foreign affiliates amounted to 530 million dollars.

In addition to being a prime source for pumping out profits, Latin America has served as an important source of raw materials, and a profitable market for U.S. goods. U.S. capitalism has a favorable trade balance from the export of goods and services. Between 1960 and 1965, the United States has had a favorable trade balance of 6.4 billion dollars with Latin America.[20] So the United States favorable trade balance doubled from 683 million in 1960 to 1.3 billion in 1965.[21] In this sense Latin America functions in the traditional colonial fashion. Traditional commodities—raw materials, foodstuffs, and nonmanufactured goods—account for about three-fourths of total sales. Latin American dependence on trade in raw materials for manufactured goods has been a problem because of the decline in prices of primary goods and the deterioration of the terms of trade. From 1954 to 1960, the average price of Latin imports from the U.S. rose by more than 15 per cent over the same period.[22] U.S. corporate capitalism pocketed the difference.

The colonial economies of Latin America, dependent on U.S. capitalism, continue to be highly vulnerable to sharp and sudden oscillations in commodity earnings: for example, the price of cocoa fell from 22.5 cents a pound in 1964, to 16.1 cents in 1965; sugar worth 8.3 cents a pound in 1963, was worth a *fifth* as much by 1966.[23]

Latin America ranks next to Western Europe as the largest market for U.S. goods. The category of "machinery and vehicles" has been accounting for about one-third of total U.S. exports and in turn, twenty-six to thirty-six cents out of each dollar received from U.S. exports of commercial (nonmilitary) machinery and vehicles have come from Latin America.[24]

U.S. control over strategic raw materials in Latin America allows for the development of the United States as a world military and political power. Strategic raw materials are vital to the growth of a multiple of U.S. industries whose earnings and products have far-reaching effects in terms of the overall performance of the U.S. economy. Copper production in Chile, over 90 per cent of which is owned and controlled by U.S. corporations, is an important component of U.S. expansionist war efforts. It also leads to development of refineries, processing plants, electrical manufacturing, etc.

In summary, we can say that U.S. business has an enormous profitable stake in Latin America. The status quo—underdeveloped, dependent, colonial economies—provides valuable sources of profit and resource payoffs to U.S. capitalism. This leads to some key questions. What sort of individuals preside over this North American empire? Are U.S. advisers and policy-makers on Latin America disinterested Pan-Americans promoting freedom and progress, or are they the guardians entrusted by the social-economic-ruling class to defend their profits and investments against Latin American development and reform aspirations?

Perhaps the best way to deal with the question of the interrelation of business and policy is to cite an important case in recent history: U.S. policy toward the Dominican Republic. A recently prepared study by two staff members of the North American Congress on Latin America points out that the key officials selected by President Johnson as advisers, and the key officials who made the actual decisions leading to the U.S. suppression of the popular revolution, were corporation lawyers and directors with a direct or indirect economic stake in the status quo ante:

The powerful U.S. economic interests, with a stake in the outcome of Dominican events, most certainly had access to U.S. Administration officials and most likely expressed their deep concern. For example, prominent New Dealer Abe Fortas was a director of the Sucrest Corporation for 20 years, third largest East Coast cane sugar refiner; Adolf A. Berle, Jr., known Latin American expert and advisor to several presidents, was Chairman of the Board of Sucrest for 18 years and is still a director and large stockholder; Ellsworth Bunker was Chairman, President, and 38-year Director of the second largest East Coast cane sugar refiner, National Sugar Refining Corporation (partially founded by his father), and one-time stockholder in a Dominican sugar mill; Roving Ambassador W. Averell Harriman is a "limited partner" in the banking house of Brown Brothers Harriman, which owns 5 percent of the National Sugars' stock (his brother, E. Roland Harriman, sits on the board of National Sugar); J. M. Kaplan, molasses magnate, is a large contributor and influential advisor to many Democratic Party candidates and the ADA; Joseph S. Farland, State Department consultant and ex-U.S. Ambassador to the Dominican Republic, is a Director of South Puerto Rico Sugar Company; Roswell Gilpatrick, Deputy Secretary of Defense, is the managing executive partner on the Wall Street firm of Cravath, Swaine, and Moore, legal counsel to National Sugar; and Max Rabb, partner in the Wall Street firm of Strook, Strook, and Lavan, legal counsel for Sucrest, is an influential Johnson supporter. The above sugar refiners, plus the largest U.S. refiner, American Sugar, depend directly on the Dominican sugar and molasses supply for their operations. Any disruption in the supply would seriously hamper price stability. Even without these direct economic interests, it would be difficult for these gentlemen in their "neutral" decision making roles to escape the assumptions, inclinations, and priorities inculcated by their economic and social milieu.[25]

An analysis of key U.S. policy-makers in the Latin American area as a whole sheds some light on the relationship of U.S. policy and corporate capitalism. A recent study of the socioeconomic career patterns of thirty influential policy-makers who played a substantial role in the development of U.S. policy between 1961–1965 suggests that their backgrounds hardly qualify them as supporters of a nationalist popular revolution.[26] Overwhelmingly educated in private schools—the great majority from the Ivy League —half were either directly engaged in business or were corporation lawyers prior to entering policy-making positions. Over 70 per cent of the policy-makers had been corporate directors, stockholders of major corporations, or served private corporations in a legal capacity.

The key factors which influence political decision-makers have little to do with their "social origins." Much more important in determining an individual's politics are the values and outlooks which are shaped by career experiences. Social origins, family background and upbringing may *predispose* individuals toward a particular career; but it is the career and concomitant political and social orientations and commitments that provide the frame of reference for political decisions. Institutional constraints pressure the individual to conform to the dominant values—with monetary incentives or by the threat of failure. Few if any career men escape these pressures. Corporate institutions politically socialize the upwardly mobile professionals some of whom are later recruited into the politically elite. Hence when leading policy-makers carry out policies beneficial to the corporate ruling class, it is not due to some "secret conspiracy" or "cabal," but a direct outgrowth of the prior process of political socialization and selection. The result of this "filtering" process is that top public officials tend to share the outlook, values and interests of the corporate elite and make decisions accordingly.[27]

Up to now we have indicated that U.S. corporations and an economic elite control strategic areas of Latin American economic activity and that corporate representatives play an important role as policy-makers concerning Latin America. We shall now briefly examine the actual policies adopted by those policy-makers to protect and enhance the position of the U.S. corporate rich and to maintain overall U.S. hegemony in the hemisphere.

Amidst all of the reformist rhetoric of the Charter of Punta del Este, which established the Alliance for Progress, there is a significant clause pushed by U.S. policy-makers which committed the Latin governments to the promotion "of conditions that will encourage the flow of foreign investments." To secure investors, Congress passed the Foreign Assistance Act in 1961, and a 1963 amendment which prohibited the use of congressional appropriations to benefit a state that fails to make "speedy compensation . . . in *convertible* foreign exchange . . . to the full value," of any property expropriated from U.S. citizens.[28] Any Latin country, not submitting to the guarantees of U.S. investors and to their "rights" to convert their profits to dollars and to remit their profits, was to be cut off from all aid as of December 31, 1966.[29] According to the Foreign Assistance Act of 1961, as amended in Section 620 (d), U.S. aid is not to be furnished to any enterprise that will compete with a U.S. business, unless the country concerned agrees to limit the export of the products to the United States to 20 per cent of output.[30]

Most of the so-called aid does not go for development and reform. Speaking at a recent U.N. Development Program session, Paul Hoffman, its chief administrator, stated: "the *gross* flow of such (development) assistance in 1966 . . . was 12 billion. However, deducting from the gross figure repayments on loans, interest payments, dividends, private investment, and other relevant items, we find . . . only about $3.2 billion."[31] Even on the level of trade and aid, the colonial economies continue to receive the short end of the stick. The U.N. Conference on Trade and Development (UNCTAD) agenda in 1968 took note that the "non-tariff barriers, of special importance to low income countries, have not been significantly reduced."[32] Regarding aid, UNCTAD noted, "Taking the developed countries as a whole, their aid—mostly in the form of loans—declined from 8.7 per cent of GNP, to 7.2 per cent in 1965 and the downward trend continues."[33]

The 1961 Foreign Assistance Act stipulated that U.S. aid be used to favor the U.S. economy. Latin Americans cannot even shop in other markets since virtually all loans from the United States are now tied to purchases of goods and services in the United States. Ninety-five per cent of AID expenditures for machinery and vehicles were made to U.S. corporations.[34] Ninety per cent of all AID commodity expenditures were made to U.S. corporations. The same practice is followed by the Inter-American Development Bank.

The Alliance for Progress, as a policy device, was used to further the interests of U.S. investors. Essentially, Alliance policy, implemented through a variety of legislative and administrative measures, was concerned with creating a favorable climate for U.S. investment.[35] The social reform and economic development goals of the Alliance were assumed to be compatible with the larger purposes of securing a primary role for U.S. investment. In operational terms, the position and advantages sought by foreign investors formed the "parameters" of the discussion of other goals. Evaluating the Alliance for Progress from this vantage point, one could agree with one of the United States' "foremost international bankers," David Rockefeller, when, in 1965, he said, "The climate of investment is improving."[36]

Regarding its primary function, the Alliance dealt with two specific issues: *protecting* existing investment and its earning power, and *creating* new opportunities for profit making. The Alliance for Progress was a Government-administered welfare program for the U.S. investors. The Alliance operation functioned on two interrelated levels. Increased U.S. government funds were utilized in subsidizing Latin governments whose base of support and internal situation were insecure and were not capable of implementing internal change. Latin governments who were recipients of Alliance funds made concessions and agreements with the U.S. government and U.S. firms which created a favorable climate for investment and increased their profit returns.

At the time of the inception of the Alliance for Progress, the Cuban Revolution had created a great fear among the international community of investors. Capital flight of considerable proportions (estimates ran as high as one billion dollars per year) threatened to bring down the already bankrupt Latin economies. In the fiscal year prior to the Alliance for Progress, 1960–61, private direct investment had been 214 million. In 1961–62 (the year the Cuban Revolutionaries defeated the U.S.-directed mercenaries at the Bay of Pigs, and Castro moved toward socialism) investment was minus 24 million; in 1962–63, it was 11 million; in 1963–64, 90 million; in 1964–65, 207 million.[37] U.S. investment "recovery" —still less than 1960–61—coincided with three interrelated events which created a more encouraging climate for foreign investment: (1) The installation of military dictators who were closely identified with the outlook of U.S. investors; (2) the repression and defeat of several reform and revolutionary movements in Latin America; and (3) the introduction of a series of policies designed to guarantee U.S. investments, increase profits, and liberalize profit-remittance opportunities. This essay will take up and discuss only points (3) and (1), in that order, leaving part two for another discussion.

It should be pointed out that there were divergent approaches among U.S. policy-makers over the best way to promote investor interests. There were heated debates between the Department of State and Congress over the timing and way in which a favorable climate could be successfully reestablished. Some congressmen took a hard line which involved issuing ultimatums to Latin governments stipulating that either they proceed immediately according to a prescribed path or face severe sanctions. For the State Department, it was more a matter of taking a strategic view—the adoption of flexible tactics in the face of adverse circumstances—in order to gain time until a particular situation could be changed to advantage. In 1962, in his opposition to the inflexible approach to defending U.S. investors abroad, Dean Rusk remarked: I don't believe the United States can afford to stake its interests in other countries on a particular private investment in a particular situation. We have to keep working at these things."[38] The Secretary of State took the long view: ". . . I would hope we would not use legislative mandates which in effect would cause us to break relations with important countries over particular points of policy, because in the longer run, it seems to me, that leads to blind alleys."[39] Translated into policy, the State Department's mode of operation was quite successful. The Brazilian case can illustrate the point. On February 16, 1962, Governor Brizola expropriated the property of the International Telephone and Telegraph Corporation. Congress clamored for economic sanctions in order to protect foreign investors. The State Department did better. The State Department pressured Brizola to pay the companies the price they desired in turn for which the U.S. government agreed to reimburse the Brazilian Government out of Alliance for Progress funds.[40]

U.S. corporations dictated State Department policy and substantially benefited. Rusk himself admitted that the policy adopted was the result of U.S. investor influence. The key to the apparent paradox of U.S. corporations supporting the expropriation action of an apparently Latin left-wing nationalist was explained by Rusk: "A number of them (U.S. corporations) would prefer to sell out their utility holdings and then reinvest in industries in the same country that have access to a free market situation. This is on the initiative of some of the companies."[41] Because U.S. corporations determined U.S. policy, Alliance for Progress funds were spent in expropriating unprofitable U.S. firms at above market prices. In turn, U.S. corporations used the funds procured to invest in more profitable activities, receiving special dispensations on the amount of profit which was remitted. Following the flexible handling of the incident, the State Department was in a position to continue toward its strategic goal, elimination of the Brazilian nationalist government. A sudden break in relations in 1962 as advocated by parochial congressmen might not have secured either the benefits to the utility investors or created a favorable situation for the rest of the U.S. corporate community. By staying and working within Brazil, the U.S. was able to participate in the overthrow of the Brazilian government and influence the new military dictatorship. The outcome was a government that more than met the criteria of the U.S. congressmen regarding the protection and encouragement of U.S. corporations.[42] An investment guarantee treaty was signed in which Brazil agreed to surrender its right to nationalize U.S. property. Control on profit remittances and tax concessions was considerably loosened. In a word, the flexible approach of the State Department, aided by the manipulation of Alliance funds, was successful in creating a favorable climate for foreign investment in the period of two years.

The Alliance for Progress aids U.S. investors by servicing the past debts of the Latin countries. In their striving to maximize profits in Latin America, U.S. and foreign creditors had over-extended themselves. The level of external debt of the Latin countries had reached the point where most of them were unable to meet their payments. The Alliance for Progress stepped in and rescued the financiers. Estimates of the proportion of Alliance funds, used to benefit foreign creditors, run from 25 to 40 per cent of Alliance disbursements during the first four years.[43] By maintaining the appearance of solvency in Latin America, the Alliance attempted to maintain a favorable climate for foreign investments.

Alliance loans to cover external debts, of course, meant new debts and new loans. The margin of autonomy that Latin economic policy-makers had was further circumscribed. The leverage that U.S. policy-makers had for promoting a favorable climate for U.S. investors increased. This can be seen by comparing the list of countries which signed the Investment Guarantee Program in 1963 and 1966.[44]

In 1963, Argentina did not approve the Program's sections regarding expropriation and war risk. By September 1966, the whole Investment Guarantee Program had been accepted.

In 1963, Brazil had not signed. By 1966, it had approved the whole program.

In 1963, Bolivia refused to sign sections guaranteeing investments against revolution and insurrection. In 1966, it was signed.

In 1963, Guyana had not signed. By 1966, the whole program had been accepted.

In 1963, Chile refused to sign sections dealing with investment guarantees against expropriation, revolution, insurrection, etc. In 1966, under Frei and the Christian Democrats, it approved the whole Investment Guarantee Program.

Similar changes occurred with Ecuador, Honduras, and Paraguay.

The installation or promotion of friendly governments by U.S. policy-makers was instrumental in increasing the number of signators. The military dictators of Brazil, Argentina, Bolivia, Honduras, and Ecuador have proved to be staunch defenders of U.S. investors and upholders of U.S. investment guarantees to such a degree that AID has been able to reduce its insurance rate in the Program.

The Chilean President Frei not only guaranteed the giant U.S. copper companies against nationalization, but significantly lowered their tax rate, overpaid for Chile's share of one of the least profitable and smaller mines, and provided the national armed forces to guarantee that the copper workers' wage demands do not cut too deeply into earnings.[45]

In so-called democracies (and in the dictatorships), U.S. policy-makers have in the past few years succeeded in utilizing the Alliance for Progress as an effective financial instrument for furthering the interests of private U.S. investors. Through political and military means, U.S. policy-makers have, in the post-Cuban Revolutionary period, re-created a favorable climate for foreign investors: between 1961 and 1965, profit remittances increased by some 200 million a year and royalties and fees increased by some 60 million per year.[46] Latin America's debt increased to 11 billion by 1964, and the foreign debt servicing burden rose from 5.5 per cent of balance of payments receipts on current account in 1956, to 15.4 per cent in 1964.[47] It is no wonder that David Rockefeller can say that the program of the Alliance for Progress is succeeding. But not for everyone.

The AID Specific Risk Investment Guarantee Program as of September 1966 covered seventy-five countries. Under its terms, the President of the United States assures U.S. investors protection in whole or part against any or all of the following risks: (1) inability to convert into U.S. dollars other currencies, or credits in such currencies, received as earnings or profits from the approved project, as repayment or return of the investment therein, in whole or in part, or as compensation for the sale or disposition of all or any part thereof; (2) loss of investment, in whole or in part, in the approved project due to expropriation or confiscation by action of a foreign government; (3) loss due to war, revolution, or insurrection.[48]

The Guaranteed Investment treaties are, for all intents and purposes, a guaranteed annual profit for investors. The supposed "risk" which investors make and for which they "earn" their profits is nonexistent.

Specific clauses of the Investment Guarantee Program have larger implications: for example, in order for a corporation to be eligible, a U.S. citizen must own over 50 per cent of the stock— thus encouraging U.S. ownership and control.[49] Under the Investment survey section of the Guarantee Program, and in pursuit of its major goals of promoting capitalist expansion and corporate profits, AID has authority, under Section 231 of the Foreign Assistance Act of 1961, to pay up to 50 per cent of the costs of a survey of profit-making opportunities in the less developed countries. Among the criteria that AID stipulates as governing its investment guarantee policy, it mentions that "The investment must benefit the economy of the foreign country, with emphasis on the private sector." A judge in this matter of "benefits" is the same private investor: "In evaluating the effect of each investment upon the economy of the underdeveloped country, heavy reliance will be placed upon the representations of the investors and upon views of the AID mission."[50]

In addition to the Specific Risk agreements protecting investors against losses from war, revolution, or insurrection, there are now "extended risks guarantees which protect investors against losses occurring from any normal business risk in certain situations."[51]

The U.S. government has committed itself a long way in a great many countries to "create a favorable climate for foreign investment." The linkage of the U.S. government and U.S. investors vis-à-vis the Latin American governments and all the rest of the so-called third world is explicit and concrete. Any attempt by these governments to exercise their sovereignty by expropriating private U.S. investors, becomes an action involving interstate affairs. The U.S. government has escalated the "class struggle" to the point where every policy affecting U.S. investors within a country becomes "international." In this specific concrete sense, the class struggle has become "internationalized."

In summary, U.S. business interests are strongly represented in important policy-making positions and are in a position to direct national resources and legislation to increasing their sales, profits, and control over Latin America. U.S. policy-makers are not merely a reflection of business interests. The strategists in Washington actively promote policies which transcend the interests of any particular group. They seek to provide a long-term institutional framework for creating stable satellites throughout the hemisphere.

Official governmental agencies are not the only means of implementing U.S. corporate capitalism's policies. The U.S. trade union leadership, AFL-CIO, in cooperation with the CIA and U.S. corporations in Latin America, has played a complementary role. Together, they have trained and financed an apparatus to subvert and destroy militant unions that defend their nation and members' interests and to collaborate with dictators and pro-U.S. business interests. The National Student Association financed by, and in association with U.S. governmental agencies, served as a transmission belt for propaganda and as a means of subverting Latin organizations and their leaders. The Congress for Cultural Freedom, partially financed by the CIA, operated on the intellectual front, its intellectuals in uniform driving home the "lessons" of anticommunism. U.S. universities strive mightily to "depoliticize" Latin American universities, attempting to reduce opposition to repressive governments and robbing the downtrodden populace of one of its important tribunes. From the Latin side, the most successful transmission belts of U.S. policy are military dictators, like

Barrientos and the late Castelo Branco, and in general, the status quo oriented politicians and social forces.

What are the results of policies drawn up by the representatives of corporate capitalism and designed to promote a favorable investment climate for the interests of U.S. investors in Latin America?

Over two-thirds of the Latin countries are ruled by military dictators or military controlled civilian governments. Assassination is a prominent political feature of two products of direct U.S. intervention (Guatemala and the Dominican Republic).[52] Little has been done in the way of agrarian reform: five per cent of the landholders still own over 70 per cent of the land. In Chile, the latest U.S. showcase, only 10,000 families have received land in five years—leaving 342,000 families still waiting for Frei's revolution in liberty—to mature.[53] Despite all the State Department's propaganda and guarantees to "free enterprise," the latest figures on the Latin economies indicate continuing stagnation: overall per capita GNP growth for Latin America for 1966 and 1967 was 1.6 per cent, well below the *minimum* goal of 2.5 per cent per capita growth called for in the Charter of Punta del Este.[54] Of the eighteen countries, only five reached the minimum goal, while several countries (Venezuela, Argentina, Uruguay, Paraguay, Haiti) had negative growth rates for the two-year period.[55]

U.S. policy in promoting and furthering the interests of U.S. corporate capitalism constricts Latin economic and social development and promotes Latin instability and authoritarian governments. The Latin American poor get poorer; and the rich, especially the foreign rich, get richer. The U.S. multinational corporation has developed a global perspective, necessitating the U.S. government to develop a global foreign policy. The main concern of the multinational corporations is profit and economic hegemony; any economic development that takes place in the underdeveloped countries is incidental. It is a myth that Latin America needs U.S. foreign investment since the multinational corporations mobilize most of their capital in Latin America through earnings and loans, and since the export of capital from Latin America is greater than the net inflow.

In summary, the net results of the various forms of intervention in Latin America are clear: continued hegemony of the metropolitan power and continued underdevelopment, dependency, and subordination on the part of the satellites. Intervention has not withered away. Only its outward manifestations have changed.

NOTES

1. The Hickenlooper amendment is an example of the levers of pressuring governments. A variety of economic measures were threatened in the conflict between International Petroleum Company and the Peruvian Government during the most recent period.

2. Gordon Connell-Smith, *The Inter-American System* (New York: Oxford Press, 1966), chaps. 1 and 2.

3. Tenth Inter-American Conference, *Documents of the Plenary Sessions*.

4. Eduardo Galeano, *Guatemala: Occupied Country* (New York: Monthly Review Press, 1967).

5. James Petras, "Dominican Republic: Revolution and Restoration" in Marvin Gettleman and David Mermelstein, *The Great Society Reader* (Random House: New York, 1967), pp. 390–412.

6. The information is gathered from private correspondence, collected in a folder entitled *The Boston Panama Company*.

7. John Hickey, "The First Year: Business," *Inter-American Economic Affairs,* Summer 1962.

8. Associated Press, April 20, 1961.

9. *Survey of Current Business,* 46, No. 9 (September 1966).

10. *Ibid.*

11. Mario Vera Valenzuela, *La politica economica del cobre en Chile* (Santiago: Ediciones de la Universidad de Chile, 1961).

12. *Survey of Current Business, op. cit.,* p. 30.

13. *Ibid.*

14. *Survey of Current Business, op. cit.,* p. 35.

15. *Business Latin America* (weekly report to managers of Latin American operations), May 25, 1967, p. 161.

16. *Ibid.*

17. *Survey of Current Business, op. cit.,* p. 35.

18. *Ibid.,* p. 38.

19. *Ibid.,* p. 35.

20. *Ibid.,* p. 37.

21. *Survey of Current Business,* June 1966, pp. 36, 37.

22. David Pollock, "Development of Commodity Trade Between Latin America and the United States," *Economic Bulletin for Latin America* (ECLA-UN, 6:2 Santiago, Chile), p. 59.

23. *Alliance for Progress Weekly Newsletter,* 6, No. 3, January 15, 1968.

24. Pollock, *op. cit.,* p. 62.

25. Fred Goff and Michael Locker, *The Violence of Domination: U.S. Power and the Dominican Republic,* mimeographed (North American Congress of Latin America, Box 57, Cathedral Station, New York City).

26. These data were compiled by Kraig Schwartz and are found in an unpublished research report "The Socio-Economic Career Patterns of 30 Persons Who Helped Shape U.S. Policy Toward Latin America 1961–1965." The study is based on an examination of seventeen policy positions and the individuals who held them. The Department of Defense, the Department of State, and Presidential appointees are included.

27. *Ibid.*

28. The Foreign Assistance Act of 1961 as amended. Section 620(e)(1) *Regional and Other Documents Concerning United States Relations with Latin America,* House Committee on Foreign Affairs (Washington: U.S. Government Printing Office, 1966), p. 143, quoted in J. P. Morray, "The United States and Latin America," in Maurice Zeitlin and James Petras, *Latin America: Reform or Revolution?* (New York: Fawcett, 1968). p. 109.

29. *Ibid.*

30. *Ibid.*

31. *Alliance for Progress Weekly Newsletter,* 6, No. 7, February 12, 1968.

32. *Alliance for Progress Weekly Newsletter,* 6, No. 3, January 15, 1968.

33. *Ibid.*

34. *U.S. Statistical Abstract* 1967, p. 827.

35. Fowler Hamilton, head of AID, stated "there will *have* to be a climate in the area that will attract foreign capital and keep domestic capital at home." Quoted in Hickey, *op. cit.,* p. 50.

36. "The Fourth Year: The Role of Private Business," *Inter-American Economic Affairs,* 20 (Autumn 1966): 71.

37. *Ibid.,* p. 73.

38. Quoted in John Hickey, *op. cit.,* p. 56.

39. *Ibid.*

40. *Ibid.,* p. 59 *passim.*

41. *Ibid.,* p. 64.

42. See Carl Oglesby, "Free World Empire," in Oglesby and Shaull, *Containment and Change* (New York: Macmillan, 1967), esp. pp. 83–97.

43. "The Fourth Year: The Fatal Barrier to Growth and Reform: Latin America's Economic Philosophy," *Inter-American Economic Affairs,* 20 (Autumn 1966): 63.

44. Material for the comparisons was drawn from the U.S., Department of State, Agency for International Development, Memorandum to Businessmen, *Aids to Business (Overseas Investment),* (U.S. Government Printing Office, 1963), p. 44; U.S., Department of State, Agency for International Development, *Specific Risk Investment Guaranty Handbook,* rev. ed. (U.S. Government Printing Office, October 1966), pp. 50–51.

45. James Beckett, "Chile's Mini-Revolution," *Commonweal,* December 29, 1967, pp. 406–408. "The Fourth Year: The Fatal Barrier to Growth and Reform," *op. cit.,* p. 68; James Petras, *Chilean Christian Democracy,* (Berkeley: Institute of International Studies, University of California, 1967).

46. "The Fourth Year: The Fatal Barrier to Growth and Reform," *op. cit.,* p. 73.

47. *Ibid.,* p. 58.

48. *Specific Risk Investment Guaranty Handbook, op. cit.,* p. 41.

49. *Ibid.,* p. 5.

50. *Aids to Business, op. cit.,* 1966 edition, p. 8.

51. *Specific Risk Investment Guaranty Handbook,* rev. ed. (October 1965), *op. cit.,* p. 13.

52. On Guatemala, see Eduardo Galeano, "With the Guerrillas in Guatemala," in Zeitlin and Petras, *op. cit.* On the Dominican Republic, see Petras in Gettleman and Mermelstein, *op. cit.*

53. U.S., Department of State, Report of the Inter-American Committee on the Alliance for Progress (CIAP), November 1967.

54. *Alliance for Progress Weekly Newsletter,* 6, No. 4, January 22, 1968.

55. *Ibid.*

8

COMSAT: THE TECHNOLOGY FOR RULING GLOBAL COMMUNICATIONS • *James L. Weeks*

Introduction

The international political system has undergone numerous changes in the past twenty-five years, many of them closely related to revolutions in science and technology. Communications by satellite are further changing the international system and necessitating decisions in a new arena: who will rule global communications?

Rapid global communications have existed ever since ocean spanning cables linked together the continents, but communication by satellite offers a much greater volume of communication than can be carried by cable and, more important, it also offers many more different types of communication such as radio and television that cables cannot economically provide. Since television and radio are a potent means of maintaining an influence and presence outside one's own country, the question "Who will rule?" gains added significance.[1]

Communications satellites make possible an increased volume of communication because of their greater channel capacity and lower costs. Most cables have a channel capacity of around 150 voice channels, though research and development is being done on cables with channel capacities of around 1200.[2] Satellites, on the other hand, begin with a channel capacity of about 1200, and satellites with 50,000 voice channels are being developed.[3] As a rough estimate, a satellite costs about $2.5 million to build and about $3.9 million to launch, whereas the cable that AT&T recently laid from New Jersey to France was about $56 million.[4] In addition, telephone rates are not proportional to distance in satellites as they are in cables.

Communications via satellite operate on radio signals which have a band-width larger than that offered by cables, thus enabling different types of communication, including television. Virtually anything that can be sent on a radio signal can be communicated via satellite including radio, television, computer hookups, facsimile drawings, telephones, and others.

The idea of communications satellite is not new, nor is it very complicated. The idea was first discussed in a speculative article written by a researcher at Bell Labs, Arthur C. Clarke, in 1945.[5] Radio signals, though they can carry many different types of messages, travel in straight lines. Because of the curvature of the earth, they can only normally be picked up within about a thirty mile radius of a transmitter; therefore, in order to send a radio signal over a great distance, it must either be reflected or relayed by some means. Reflection is inefficient and unreliable for most communications use, so relay stations, which receive a signal and send it on to a receiver or another relay station, are usually employed. For transoceanic communication, the cost of establishing relay stations is prohibitive, so cables have been laid instead, which exchange variety and flexibility for cost and reliability. To overcome this shortcoming, Clarke suggested putting a relay station on an artificial earth satellite which would receive signals from a transmitter on the earth, amplify them, and send them back, thereby covering a wide portion of the earth's surface with its signal. He calculated that if a satellite were placed in an orbit at about 22,300 miles over the equator, it would have a twenty-four hour period, the same as the earth's, and would appear to remain stationary over one portion of the earth's surface. Such a satellite in this "synchronous" or "geostationary" orbit could be considered as a relay station 22,300 miles up. It would take only three such satellites to completely cover the globe, save for some polar areas. Since then lower, "random orbit" satellites have been considered as suitable for use as well. Current systems are based on the synchronous satellite.

Ground stations are presently an integral part of a communications satellite system, though they will become obsolete in the future. Ground stations consist of transmitters and receivers which hook the satellites into the existing communications network. It is becoming possible, however, for satellites themselves to have big enough power sources to transmit directly to home receivers or to much smaller antennas and bypass large ground stations altogether. These "direct broadcast" satellites are still in the development phase but it is only a matter of time before they become a reality.

The idea of a communications satellite, however, had to wait for the development of electronics and space technology in order to make the satellite and to place it into orbit. These developments came with the United States' space program in the 1960's and were demonstrated with the launching of the random orbit TELSTAR and the synchronous orbit SYNCOM.

Shortly thereafter, when communications satellites were shown to be economically as well as technically feasible,[6] the communications industries in the United States made concrete efforts to exploit this technology and expand their networks around the globe. Yet they could not do so alone because only the U.S. government by way of the National Aeronautics and Space Administration (NASA) had the rocket capacity to put communications satellites in orbit. After much debate, the mixture of the ambitions of the private corporations and the capabilities developed by the government was blended into the Communications Satellite Corporate (Comsat), a government chartered private corporation created by the "Communications Satellite Act of 1962" passed by Congress on August 31, 1962.

Comsat has been described as the "inevitable anomaly"[7]—a mixture of private industry and government in the United States. Some of the board of directors are appointed by the President while the majority are elected by the stockholders. Half of the stock, by law, is sold only to the communications corporations while the other half is sold to the general public. Comsat has an absolute monopoly on international communications satellites in the United States; no other U.S. firm may compete with it in international communications by satellite. Yet, with all its roles as a private corporation, it is the "chosen instrument" of the stated U.S. policy which is "to establish, in *conjunction and in coopera-*

tion with other countries, as expeditiously as practicable a *commercial* communications satellite system, as part of an improved *global* communications network, which will be responsive to public needs and national objectives."[8] Comsat negotiates with other countries, pursues commercial objectives, and works to develop an improved global communications network, all as a matter of public policy.

The Congress bitterly debated the Comsat legislation, including an unprecedented filibuster by liberal senators in coalition with conservative southern senators. The crucial issues concerned the monopolistic character of Comsat, and its exploitation, as a private corporation, of government-developed space capabilities. These domestic politics, however, are beyond the scope of this paper.[9] We are interested here in the international behavior of the United States via Comsat.

The thesis of this essay is that within the context of this global technology, the United States via Comsat has pursued a nationalistic policy, using its superiority in space technology to enhance its position in the world. Technology is being used, in this case, as an instrument of national power and expansion.

Both the Europeans and the Soviets have strongly opposed U.S. actions and have used many means to compete with the United States. The poor countries of the world have for the most part been impotent and ignored. To the question, "Who will rule?" we must answer, Comsat has ruled until now and will probably continue to do so.

To a great extent, this is an old story; the rich and powerful have almost always in the past used their wealth and power to their own advantage. Further, extensive communications networks have historically been concomitants of nationalist or imperialist expansion; the British Empire at its height in the nineteenth century was held together by an extensive cable network. What is new now is that this particular technology is inherently global and therefore offers a means of greatly extending American influence around the world.

The institutional context in which Comsat has ruled is the International Telecommunications Satellite Consortium (Intelsat), an organization of some sixty nations (by mid-1968) designed to "establish a single global commercial communications satellite system."[10] This paper will discuss events leading up to the establishment of Intelsat, and the means by which Comsat has controlled it.

Prelude to Intelsat

There have been many problems surrounding communications by satellite, but this paper will focus on the international, political, and institutional ones. The legal problems were resolved by the UN Committee on the Peaceful Uses of Outer Space in December 1963 in a resolution concerning general principles for the use of outer space.[11] The controversial technical problems relating to the allocation of radio frequencies were resolved by the seventy nation Extraordinary Radio Administrative Conference in Geneva in October-November 1963,[12] which set aside a portion of the radio frequency spectrum for communication by satellite. Thus, the chief remaining problems have had to do with the international institutional framework that would finance, build, manage, and operate a communications satellite system.

Since the United States has a near monopoly on the technology required for a communications satellite system, it is not surprising that the United States Comsat Corporation would play a leading role in any negotiations leading up to an institutional arrangement and would be likely to dominate whatever institution was subsequently established. Indeed, Comsat was set up for this very reason.[13] This leadership role was in part a desire by the U.S. to be first, ahead of the Soviet Union, in establishing a working global communications satellite system and in part a desire to exploit its technological advantage—no one else had the booster capacity to place a satellite in synchronous orbit with the exception of the Soviet Union.

Since the greatest volume of international communication is between Europe and North America,[14] we can also expect that the most active participants in any negotiations would be the United States and European countries. International communications by satellite offers a cheaper, more efficient, and greater range of communications[15] and would thus most immediately benefit those countries with the greatest volume of international communications.

The Europeans, aware that the United States through Comsat had the power of initiative deriving from its technological monopoly and from its relatively stable financial situation, began to unite their forces to protect their common interests.

(In 1962) with a communication satellite system only a matter of time, a number of European officials in the telecommunications field began to consider the desirability of regional cooperation in Europe on such a system. They felt that European interests would best be protected if the various countries could speak with a single voice rather than many. Moreover, they felt that a larger number of ground stations could not be economically or technically feasible.[16]

After some further exploratory meetings, the European Conference on Satellite Communications (CETS)[17] was formed in London in July of 1963 on the consensus that Europe should contribute to a single system with the United States.[18] The CETS held a number of meetings, some of which Comsat and representatives of the U.S. government were invited to, in an effort to arrive at a common European position on how to develop an international satellite communications system and how to bargain with Comsat. At a meeting in Rome in November 1963, to which Comsat was invited, both the Europeans and Comsat agreed that some sort of world organization would be the best means of operating a system, but the Europeans felt that it should be established as soon as possible while Comsat wished to gain more experience in developing a system before solidifying such a world body.[19] A 1963 RAND memo reported that "to turn over the development and the establishment of the system to a supra-national agency at this time— whatever the political gains for one or another country—would undoubtedly delay the establishment of the system."[20] Given Comsat's priority of establishing a working system as soon as possible, this may have been the chief reason for their resisting the formation of an international governing agency at such a date. On the other side, the Europeans wanted to protect their interests in a formal way as soon as was possible so that major decisions concerning the type of system and service would not be preempted by Comsat.

At subsequent meetings, further disagreements appeared. The Europeans felt that seats on a board of governors of such a world body should be appointed so that no nation had more than half of the votes. The United States felt that seats should be proportional to the number of shares held by each country.[21]

As the nature and extent of the disagreements became more evident, European fears intensified. M. N. Golovine, vice president of Eurospace,[22] the European Aerospace Industry Association, said that Europe could decay into a "technologically underdeveloped area" if its space industries were allowed to atrophy because of a "subversive agreement with the U.S. Comsat Corporation."[23] In Britain's House of Commons, the view was expressed that, "according to the trend of present talks, we shall finally end by starving the transatlantic cable of telegraph communications from America and assisting Comsat to get off the ground, and Britain will merely end up renting a line from America."[24]

Yet many felt that the Europeans had no choice but to go along with Comsat and be glad that they were allowed to participate in the global system. If they did not, they would be completely subjected to a U.S. monopoly and a stream of U.S. television, radio, and other communications over which they would have little control. The British Postmaster General expressed the view that "the only way of preventing an American monopoly . . . is to join a partnership with the U.S. and other countries and so secure the right to influence the course of events."[25] The Europeans, especially the British, felt they were being *"allowed* to buy their way into the American Comsat project."[26]

The Europeans were interested in protecting their own cultural, technological, and economic interests. The specter of either a Soviet or a U.S. communications satellite beaming radio and television into Europe over which the Europeans had little control was not a welcome sight.[27] Moreover, Comsat was a commercial profit-making corporation without the accountability to the public interest that the government-run communications entities of Europe have. As one writer has noted, "Granted the commercial nature of the global satellite system and the role of private common carriers in the management of the Comsat Corporation, the problem of propaganda arises."[28] H. G. Darwin, the United Kingdom's legal advisor at the UN has said that the social interest inherent in communications would be better protected by a government than by a corporation whose loyalties lie with its shareholders.[29] Consequently, the Europeans wanted to have a voice in the establishment of the system.

Technologically, Europe did no want to fall further behind in its space industries, and they felt that they could gain valuable experience and technology from the United States by participating with Comsat in a global communications satellite system.[30] The British, for example, were willing to put up forty million dollars for the global system provided it received in return a share in the ownership *and* a guarantee that the United Kingdom would share in systems design and manufacture.[31] The French, also greatly interested in developing its aerospace industries as well as in warding off the "American Challenge" to European technology, saw development of their aerospace industries more as a means than an end: they wanted to put up their own communications satellite system and compete with Comsat.[32]

The United States wanted participation from Europe and other areas for a variety of reasons. There is, first, the inescapable need to have cooperation on the other end of the line in location and construction of ground stations, their management, and so on. Perhaps this was Europe's greatest bargaining leverage. Second, the U.S. Comsat project was organized with the clear political objective of "beating the Russians," as has so much of the U.S. space program. Moreover, European regional efforts could enable them to develop a communication satellite of their own in a few years. The United States wanted, therefore, to move quickly not only to prevent another Soviet "first" in space but also to channel European efforts to insure they would be part of the U.S. "first." The United States needed to insure what is called the Free World confidence in the strength and leadership of the United States[33] and European participation—as followers—was essential.

But, at the same time, the United States wanted only limited participation by other countries. As one Comsat official put it, sharing full responsibility with Europe would "put something of a drag on our operations."[34] A State Department official was quoted as saying at the Geneva Conference on frequency allocations, "Let's face it. The United States is acting like any space power would who wanted to get on with the job without waiting for, say, Gabon, to catch up."[35]

Comsat basically sought to retain its independence of action amid necessities for international cooperation.[36] It could retain this independence either through a loose and informal system which it preferred or through a formal system under its control. As we shall see, it ended up with the latter.

Comsat's independence was assured not only by the relatively underdeveloped nature of European technology but also by the relatively passive role of the U.S. State Department. At the Rome meeting, though the State Department was present, the chief spokesmen for the U.S. position were the representatives of Comsat.[37] The U.S. Government had made it clear that as soon as an agreement was finalized it would drop out of the picture, leaving Comsat as the sole spokesman.[38]

Thus, by the time the "Plenipotentiary Conference to Establish Interim Arrangements for a Global Commercial Communications Satellite System" was convened in Washington, in August 1964, the positions of the United States and of the Europeans were fairly well established. Both the Europeans and the United States favored an eventual world body to govern the establishment of a worldwide system. The Europeans wanted it sooner; Comsat, later. The Europeans wanted no one nation to dominate the body; Comsat wanted voting rights to be proportional to commercial interest. Comsat insisted it be a commercial enterprise. Since the United States retained a monopoly on the technology, generated the majority of international communications, and controlled the necessary wealth, it was almost a *fait accompli* that Comsat would maintain a dominant interest in whatever arrangement was established.

There were nineteen nations and the Vatican City State at the Washington conference. Most were from Western Europe, though Australia, Canada, and Japan were also represented as was the United States. (See the appendix of this chapter for a complete list of the signatories to the eventual agreements.) Both governments and communications entities from the various states were present and, among the communications entities, Comsat, as a private corporation, was unique: all the other communications carriers were government owned and operated. Because of this difference, the Europeans insisted on two separate agreements to be negotiated: an "Agreement" between the governments specifying policies and general outlines, and a "Special Agreement" between the communications entities setting up the mechanics to implement the policies.

These negotiations were something of a precedent in that a profit-making corporation, by all appearances acting as a private corporation though it was created by a public charter, was negotiating as an equal with government agencies of other countries. In behaving in this way, Comsat was in fact exercising some of the prerogatives heretofore reserved only to sovereign nation-states.[39]

Comsat wanted at the opening of the conference to set up a series of bilateral agreements with the communications entities much like what AT&T already has.[40] The Europeans refused; such an arrangement would leave all the decisions about the space system in the hands of Comsat while the Europeans would all be dealt with separately. Comsat's second proposal was that the Europeans would participate by ownership and operation of the ground segment of the system but not the space segment. This, also, was rejected.[41] Finally, the group agreed upon joint ownership of the space system with control over the makeup of the entire system to be vested in a single international governing body. This was the original European position which Comsat had consistently resisted. Consequently, Comsat insisted and the Europeans acceded that voting on the new body be proportional to shares and that shares be proportional to the volume of international telephone traffic. This left Comsat with the biggest single investment ($122 million of a total of $200 million initial capitalization) and 61 per cent of the votes. In addition, Comsat was named manager of the system. The United Kingdom with 8.4 per cent, France with 6.1 per cent, and West Germany with 6.1 per cent ownership were the next three biggest co-owners of the system. (See the appendix for a complete list of the quotas assigned to the original signatories.)

Thus the International Telecommunications Satellite Consortium (Intelsat) was established. The agreements are interim and up for renegotiation of definitive arrangements "with a view to their entry into force by January 1, 1970."[42]

There is no provision for enforcement of the 1970 deadline, a

loophole that Comsat has successfully exploited. There have been
two conferences attempting to renegotiate the agreements, one in
March 1969, the other in March 1970, neither of which came
to any conclusion except to perpetuate the interim agreements. As
long as the interim agreements remain in effect, Comsat maintains
its dominant voting strength and its role as manager, both of which
have been the key obstacles to achieving definitive arrangements.
Even so, however, a joint Japanese-Canadian proposal for definitive arrangements that is the basis for reconvening the conference
in November 1970, would still leave Comsat in a dominant position. This proposal, arrived at through many hours of debate and
bargaining, would name Comsat as manager for six more years
and would lower Comsat's vote to 40 per cent. With the growth
of Intelsat, and the continuation of the vote-proportionate-to-use
formula, the U.S. share would probably drop to 40 per cent in any
event. Meanwhile, the interim agreements remain in force.[43]

By the end of 1969, Intelsat, under Comsat's management, had
orbited and retired two generations of satellites, and completed a
global network of 1,200 circuit Intelsat III satellites—two over
the Atlantic, one over the Pacific, and one over the Indian Ocean.
These satellites serve thirty-six ground stations in twenty-four
countries. Intelsat's membership has grown from the original
eighteen to seventy-four countries and Comsat's voting quota has
dropped to 53 per cent.[44] The members nations of Intelsat account
for about 95 per cent of global telecommunications. Comsat pre-
sides over an impressive empire.

The Technology of Control

The objectives of Comsat and the United States government seem
to be threefold: to maintain its independence of action, to retain
for the United States the near monopoly position in satellite and
booster technology, and to reap the economic and political benefits
from communications by satellite. In this section, we will explore
the four basic means by which Comsat has tried to achieve these
objectives. The means are (1) through the operating philosophy

of Intelsat and through the consequences this has on the system of voting allocations; (2) through procurement and research and development contract policies; (3) through insistence on a rapid rate of expansion of the system; and (4) through policies on the exchange of technical information.

First, the Intelsat system is to be a commercial system, operated on a profit-making basis. Countries may participate in the system either through buying into the agreement or through renting channel capacity on the satellites. Most communications entities around the world are government agencies; hence they are generally not operated on a profit basis. Communications in the United States, however, are the domain of privately owned companies operating for a profit under government regulation, and Comsat is basically no different in this regard. When this philosophy is operated on the world scale, then it represents a clear bias toward the U.S. system of communications and institutional arrangement. One of these biases, perhaps the most crucial, is in the method of allocating votes.

In most commercial ventures, voting strength is based upon the amount of equity a party has in such a venture—the more a party invests or risks in such a venture, the more voting strength he has. In Intelsat, voting quotas are set according to the expected use of the system which in turn is based on transoceanic telephone traffic, which is a *commercial* criterion. Since the United States not only has the greatest volume of transoceanic telephone traffic but also has the wealth and the technology to invest in the system, making Intelsat a commercial system gives the United States a preponderant share of the votes.

However, all this assumes that the major decisions to be made by Intelsat are commercial decisions, which is simply not the case. For example, decisions about where to contract for research and development involve the problem of the geographic distribution of funds on an international scale. Where these contracts are let will influence the technologies and industries which will be stimulated. In addition, decisions about the location of ground stations have a great bearing on who has access to the system and on who controls this access. These political decisions have commercial implications, to be sure, but the structure of the decision-making machinery biased heavily in favor of commercial interests places commercial criteria in a paramount position.

As Abram Chayes, once State Department Legal Adviser, put it, after leaving the State Department,

(The vote allocation formula) is perfectly understandable in an organization operating in a commercial framework and subject to market limitations. . . . It is not necessarily the best pattern of use measured by other than commercial criteria. . . .

Once we begin to think along these lines, it becomes apparent that many of the most important decisions to be made about communications satellites systems over the next decade will be highly political, more so as satellites become powerful enough to beam directly to home receivers without the interposition of a national ground station. This growing political element must find reflection in the allocation of voting power. And the distribution of votes in proportion to use simply does not do that.[45]

Let us take a closer look at how decisions are made in Intelsat. The agreement establishes an Interim Communications Satellite Committee (ICSC) requiring a minimum ownership of 1.5 per cent —held either by an individual nation or a group—for membership.[46] The ICSC has broad responsibilities for decision-making and implementation of the system for the Intelsat Consortium. Voting on the ICSC is according to ownership percentages with, at the time the agreement was made (August 1964), Comsat holding 61 per cent. Decisions are made by the ICSC according to majority vote except for a special class of "important" matters which need the concurrence of 12.5 votes more than the "representative with the largest vote,"[47] i.e., Comsat. These special important matters include the type of satellite system to be used, the standards for earth stations, approval of budgets, rates to be charged for using the system, decisions to exceed the then $200 million capitalization, launching arrangements, the approval of new owners, and the placing of contracts.[48] However, for certain of these "important" matters (namely, decisions on the type of satellite, approval of the budget, placing of contracts, and approval of launching details), if a decision is not reached by sixty days, only 8.5 votes concurring with the largest vote are necessary for a decision to be made.[49]

These concurrence provisos were put in with the frank admission that without them, ownership participation by the Europeans would have been "unpalatable."[50] The State Department and Comsat considered "ownership participation essential to achieve effective 'receiving end' cooperation for a global system. 'We have to have someone to talk to,' said Leo D. Welch, chairman . . . of Comsat."[51]

Comsat was also designated as manager of the system on behalf of the ICSC with responsibilities to recommend plans and to operate the space segment of the system.[52]

Additional states which are also members of the International Telecommunications Union (which does not include China, East Germany, North Vietnam, and North Korea) may buy into the consortium up to a maximum of 17 per cent of the present owner-ship.[53] This proviso insures that Comsat's share will not fall below 50.6 per cent, regardless of how many more states enter into the Consortium. As of November 1967, Intelsat consisted of some fifty-nine states from around the world and Comsat still controlled 53 per cent of the votes.

Vote allocation by commercial criteria has successfully allowed Comsat to maintain its independence of action through the formal structures, at least for as long as the interim agreements have been in force. It has an absolute veto in the ICSC on all matters; it needs only minimal concurrences on important matters; it manages the system and thus has the power of initiative in recommending various courses of action for the entire system as well as in making day-to-day decisions. Comsat has successfully transformed a tech-nological advantage into a formal legal dominance.

The second means by which Comsat has controlled Intelsat, largely derivative from its voting power, is through its contracting policies, both for procurement and for research and development. Comsat first entered the Intelsat negotiations with the position that it should buy the best hardware that was available. The Euro-peans wanted to award contracts roughly proportional to the ownership in Intelsat, so that, say, Britain would receive 8.4 per cent of the contracts.[54] Comsat's position was described as "pretty inflexible"[55] by a delegate to the conference. After further negotia-tions, Comsat representatives conceded that the proportion of ownership ought to be considered in the awarding of contracts but that the prime criteria for selection of hardware and research ought to be according to technical merit—buy the best for the cheapest price.[56] In essence, technological criteria were placed above social criteria,[57] at least for the initial contracting of the system.

The setting of these criteria insures that most of the contracting would go to U.S. industries because the superior, and in some cases only, existing space technology necessary for the system is found in the United States. Consequently, U.S. space technology would receive the greatest stimulus and European space technology would continue to lag. Such a policy was exacerbating the so-called technology gap, and it was this that most worried the Europeans.

U.S. representatives were not unaware of what was most likely to happen. One State Department official was quoted as saying, "It is very unlikely that for some years to come there will be a substantial European contribution to the procurement of the system."[58]

Eurospace, in particular, was especially sensitive to contracting policies. In a 1967 report urging that Europe put together its own communications satellite system, Eurospace said that

a first consequence would be the ending of the unsatisfactory situation whereby Europe subscribes 28% of the capital of Intelsat and receives less than 4% of the money spent by the organization. [If Intelsat retains a complete monopoly on the international communications satellite programs, it will perpetuate a situation in which] European contributions finance by direct investment and not only by purchase, the development of American oriented industry.[59]

Comsat has tried to respond to the complaints of the Europeans by encouraging prime contractors in the United States to subcontract to non-U.S. firms. A Comsat spokesman related that

under a $32 million contract to TRW Systems for the first installment of six satellites TRW has . . . awarded subcontracts to eight European aerospace companies and to one Japanese concern. . . . In addition, TRW is conducting educational seminars for representatives of these firms so that they can perform the work under the subcontract. . . . Over 50% of the work on the fifth and sixth satellites will be performed by the non-U.S. subcontractors. In the second procurement buy of six, the tenth, eleventh, and twelfth satellites will be entirely developed and assembled in Europe with TRW Systems serving as manager or administrator.[60]

Subcontracts, however, are not exactly what Eurospace had in mind. Referring to the 4 per cent of contract funds that has come to Europe, Yves Dmerliac, secretary of Eurospace, said that, even of the 4 per cent, it was mainly "in the form of manufacturing subcontracts, and not in research and development. We want to acquire experience as prime contractors."[61]

Let us see how this contracting policy compares with broader policy objectives of the United States with respect to science and technology in Western Europe. According to the U.S. State Department's *International Science Notes,* a "principal policy objective in Western Europe" is to "insure a *strong, economically and politically integrated region,* socially compatible, outward looking and *maintaining close ties with the U.S."* (emphasis added)[62]

It appears that Intelsat's contracting policies as defined by Comsat, are subordinating the economic development of a region to the maintenance of close ties with the United States. From the above discussions dealing with Europe's slight share of the contracts, it should be clear that European aerospace industry is not being strengthened, at least not as the Europeans want. Close ties with the United States are being maintained in this contracting policy by two ways: first, through European firms receiving primarily subcontracts and, second, through U.S. firms training and educating the European firms.

Both subcontracting and training integrate the European firms into U.S. space technology and maintain close ties within that framework. Training integrates them into an administrative framework, subcontracts into a technological framework. If they wish to participate at all in communications satellite technology within Intelsat, they will be dependent on U.S. aerospace industry.

But these policy objectives in turn are of secondary importance to the objective of establishing a working communications satellite system as soon as possible. The same RAND study quoted above expressed the viewpoint that

the value of foreign technical contributions . . . has to be considered in relation to the need for early establishment of a working system, a prime objective of both the United States and the Corporation (i.e., Comsat). Foreign participation in the research and development phase could delay the effective initiation of the system long enough to permit the Soviet Union to gain another "first" in space. Moreover, the sharing of decisions about research and development with nations that are less advanced than the United States and have different research and development interest might prove exceedingly disadvantageous to the system at this time.[63]

"Buying the best hardware that is available" thus facilitates achievement of the objective of establishing a working system as soon as possible. Economic advantages accruing to United States industry are a by-product, convenient nonetheless, to the U.S. space industries.

This policy, however, not only has been benefiting U.S. industries, it also has influenced the direction of technological development in Europe. At first glance, the "technology gap" is being exacerbated by this policy and in those cases where European firms do receive contracts for work on the system, they are usually subcontracts. Moreover, European space technology is being integrated into the space and satellite technology of the United States, with U.S. firms retaining control over most systems decisions. European space firms, insofar as Intelsat is now influencing their direction, are becoming part of the infrastructure of U.S. space industries.

It has been suggested in the above that the early establishment of a working system was a prime objective of both the United States and of Comsat. However, once that system has been established, its rapid expansion has been a third objective in order first, to integrate as many countries into the system as possible before the interim agreements expire; second, to develop and perfect the system before the Soviets perfect theirs;[64] and third, to reap economic benefits from U.S. industrial innovations. The overriding concern has to do with the expiration of the Intelsat agreements. Once they expire, and unless whatever supersedes them closely resembles the present arrangements, Comsat will no longer have the context within which to work in order to benefit U.S. industries and implement U.S. policy in communications satellites.

The first objective, integrating many countries into the system before the interim agreements expire, is important to Comsat because the more countries that are integrated into the system, the more vested interest there will be in maintaining the system and, consequently, the more vested interest there will be in U.S. space technology.[65] It represents one way in which U.S. influence can be spread.

The second objective, beating the Soviets in space, has been a particularly important objective of the U.S. space program ever since Sputnik. Vernon Van Dyke, in his *Pride and Power* found that

the most powerful motives of the space program—above all in political circles—are of a competitive sort. When people abroad compare our achievements in space with those of the Soviet Union, we want to come out on top. Even more important, when we ourselves make the comparison, we want to be able to credit ourselves with first place; to be second is bad and to be second rate is intolerable.[66]

Third, economic advantages also accrue to the U.S. by rapid expansion of the capacity of the system. As long as Comsat retains its controlling position in Intelsat and before that position changes when the present agreements expire, it stands to benefit U.S. industry and seems intent on doing so.[67] Rapid expansion means that expenditures for U.S. hardware will be made before the agreements expire, which will not only benefit U.S. industry in the short term but will also establish the presence of more U.S. hardware in the system as a whole, thus insuring U.S. presence in the long run as well.

Rapid system expansion has been opposed by the Europeans, however, not on the grounds that it unduly benefits the U.S. but on the grounds that the projections for traffic growth do not make such expansion necessary. The Europeans have bitterly fought Comsat in the ICSC on these grounds.[68]

Thus by insisting on a rapid rate of expansion, a seemingly innocuous position, Comsat has been attempting more firmly to establish itself and U.S. industry in the entire system before the interim agreements expire. This represents still another way in which technological advantage is used to corporate and national self-interest and the perpetuation of that advantage.

Within Intelsat we have a concrete example of what is often referred to in the phrase "knowledge is power." The fourth issue we will discuss here has to do with the control over the transfer of knowledge—technical information—both within and outside of the Intelsat framework. As we shall see, Comsat, the State Department, and some U.S. industries have exercised strict control over the transfer of technical information.

This issue has been present in communications satellite systems since the first preliminary meetings between Comsat and CETS. At that time, "the United States flatly refused any official exchange with European countries of technical information regarding communication satellites. Industry cooperation was not barred but exactly what form such cooperation might take was not known."[69] The consequences of this refusal were widely held to be that European space-oriented firms would be frozen out of the market.

During the Intelsat negotiations in Washington, the U.S. position softened somewhat and became more ambiguous. In the Intelsat Agreements technical information is to be made available to the signatories of the agreement but only for use by them or firms in their countries for work on Intelsat contracts. Use for their own national projects or any other non-Intelsat projects is prohibited.[70] Even then, however, the technical information that can be transferred is only that which arises from work that Intelsat acquires through its contracts.

This policy represents the transfer of an institutional style that the U.S. government uses when it contracts in the United States. That is, the government acquires invention and information rights from domestic contractors for use on other government contracts.[71] When another contractor works on related matters, he has access to that invention information from the government. What is being transferred, in this instance, from the U.S. to European and other countries is a style of institutional technology that has been developed in the United States.

A recounting of some incidents involving transfer of communications satellite technology illustrates how this policy has worked out in practice. In mid-1967, French aerospace industry had asked for technical assistance from U.S. companies for use in developing their own satellite system to use in countering the dominant role of Comsat within the international system. The specific technology involved had to do with travelling wave tubes and total systems integration. "Travelling wave tube" technology is a key element in developing communications systems. Systems integration is a key element in developing Europe's technology, since many in the United States think that the "technology gap" between the United

States and Western Europe involves mainly differences in managerial skills. The United States now has a monopoly on travelling wave tube technology and the U.S. companies must obtain permission from the State Department in order to assist the French. For this reason, and because the French government intended to use the technology to counter U.S. dominance in Intelsat, it was expected that the State Department would refuse permission. The issue was complicated by suggestions that the French would turn to the Soviets for substitute assistance; consequently, the State Department acquiesced and approved limited assistance.[72]

The State Department has balked in another instance in which Mexico had asked Hughes Aircraft to make a study on the possibility of using direct broadcast satellites for domestic use. Again, this technology would not be directly integrated into the Intelsat system but woud not pose as explicit a challenge as would the French plan. Also, the United States has a monopoly on such high powered satellites and only the U.S. government through NASA has the capacity for launching them into synchronous orbit. Robert Lewis Shayon, writing in the *Saturday Review* relates the following:

Hughes Aircraft has made a study at the request of the Mexican government for a domestic satellite; it took the company two years to get the State Department's permission to make the study. The State Department's Office of Munitions Control has forbidden the export of communications satellite technology. And now that the study has finally been made, permission has not yet been granted to Hughes to show the study to the Mexican Government.[73]

Shayon relates that the reason for this resistance is that domestic satellites do not fit into Intelsat's conception of how communications satellites ought to be used. "They do not fit the pattern of Intelsat's development of high-profit routes for the point-to-point movement of telephone calls, data, and television programs."[74]

In still another instance involving the British, the State Department has delayed in assisting them to put up a military satellite system that would link Britain with Australia. In this instance, there was minimal competition with the Intelsat system, yet the State Department was perceived by the British to have unnecessarily delayed the launching of the system.[75] Again, only U.S. technology has the booster capacity to put up the kind of satellite system that the British wanted.

Not only the State Department but also some U.S. aerospace firms have resisted transfer of communications satellite technology to Intelsat. It was written in *Aviation Week and Space Technology*, the aerospace trade journal, that "U.S. aerospace firms are balking at a requirement that Intelsat be given patent rights to all patents used on Intelsat contracts."[76]

From the above discussion of contract policies, it appears that transfer of technological information and techniques within the Intelsat framework is proceeding according to the agreements. But any initiative by other nations and firms that does not correspond to Intelsat's (and, hence, Comsat's) preconceptions of what communications satellites are to be used for has been frustrated. Through this policy, Comsat, the U.S. State Department, and some U.S. industries have retained not only the U.S. technological monopoly but have also directed the development of the system to their own advantage.

Conclusion

It is clear that Comsat has taken the superiority of U.S. space technology and economic capital and used it, first of all, to gain a controlling position within Intelsat, a functional supranational organization, and second, has used this controlling position to advance its own aims, those of the U.S. government, and of U.S. aerospace industries. Moreover, it has done this in a context requiring international cooperation.

The West Europeans and the Soviets have responded to this U.S. dominance in somewhat similar ways, even though the Soviets remain nonparticipants in Intelsat and the West Europeans constitute the largest bloc outside of Comsat. Both have objected to Comsat's dominant position and both have made efforts at establishing independent communications satellite systems, partly to gain bargaining leverage with Comsat.

There have been suggestions in the United States that all parties involved in international communications—Comsat, AT&T, ITT, RCA, Western Union International and some others—merge to form a single entity in order to bargain more effectively with other communications entities around the world. This proposal, however, has been resisted by the major carriers.

Meanwhile, the renegotiations around Intelsat continue. It appears likely that Comsat's position will change, though to what extent remains unclear. Intelsat in one form or another will probably persist, and the United States is in a strong position to affect its future and the future of global communications.

NOTES

1. For discussions of the social and political influence of communications, see Wilbur Schramm, ed., *The Process and Effects of Mass Communications* (Urbana: University of Illinois Press, 1960), which contains numerous essays on a wide variety of subjects and an extensive bibliography.

2. Katherine Johnsen, "Shortage of Frequencies Threatens Satellite Communications Growth," *Aviation Week and Space Technology,* May 9, 1966, p. 32.

3. Katherine Johnsen, "Intelsat Vote Expected for New Satellites," *Aviation Week and Space Technology,* January 1, 1963, p. 33.

4. "The Room Sized World," *Time Magazine,* May 14, 1965, pp. 84-88.

5. Arthur C. Clarke, "Extra Terrestrial Relays, Can Rocket Stations Give World Wide Radio Coverage?" *Wireless World,* October, 1945, p. 305.

6. William Meckling, "Economic Potential of Communications Satellites," *Science,* 133 (June 16, 1961): 1885.

7. Roger Kvam, "Comsat: The Inevitable Anomaly," in Sanford Lakoff, ed., *Knowledge and Power* (New York: The Free Press, 1966), p. 271.

8. U.S. Congress, *Communications Satellite Act of 1962,* Sec. 102 (a), Public Law 87–624, 87th Cong., H.R. 11040, August 31, 1962 (emphasis added).

9. For a collection of articles on the domestic politics of communications satellites, excerpts from congressional hearings and deliberations, as well as selected documents, see Lloyd L. Musolf, *Communications Satellites in Political Orbit* (San Francisco: The Chandler Publishing Co., 1968).

10. Plenipotentiary Conference to Establish Interim Agreements for a Global Commercial Communications Satellite System, *Agreement Establishing Interim Arrangements for a Global Commercial Communications Satellite System* (hereafter referred to as *"Agreement"*), Preamble, Reprinted in U.S. Senate, Committee on Aeronautical and Space Sciences, *International Cooperation and Organization for Outer Space,* 89th Cong., 1st sess., August 12, 1965 and in *U.S. Department of State Bulletin,* August 24, 1965.

11. A/RES/1962/XVIII, December 13, 1963.

12. For a summary of these arrangements, see R. L. Smith-Ross, "Allocations of Frequencies for Radio Astronomy and Space Sciences," *Nature*, 203 (July 4, 1964): 7–11.

13. *Communications Satellite Act of 1962*, Sec. 102 (b), (c).

14. See Wilbur Schramm, *Mass Media and National Development*, (Stanford: Stanford University Press, and Paris: UNESCO, 1964), pp. 58–69.

15. Meckling, *op.`cit.*, pp. 1885–1886.

16. U.S. Senate, *International Cooperation in Space*, p. 117. See note 10.

17. I have used the form "CETS" from the French title, Conférence Européenne des Télécommunications par Satellite, to avoid confusion with ECSC of the European Coal and Steel Community.

18. U.S. Senate, International Cooperation in Space, pp. 118–119.

19. "Comsat in Europe," *New York Times*, February 16, 1964, p. 28.

20. Murray L. Schwartz and Joseph M. Goldsen, *Foreign Participation in Communications Satellite Systems: Implications of the Communications Satellite Act of 1962*, (Santa Monica, California: The RAND Corporation, 1963), RAND Memorandum, RM-3484-RC, pp. 78–79.

21. Frank G. McGuire, "Europeans Shying at Possibility of U.S. Dominated Comsat Corporation," *Missiles and Rockets*, May 4, 1964, pp. 28–29.

22. Eurospace "enlists some sixty or seventy companies on the continent and in the United Kingdom in activities calculated to raise the sights of the European governments in their space planning." Arnold Frutkin, *International Cooperation in Space*, (Englewood Cliffs, N. J.: Prentice-Hall, Inc., 1965), p. 162. Eurospace appears to be something of an international lobby.

23. McGuire, *op. cit.*, p. 29.

24. United Kingdom, House of Commons, *Parliamentary Debates*, February 26, 1964, col. 124. Referred to in Ivan Cheprov, "Global or American Space Communications System?" *International Affairs* (Moscow), December 1964, p. 71.

25. *Ibid.*

26. "Buying into Comsat," *Economist*, 212 (August 1, 1964): 490 (Emphasis added).

27. "Persuaders from Outer Space," *Economist*, 218 (March 26, 1966): p. 1206.

28. Neil P. Hurly, S.J., "Satellite Communications: A Case Study of Technology's Impact on Politics," *The Review of Politics*, 30 (April 1968): 184.

29. Quoted in Donald E. Fink, "Eurospace Urges Regional Comsat System," *Aviation Week and Space Technology*, August 28, 1967, p. 29.

30. Elinor Langer, "Comsat: Europeans Wary of U.S. Plan for American Dominated Commercial Satellite Enterprise," *Science*, 142 (December 27, 1963): 1638.

31. McGuire, *op. cit.*, p. 29.

32. Robert Gilpin, *France in the Age of the Scientific State* (Princeton: Princeton University Press, 1968), p. 581. See also Jean Jacques Servan-Schreiber, *The American Challenge*, (New York: Atheneum, 1968).

33. For a fuller discussion of this perspective, see Arnold Frutkin, *op. cit.*, pp. 74–79 and Don E. Kash, *The Politics of Space Cooperation*, (West Lafayette, Indiana: Purdue University Press, 1967), pp. 10–12.

34. Quoted in Langer, *op. cit.,* p. 1639.

35. *Ibid.,* p. 1638.

36. Eugene B. Skolnikoff in his *Science, Technology and American Foreign Policy* (Cambridge: MIT Press, 1967) writes, "The increasing prevalence of technology with . . . global implications represents a trend in current technological development, a trend that can confidently be predicted to intensify in the future. Such a trend has important long-term implications for this country's foreign policy, implications that deserve explicit recognition and extended analysis. . . . The steady diminution of a nation's freedom of action to apply science and technology as it sees fit even at times within its own borders, is one such implication." (p. 303).

37. Elinor Langer, "Comsat: Private Satellite Firm Working out Ties with Government: Basic Decisions Still Open," *Science,* 142 (December 20, 1963): 1559.

38. "Satellite on the Dotted Line," *Economist,* 211 (June 27, 1964): 1454.

39. For a fuller discussion of the issue of nongovernment entities taking on roles heretofore reserved to sovereign nation-states, see Don K. Price, *The Scientific Estate,* (Cambridge: Harvard University Press, 1964), chapter II. For a discussion of Comsat in particular, see Herbert I. Schiller, "The Sovereign State of Comsat," *Nation,* January 25, 1965, p. 71.

40. Elinor Langer, "Comsat: U.S. Satellite Company Leads New International Venture: System to be ready around 1966," *Science,* 146 (November 30, 1964): 624.

41. *Ibid.*

42. *Agreement,* Article IX (c).

43. Cf. *Telecommunications Reports,* March 23, 1970, pp. 5–7.

44. Communications Satellite Corporation, *Annual Report,* 1969.

45. Quoted in Richard G. O'Lone, "U.S. Dominance Seen Hindering Intelsat," *Aviation Week and Space Technology,* August 28, 1967, p. 31.

46. See the *Agreement,* Article IV.

47. *Ibid.,* Article V (c).

48. *Ibid.*

49. *Ibid.,* Article V (d), (e).

50. Katherine Johnsen, "International Comsat Agreement Reached," *Aviation Week and Space Technology,* August 3, 1964, p. 25.

51. *Ibid.*

52. *Agreement,* Article VIII. See also Plenipotentiary Conference, *Special Agreement,* Article 12. (Hereafter referred to as *"Special Agreement."*)

53. *Agreement,* Article XII (a), (b), (c).

54. Cecil Brownlow, "International Comsat Agency Considered," *Aviation Week and Space Technology,* February 17, 1964, p. 34.

55. "Russia Delays Comsat Team Commitment," *Aviation Week and Space Technology,* June 22, 1964, p. 24.

56. See the *Agreement,* Article X.

57. These categorical distinctions between social and technological criteria are taken from Alvin Weinberg's "Criteria for Scientific Choice," *Minerva* (Winter 1963): p. 159. Though Weinberg did not elaborate on his social criteria, the issue of geographical distribution of funds for scientific work seems to be an example of social criteria for scientific choice. The conflict between criteria, in this case, is a *political* conflict. It is be-

tween geographically defined political units (i.e., states and nations) and political units defined with respect to science and technology (i.e., aerospace and communications companies and Intelsat), to which geographical distinctions are of secondary importance.

58. Langer, *op. cit., Science,* November 30, 1964, p. 682.

59. Donald E. Fink, "Eurospace Urges Regional Comsat System," *Aviation Week and Space Technology,* August 28, 1967, p. 30.

60. Johnsen, *op. cit., Aviation Week,* January 23, 1967, p. 33.

61. William D. Hartley and Jerry Bishop, "Comsat on the Spot," *The Wall Street Journal,* September 12, 1967, p. 1.

62. U.S. Department of State, "The U.S. and International *Science Notes,* No. 20, August, 1968, p. 6.

63. Schwartz, *op. cit.,* p. 31.

64. "Satellites: A Fight at Home, A Hard Sell Abroad," *Business Week,* May 21, 1966, 47.

65. See Kash, *op. cit.,* who argues that international cooperation in space programs with the non-Communist world gives those peoples a stake in U.S. successes and failures in the space program. If they are not related by some sort of cooperation, Kash argues, they then tend to be swayed by the press which relates more of the U.S. program's failures than it does failures of the Soviet Union. "The expectation was that by helping other countries get various kinds of satisfaction from space activities, the United States could gain their good will and support." pp. 16–17. See also E. J. Moulton (manager for African development in the Comsat Corporation), "Satellite Over Africa," *Africa Report,* 12 (May 1967): 13, who, after noting that several African countries had bought into Intelsat, suggests that "since they pay a continuing share of the costs of establishing and maintaining the system, these countries have a direct interest in the success of each launch." See also Frutkin, *op. cit.,* pp. 74–79.

66. Vernon Van Dyke, *Pride and Power, The Rationale of the Space Program,* (Urbana, Illinois: University of Illinois Press, 1964) p. vii. See also Richard N. Gardner (Deputy Assistant Secretary of State), "Cooperation in Outer Space," *Foreigng Affairs,* 41 (January 1963): 354, and Schwartz, *op. cit.* for a fuller discussion of this general objective.

67. Johnsen, *op. cit., Aviation Week,* January 23, 1967, p. 33.

68. *Ibid.*

69. "Global Comsat Expansion Delayed Two Years," *Aviation Week and Space Technology,* May 30, 1966, p. 31.

70. *Special Agreement,* Article 10, (f), (g); Article 12, (g).

71. Johnsen, *op. cit., Aviation Week,* August 3, 1964, p. 25.

72. Donald E. Fink, "French Ask U.S. Help for Comsat," *Aviation Week and Space Technology,* June 5, 1967, p. 22.

73. Robert Lewis Shayon, "Satellites: Orbit for the Future," *Saturday Review,* June 8, 1968, p. 74. I have not encountered this incident in other sources and, since Shayon does not reveal his sources, I cannot vouch for its accuracy. Nonetheless, it seems to indicate resistance in the State Department to transfer of communication satellite technology.

74. *Ibid.*

75. "Persuaders from Outer Space," *The Economist,* 218 (March 26, 1966): 1207.

76. Johnsen, *op. cit., Aviation Week,* January 23, 1967, p. 33.

List of Original Signatories to the
Agreement and to the *Special Agreement*

TABLE 8-1

Country (Governments signed the *Agreement*	Communications Entity designated to sign the *Special Agreement*	Quota
United States of America	Communications Satellite Corporation	61.0
United Kingdom of Great Britain and Northern Ireland	Her Britannic Majesty's Postmaster General	8.4
France	Government of the French Republic	6.1
W. Germany	Deutsche Bundespost	6.1
Australia	Overseas Telecommunications Commission	2.75
Italy	to be designated	2.2
Japan	Kokusai Denshin Denwa Company Ltd.	2.0
Switzerland	Direction Générale des PTT	2.0
Belgium	Régie des Télégraphes et Téléphone	1.1
Spain	Government of the State of Spain	1.1
Netherlands	Government of the Kingdom of the Netherlands	1.0
Sweden	Kungl. Telestyrelsen	.7
Denmark	Generaldirectoret for Post og Telegrafvesenet	.4
Norway	Telegrafstyret	.4
Portugal	Administracão Geral dos Correios, Telegrafos e Telefones	.4
Ireland	An Roinn Poist Agus Telegrafa	.35
Austria	Bundeministerium für Verkehr und Electrizitätschaft, Generaldirection für die Post und Telegraphenverwaltung	.2
Vatican City	Government of the Vatican City State	.05

IV

*POLITICAL
SCIENCE AND
THE PROFESSIONAL
MYSTIQUE*

Most *dissenting political scientists face a paradox: on the one hand, many leading administrators and presidents of key institutions of higher learning in America were trained as political scientists; but on the other, the discipline had contributed very little—actually, almost nothing—to the questions which eventually came close to destroying those institutions. Political science has long been an inward discipline more concerned with applying trivia to its trivia than using its knowledge outside the discipline. To break the search for trivia is also to say something about this use of knowledge. The contributions in this section seek to clarify the uses of knowledge by examining the relationship between the discipline and the academic world surrounding it. By showing how little the discipline has contributed to an understanding of that world and how much it has blocked attempts to gain an understanding, they prepare us all for a more proper use of political science knowledge.*

9

DEATH AT A LATER AGE: POLITICAL SCIENCE VERSUS THE COLUMBIA REBELLION • *David Underhill*

Introduction

Almost everyone perplexed by some problem has had the experience of dreaming a solution which reconciles every difficulty, fits every loose piece into a comfortable niche, smooths all the rough edges. Then the dreamer awakes, and as he watches helplessly his grand solution dissolves like a unit of the South Vietnamese army under attack. Students of political science at Columbia underwent a similar experience beginning in April 1968. After studying politics for several years, politics suddenly engulfed them right on the campus in the form of the first Columbia rebellion.

It dumped them into a sea of data and besieged them with the problem of understanding what was happening so that they could decide what personal roles to take in the events around them. But when they tried to apply their training and talents, many of them discovered, and have continued to discover in the quieter months since the spring of 1968, that their backgrounds gave them no

better grasp of the Columbia events than training as a physicist
or a plumber would have given them.

Beyond this vexing discovery, these students had to face and
account for the roles taken and attitudes displayed by the certified
political scientists on campus. At Columbia even more than at
most other universities, political scientists and the seats of institutional power have exercised a magnetic influence on each other.
In April 1968, the president of the university Grayson Kirk, the
vice president and heir apparent David Truman, and Kirk's
eventual successor Andrew Cordier, then dean of the School of
International Affairs, were all members of the faculty in the Department of Political Science and had actually taught in earlier
years. Another member of the department's faculty was the dean
of the university's graduate division and one of the administration's
stalwarts during April and May. Among the university's entire
faculty, another professor of political science became the most outspoken ally of a quickly formed student group inaccurately calling
itself the Majority Coalition. This group's main dispute with the
administration was over the administration's initial reluctance to
crush protests quickly and forcefully. Another political scientist became the chief organizer and one of the main spokesmen for an
assemblage called the Ad Hoc Faculty Group that tried to mediate
between the administration's camp and the protesters. The effect
of the AHFG's activities was to undermine the protesters' position,
as will be shown later. Another political scientist became a
spokesman for a small, short-lived, and impotent band of faculty
members who gave slightly more sympathy (but no forthright support) to the protesters than to their opponents. In short, the
political scientists at Columbia not only failed without exception
to support the protests but actually were the leading figures in the
campaign to end the protests and restore the administration's
authority on campus.

The issue that arises, therefore, is why Columbia's students of
political science generally found themselves incapable of applying
their training usefully to the events around them and why their
professors largely lined up forcefully against the protests. The
discussion which follows points toward the conclusion that political
science as presently taught, learned, and used generates more

confusion, distortion, and verbose inertia—if not canonization of the established order—than understanding.

The Triple-Ply Blindspot: Data, Language, Method

The use of the word "science" in the name of the discipline and of most university departments where political scientists teach or study implies objectivity and impartiality. This ideal is an elusive one even under the best circumstances, which as a mere beginning, must include a body of impartial and objective data. A quick look at the data available on the Columbia events shows that any selection from among these data for a scholarly study must inevitably be at least as arbitrary as it is impartial and objective.

Even a casual search for data in the form of speeches, press releases, pamphlets, leaflets, articles, interviews, and personal observations would quickly turn up enough material to keep any researcher chained to his desk for weeks simply reading it. Stripping this heap of data down to manageable size is a problem that an astrologer could handle easier than a scientist.

Political scientists are trained to be suspicious of radicals and ideologues. So anything issued by the Strike Coordinating Committee falls very easily under suspicion. But the administration's view of events, ex-President Kirk's "Message to Alumni, Parents, and Other Friends of Columbia," contains, by this writer's careful count, no less than sixty-three outright lies (or innocent errors, perhaps) and artfully misleading or highly dubious passages.

Off-campus sources are no more reliable. The daily press is stuffed with data, but in its rush to meet deadlines, if for no other reason, it falls into many errors of omission and commission. It also harbors biases which color its reporting regardless of deadlines. In some cases, like the underground press, these biases are explicit and unmistakable. In others, like *The New York Times,* whose grey layout and language convey an impression of languorous impartiality, the bias is not so obvious. The innate tendency of reporters and editors for established papers to take established leaders seriously, if not sympathetically, does not necessarily make their stories inaccurate. It may only make their stories carry more of the established authorities' views and opinions, clearly labeled as such, than the other side's. This bias makes the established press a handy reference for official statements and documents, but it can also lure or numb a researcher into adopting the authorities' views of what has happened. He needs a nearly religious devotion to giving the insurgents' side a fair hearing if he expects to give that side a fair hearing.

This highly selective reporting—and many examples could be cited from the *Times* and other "impartial" sources—often did no more than make the other side of the story hard to find. Sometimes, however, the tendency to view the contest from the administration's lines produced stories that err in more than omission and lopsided emphasis. Stories that the *Times* ran on damage done inside university buildings during student occupations and police busts adopted as fact the administration's charge that students had done the damage, even though evidence existed suggesting that the police were, at least, partly responsible. The *Times* also offered very subtly distorted views of events even when it did not cater to the administration's views. A story of May 23 on the second bust said that police "swept through the university grounds clubbing, kicking, and punching student protesters who flung back rocks, taunts and obscenities."[1] The chronology of the sentence indicates that the police were the aggressors. But it also pictures the students as putting up a fierce and spirited resistance as the police shoved them across the campus. In fact, nothing like the skirmish evoked in the story occurred. The great majority of students receiving the cops' kicks, clubs, and punches were not taunting and throwing but were trying to run and hide.

There is no way of knowing what was on the mind of the reporter who wrote the story that way or the editor who altered it. But the story, as printed, had the effect, intentional or not, of justifying to some degree the police behavior and thereby, to the same degree, absolving the university authorities of blame for wanton injuries inflicted by the cops whom those authorities had asked to clear the campus. Thus, even reporting which seems to present a balanced view of an event like the second bust actually distorts that event in a way that could very easily delude a researcher, both in his search for the simple facts of what happened and in his appraisal of the contending sides.

It shouldn't be surprising that crowds of students booed the *Times* delivery trucks making their stops at newsstands near the campus during May or that many of these same students trusted the news in underground papers like the *Rat* and *New York Free Press* or radical papers like the *Guardian* more than the news in an objective source like the *Times*. A political scientist who, in his search for data, ignored or belittled this judgment by the masses would make his job easier, his conclusions neater, and his work much less scientific than a nonprofessional's who took this judgment seriously.

After a researcher has decided how to solve, evade, or overlook these problems with the data, he then has to decide how to couch his analysis. The problem arising here is that his analysis cannot be carried out in the English language (or any other for that matter) without imposing one bias or another upon his work and, therefore, upon his readers. Did the people who moved into the campus buildings for six days "seize" those buildings or "liberate" them, "occupy" them or "free" them? Was the mass failure of students to appear in class during the days after the first police action a "high absence rate" or a "strike"? Have the students who were suspended from school or otherwise punished been judged and found guilty by "disciplinary proceedings" or have they been "purged"? The two times that the police came onto campus did they "restore law and order" or did they carry out a "seize and hold" pacification campaign? Should the whole series of events which began near the end of April 1968, he described as "turmoil" or an "insurrection," as "disruptions" or a "rebellion"?

There is no escape from these verbal dilemmas, and choices must be made. The trend of the choices made by this writer will become clear as the paper progresses, but there will be no elaborate attempt to justify these choices. In the absence of any objective basis for making such choices, they must be arbitrary. Perhaps a new incarnation of political science could establish some scientific means of making these choices. Political science as it now exists cannot do this because it cannot, as this paper intends to show, carry out an objective analysis of the Columbia insurrection. Only if political science were capable of such an analysis could the discipline provide guides for choosing between contradictory sets of words and for separating valid and significant from faulty and irrelevant data.

Of course, the discipline does attempt, in its fashion, to carry out objective analyses and to provide such guides. This is done under the direction of various methodologies, "analytical constructs," and "tools of the trade." They have names like systems analysis, behavioralism, communications theory, pluralism, input-output analysis, decision-making theory, etc. Since no analysis of a subject can include and comprehend everything, any analysis must begin by setting aside most of the information and issues bearing on the subject. The various branches of political science achieve this winnowing by adopting one of the methodologies or another, which automatically excludes (or drastically subordinates) certain issues and information. Thus, many of the problems arising from the volume and the contradictions in data disappear, since much of the data drop out of sight. Many of the problems over deciding which words to use also disappear. For instance, a researcher's chosen method may tell him that certain kinds of conduct are the typical forms of political competition and other kinds of conduct are not. If his chosen method says it's not the norm for students to take over university buildings, then he knows that the buildings were seized rather than liberated.

Political scientists often try to justify these effects of adopting one method or another by conceding that the effects occur but denying that they produce any bias. To use one method, so the argument goes, is not to deny the validity of other methods. The chosen method simply deals better with the issues that a certain researcher is interested in than another method would. Other researchers could use other methods to deal with other aspects of the same general subject—the Columbia rebellion, for instance—and get equally valid results. The presumption behind this catholic attitude is that the sum of the efforts by the various sects within political science will amount to an overall analysis that is a thorough, accurate, and objective presentation of all sides of the subject at hand.

It is possible, however, that the sum of such efforts is a thorough presentation of a fairly narrow set of attitudes and conclusions.

In such a case, the medley of methods would, far from presenting an unbiased picture of some subject, actually be giving narrow orthodoxy the appearance of an exhaustively verified objective outlook. So the issue that has to be examined is what the biases of the various methods are and whether these biases offset or actually reinforce each other. This will be done by choosing a few questions that appeared during the Columbia insurrection and examining what difficulties and distortions arise through trying to answer them according to the canons of political science.

Questions and Nonanswers

Questions could be chosen by deciding to analyze the insurrection via one of the existing outlooks or methods of political science. The so-called tool chosen would be better suited to answering some types of questions than others. Therefore, this choice of a tool would also amount to a choice of the questions to be answered. This method of selecting questions is professionally quite acceptable, but it will not be used here because it bases the selection on the harmony between the tool and the questions rather than on the importance of the questions themselves. Questions will be selected instead by the very simple method of choosing those which arose prominently from various quarters during the insurrection and which continue to cry out for answers.

1. Among all these questions, the first in magnitude, if not also in importance, is the very fundamental puzzle of what caused the insurrection. The type of answer that anyone gives to this question will depend critically on where his analysis starts in history and on what issues he believes were involved in the rebellion.

For instance, an analysis which began on April 23, 1968, would tend to conclude that SDS caused the insurrection, with the assistance of clumsy tacticians in the administration. One which began a few years earlier would tend to conclude that administrative decisions like planning to build a gym in Morningside Park and affiliating with the Institute for Defense Analyses, plus the war against Vietnam, perhaps, caused the insurrection. One which began in the Middle Ages would conclude, much more readily than one which began in this decade, that the great change in the nature of universities since that time caused the insurrection. If the choice of where to start is arbitrary, then so are the conclusions which flow from that choice.

Decisions about what issues were involved in the rebellion will have an equally powerful impact on a researcher's conclusions about what caused the rebellion, since deciding what the issues were amounts, in large part, to deciding what motivated the various participants in the rebellion to take the roles they did. Was student power versus autocratic authority on the Columbia campus the issue, or was it university expansion into the surrounding community, or affiliations with national government and business, or connections with international wars, institutions, and businesses? Was student discontent with this particular university the issue or was it national or international student unrest? Were student unrest, the alienation of youth, and the generation gap issues at all, or were racism, the American economic and political system, and a latter-day Luddite rebellion against automatonization the issues?

In cases like the Columbia insurrection where the data do not point irresistibly toward certain historical starting points and issues as the appropriate ones—and this includes most subjects worth studying—then the various methods of analysis current in the discipline intervene to make the arbitrary choices that are necessary. The method or methods decided upon will, in effect, declare certain issues and events relevant and others irrelevant. The profound effects which these allegedly methodological decisions will have upon a researcher's conclusions turn the decisions themselves into data, since these decisions will shape an analysis and its final "findings" as much, if not more, than will the data available on the subject under analysis.

Therefore, if it's pertinent in studying the Columbia rebellion to collect data about decisions made within the Strike Coordinating Committee, the administration, and the various faculty councils, along with data about the purposes these decisions served, then it's equally pertinent to inquire closely into methodological decisions and the purposes they serve. The purposes woven through the methods which political scientists generally choose can be perceived in part by recognizing that a researcher who desires to minimize the political significance and emphasize the irrational or conspiratorial character of the Columbia insurrection would make the choices which tend to confine his analysis to recent dates and to the Columbia campus. One who desired to emphasize the political significance of it would make the choices which spread his analysis out historically and geographically.

A political scientist is not supposed to begin his work with the desire of pursuing one of these angles or the other. Nevertheless, the methods of the discipline strongly encourage him to take the narrowest perspective. In other words, they propel him in the same direction he would take if he began his analysis not by resolving to proceed as a political scientist but instead by deciding to analyze the insurrection in a way that would confine it as closely as possible to the campus and recent times, thereby making it seem like a rather limited and local affair stirred up by agitators and suggesting that a resolution of the conflict could be found at the same level.

Systems analysis is one of the tools which does this, and it has this compressing effect, even though it seems in some formulations to be an extremely expansive tool. But a systems analysis which tried to find the cause of the Columbia insurrection in a system of national or worldwide scope would still have two major limitations. First, any systems analysis, no matter how expansive, has an historical depth approaching zero. Although some forms of systems analysis speak of system transformations and try to trace such changes through history, nevertheless, when it comes to explaining the cause of a particular event, the explanation is usually phrased in terms of the interactions among the system's components existing at the time the event occurred. Thus, systems analysis allows scarcely any room for finding the causes of the insurrection in the changes that universities have undergone since the Middle Ages or even in the changing relationships between universities and government during recent decades.

Second, the difficulties in constructing the outlines of a coherent and credible system of national or worldwide scope virtually force the analyst not to construct a system and then fit the Columbia insurrection into it but rather to adopt some system already current in academic circles. This adoption has two limiting effects upon analysis. It discourages the development of ideas and analogies that clash with those acceptable within the adopted system. For instance, some of the striking students contended that their struggle was the same as the struggle being waged by oppressed people in the Third World and that the insurrection was not a complaint about certain conditions on and near the campus but an attack on capitalism and its fraudulent facade of democracy. If the adopted system does not postulate a similarity between Third World struggles and insurrections like the Columbia one and if it does not recognize the existence of substantial forces inside the country seeking to overthrow capitalism and the brand of democracy attached to it, then an analysis founded on such a system would have to dismiss the strikers' contentions as mere rhetoric, if not propaganda or demagoguery. The analyst's inability to attach these charges plausibly to any part of the system he has adopted leaves him no choice but to handle them in this fashion. The second limiting effect of adopting some current system is that the analysis based on it tends to shrink down into an analysis of Columbia as a subsystem, regardless of how expansive the entire system that it fits into may be. This happens because adopting the larger system means accepting it as an accurate scheme for explaining events. Therefore, the workings of the larger system are viewed as rather ordinary and commonplace, and the issue which warrants special attention is not those workings but instead something unusual and extraordinary, like the Columbia insurrection. Thus, both an expansive type of systems analysis and an initially constricted type result in an analysis of a subsystem to answer the question of what caused the insurrection.

On top of these historical and spatial limitations lies still another limitation derived from the logical requirements of systems analysis. The analysis concentrating on Columbia may indeed find a tempest in this subsystem. But that is all the disorder it is likely to find, and it will also foresee the withering of this tempest, with the larger system easing simultaneously back toward equilibrium, though perhaps an equilibrium slightly different from the previous one. This bias infuses systems analysis because the method can handle departures of a subsystem from normal behavior, the resultant disequilibration of the larger system, and a subsequent return to equilibrium. But it cannot handle pervasive or permanent departures from equilibrium. Systems analysis must be able to discern rather precisely the structure, functions, and boundaries of the components of any system under consideration. A system in equilibrium can, theoretically at least, have these characteristics. But a system moving out of equilibrium cannot have them, for the chaos that begins to erupt at such times makes it virtually impossible to discern these characteristics any longer. Since systems analysis could not operate if these chaotic conditions persisted, its logic induces the practitioners to concentrate on the factors which pressure the dysfunctional subsystem back toward more normal behavior and the larger system back toward equilibrium. The result will be an analysis destined to discover that the causes of the Columbia insurrection can be found in neither a disorder of the larger system that Columbia is a part of nor in a genuine revolutionary attack on the existing system and simultaneous attempts to erect an alternative.

2. The question of why the rebellion received as much student support as it did is closely linked to the question of what caused it, for in the absence of this support the revolt would not have begun or mushroomed as it did. All parties to the rebellion desperately desired an answer to the question, because the answer forms a crucial guide to means of increasing or decreasing the amount of support.

Any answer that political science might supply would first have to confront the fact that the contending parties to the rebellion disagreed wildly both among and within themselves on this question. Within the rebel ranks particularly the answers ranged from highly political (and often conflicting) ones to responses of the "This is where the action is" variety solicited by various media reporters. Under these circumstances, a political scientist searching for an explanation of why so many students supported the strike can conclude very little from sources at the scene of action and must rely almost exclusively on his own resources. This means adopting some model or framework or analogy for explaining the rebellion as a whole. The adopted scheme then provides a guide for deciding which, if any, of the many confused and contradictory reasons offered by the contending parties for the size of the support are the correct ones.

Unfortunately, no scheme currently in fashion among political scientists of good repute in the profession makes any room for popular uprisings as a part of the American political process. Politics is instead the interplay of interests within or very near the councils of power, the mobilization of arguments and public opinion, the bloodless clash of conflicting elites, the private mysteries of the polling booth. When activities of this sort constitute the definition of politics, then any other types of activity, are, by definition, nonpolitical. If these other activities steer clear of the political realm, then they are dubbed economic, or social, or cultural, or whatever. If they don't and insist instead on intruding into politics, they have, like a whale swimming ashore, forced themselves into a realm where they don't belong and become, thereby, a brand of madness.

This explains why not only opponents seeking to discredit the rebellion but also political scientists and other academics have frequently couched their accounts of the rebellion's size in terms of psychology, if not psychoses. Accounts of this type take advantage of the confusions, contradictions, and uncertainties in the rebels' own explanations for their conduct by saying that people have serious flaws in their personalities when they engage in highly peculiar, dangerous, and possibly self-destructive activities for reasons that they have difficulty explaining even to themselves. This outlook is unfair and delusive.

It is unfair because it applies to participants in the insurrection a standard of judgment which is not usually applied to people engaging in more ordinary political activity. When an opinion survey asks a person what he thinks of some policy or candidate, or when a citizen steps into a polling place to cast his vote, he is not asked to justify his words and acts. They are automatically accepted as sane and pertinent, almost regardless of his reasons or lack of reasons. Demanding higher standards of rebels may be a wise tactic for opponents who wish to label them daffy, but it cannot be justified on any other grounds.

It is delusive because it blinds (willfully?) the observer to reasons for the insurrection which are more fundamental and powerful than the rebels' alleged psychoses. If mass insanity did occur, calling the rebels nutty makes less sense than applying the same word to a society and political system that drive large groups of its people out of their minds.

In any case, to the extent that the diagnosis of madness depended

upon the rebels' sometimes harelipped attempts to explain themselves, the diagnosis lost much of its validity (assuming that it
ever had any) as the rebellion proceeded. People who entered
the buildings or joined the subsequent strike motivated by little
more than vague feelings of discontent and anger or by a simple
desire to be where the action was began to acquire verbalized
reasons for their behavior. To some extent they merely adopted
reasons already worked out and presented to them by others who
had been in the struggle longer and stood closer to the centers of
control (such as they were). An enemy of the rebellion could
easily picture this process as manipulation of the innocent and
credulous rather than the development of reasons for rebellion
appropriate to the circumstances and participants. But giving this
sinister tint to the process is merely a throwback to the insanity
argument, for it assumes that the people who joined in without
having an articulate rationale for their conduct were intellectual
fools and psychic cripples who would desperately and thankfully
believe whatever the manipulators told them.

Saying that the rebels had or acquired sane reasons for what
they did and therefore cannot be dismissed as psychiatric cases,
nevertheless, does not answer the original question of why so
many people supported the insurrection. Recognizing this redirects
the inquiry, for it now becomes necessary to ask what the issues
were that gave the rebels the motives and rationale to do what
they did.

3. Trying to answer the question of what the issues were immediately raises the same problem met in trying to answer the
previous question about the size of the support for the rebellion.
There are too many answers already on the record to cope with.
Consider, for instance, the matter of whether the university should
build a new gym in a city park lying between the campus and
Harlem. For some of the rebels, stopping the gym was a prime
concern. For others, the gym was important mainly as a symbol
of the administration's general policies toward the surrounding
communities. And some opponents of the insurrection called the
gym a "fake," "false," or "dead" issue at various times after
April 23. A similar spread of opinions could be shown for almost
every other matter that someone called an issue during the rebellion.

Once again, the accepted methods of the profession offer a very poor guide for deciding how to separate the real from the bogus. According to the ideology of pluralist democracy, which provides the philosophical justification for the standard American methods of analyzing domestic politics, an issue is a difference of opinion among groups competing for the authoritative allocation of the limited values dispensed through the political system. This formulation implies two corollaries for deciding what the real issues were at Columbia. First, that groups pursue their own interests in the competition and that when they apparently seek to pursue others' interests, then they are not raising an issue but are indulging in either apolitical or somewhat sinister activity, or both. Second, when groups attempt to operate outside the established rules of the competition, they are not raising an issue but are engaged in nihilistic practices which must be crushed. Otherwise, the political system (i.e., Columbia and, in some of the more megalomanic views, higher education in the U.S. or, occasionally, Western civilization as well), will contract a rapidly terminal corruption.

Accepting this kind of guidance about what the issues were leads very easily to conclusions of the following sort: The gym was not a real or even symbolic issue, because the students who rose to oppose it (with the possible exception of the black ones) were not acting in their own interests but on the alleged behalf of Harlem residents, who had hardly organized at all to oppose it, and, therefore, presumably approved of it. The university's affiliation with the Institute for Defense Analyses was not a real issue because it involved the university and various of its faculty members in activities with no practical effect upon students, and, hence, neither offered nor denied students any of the values that groups can compete for. Amnesty was not a real issue either. Since the demand for amnesty amounted to a demand for monumental changes in the rules of the competition, this demand was, by definition, not an issue. It follows that there was no reason for even discussing the argument advanced by the rebels: that amnesty was proper under the circumstances, because the political reasons for rebelling against the administration were just. If amnesty can't even be seen as an issue, it certainly cannot become one of the terms of a settlement. It had to be denied and its proponents squashed.

Even when political science can recognize some questions as

real issues, it has great difficulty dealing with them sensibly. Consider, for instance, the issue of whether Columbia is a racist, imperialist institution. This charge formed a large part of the rebels' basic argument from which the issues of the gym, the administration's expansion policies, and the IDA affiliation are logically derived.

Political science, when applied to international relations and comparative government, teaches much about classical military imperialism but relatively little about economic imperialism and neocolonialism. When it doesn't dismiss these last two concepts outright, it calls them by a different name—nation building—which casts them in a very different light and encourages very different conclusions about their character and benefits. Therefore, if Columbia is not dispatching troops into the surrounding territory and not setting up a colonial administration, then regardless of what other means the administration might be using to accomplish similar results, the political scientist has great difficulty in thinking that the university is imperialistic in any sense.

The racist part of this charge gets sluffed off with equal ease. At the end of slavery and reconstruction, racism ceased to be a major issue in national politics, and respectable scholarship began dealing with it as primarily a psychological problem. Most academic studies of it since then have been confined to the compartments of the universities that probe the mind and the sociology of small groups. Hence, political scientists (among others) have great difficulty recognizing its existence except in its most bold, malevolent, and KKK forms. That an institution which deliberately seeks black students and black employees for white collar positions could simultaneously be a racist institution becomes a virtually unthinkable concept. Therefore, policies that quietly but systematically force black and brown residents out of the university's immediate vicinity and that aid the development of counter-insurgency warfare do not deserve the label "racist," because they are not carried out with frenzied malevolence. When thought is constricted in this fashion, the presence of a few black faces on the campus produces the grotesque conclusion that nothing the university does quietly off the campus can be construed as racism.

4. The issues that actually motivated the rebels—as opposed to what political science would readily recognize as issues—did not

mix well with compromises. The administration was also reluctant
to compromise. Under these circumstances, a question that arose
frequently was whether more flexible and moderate leadership,
especially within the administration and the strike coordinating
committee, could have ended the conflict short of the drastic
measures that finally were taken. This question, particularly when
raised by the Ad Hoc Faculty Group in its attempts at mediation,
often took the form of an exhortation calling on the administration
and the rebels to be more moderate and flexible. In this form it
embodied the assumption that some common ground for compromise existed.

Superficially, an analysis of whether this exhortation was a practical suggestion would be an ideal task for a political scientist to
undertake. The exhortation implicitly contains several subsidiary
assumptions which all run congruent to ones that are an ordinary
part of the political scientists' trade. But once again the discipline's
assumptions and the methodology which employs them lead its
practitioners toward highly biased and unwarranted conclusions.

First, the exhortation assumes the existence on both sides of
distinct groups and leaders within them or of leading elites and
followers who recognize and accept leadership by the elite. Once
this assumption has been made, the analytic techniques derived from group theory and elite theory can be called into action.
The mere fact that these techniques exist constitutes a strong
inducement to make the assumption so that the techniques can
justifiably be used. But beyond this, both the political scientist and
the exhorters of moderation and flexibility *must* make the assumption in order to believe that moderation, flexibility, and eventual
accommodation are possible. If the rebellion were a mass uprising
rather than an organized movement with leaders or elites, there
would be no sense in making the exhortation. There would have
been no leaders to whom it could be directed and who could then
tell or persuade their followers to heed it. Political science teaches
so consistently that leaders or elites always emerge quickly to take
control even of initially mass movements, and the mass media
create leaders so compusively that conceiving of contrary circumstances requires an exertion of will bordering on sheer cussed-
ness. But the truth is that despite strenuous efforts by various
loose factions to seize control of the rebellion and direct it from

the strike committee's headquarters, no one ever accomplished this. So-called leaders of the strike frequently had so scrambled a comprehension of what was happening around them and exercised so little control over their followers that the leaders were led, rather than the followers. The most graphic demonstration of this chronic condition is the fact that the leaders were repeatedly surprised (astonished and shocked might be more accurate words) at the size and vehemence of the crowds that came out to liberate the buildings, confront the police, attend rallies, join the liberation school, etc. Under such conditions, exhorting the "leaders" of the strike to become more flexible or conducting an analysis that assumes they could have done so will generate as much confusion as understanding.

The second assumption, logically following very closely upon the footsteps of the first, is that these putative leaders could themselves make a decision to be more flexible and were not the mouthpieces of interests elsewhere. If they weren't free to choose their own courses of action, then calling on *them* to be more flexible, or anything else, would make no sense. A political scientist who accepts the validity of this second assumption can apply some variant of decision-making analysis to the way in which the leaders decided to behave or not to behave more moderately. In doing so, he concentrates his and his readers' attention on the process of making decisions within the leadership of the contending parties. This necessarily stifles consideration of whether the actual centers of decision-making lay elsewhere, and thereby fortifies the administration's (and a large part of the faculty's) contention that the rebels were interested mainly in agitation over issues beyond the campus walls and would destroy the university to promote these outside purposes, while the administration's only concern was Columbia. If a political scientist using a decision-making analysis wanted to avoid giving unwarranted support to the administration's contention, he would have to expand the decision-making system greatly so it included much more than the university. This is a step he would instinctively be reluctant to take, since it would blur the boundaries of his decision-making unit and vastly increase the number of decision-makers and communication channels to be studied, thus making it extremely hard to conduct an analysis that would appear scientific.

Taking this step would also tend to support the more radical rebels' charge that the source of Columbia's problems—and, therefore, the solutions—could not be found in the university's central administration building. Since the requirements of the discipline's methodology, if not its ideology as well, urge that this step not be taken, the rebels' charge gets short-changed or ridiculed.

The third unspoken assumption behind the call to moderation is that both sides sought or could be persuaded and pressured into accepting a solution which restored roughly the *status quo ante,* with some marginal changes in policies and personnel. This presumes that decisions taken by the contending parties, acting in a moderate mood, would have the effect of eradicating the problems that gave rise to the insurrection.

Insofar as the war against Vietnam was one of these problems, the presumption obviously does not apply. With other issues, their immunity from the power wielded by the disputants on campus is less clear. However, it wouldn't be rash to argue that the administration's decisions to link up with the Institute for Defense Analyses and to stand firm against amnesty were not taken entirely at the administration's initiative and free will. These decisions reflected the wishes and interests of many influential individuals or agencies far removed from Broadway and 116th Street. Therefore, these were not decisions that the administration could undo easily, if at all, and thereby extricate itself from the problems that they generated.

Under these circumstances, the calls for moderation and flexibility echoing from the faculty (and later implicitly from *Up Against the Ivy Wall,* a book about the insurrection by the staff of the undergraduate daily newspaper) are not only impractical but also unfair, especially to the administration, in their failure to give accurate weight to the immense pressures reaching in from outside the university. The political scientist participates in this unfairness too if he adopts, and he can hardly do otherwise, a methodology that encourages him to constrict the range of the issues and pressures at play.

But while being unfair to the administration, he is also being subversive of the rebels' position. The administration could hardly disregard the pressures bearing on it from outside, no matter how much the faculty or others might have called on it to be more flexible. But calling on the rebels to be moderate demands, in effect, that they capitulate. At the beginning of the rebellion, the administration had a vast superiority in organization, influence, and resources both on the campus and off. The operators of these implements temporarily lost some of their grip and their cool, but the implements remained. The rebels, on the other hand, began with almost nothing and gained very little durable political power beyond this, even at the height of their so-called strength.

Asking for moderation in these circumstances, or conducting an analysis that presumes moderation was possible, calls upon the administration to give up relatively little from its warehouse of political power while suggesting that the rebels ought to surrender virtually everything they had gained, which was really not very much. Thus, even if the faculty members or potential analysts who would make the call for moderation and flexibility did not devise this approach as a disguised way of calling on the rebels to surrender, the call nevertheless amounts to precisely that.

5. When participants and observers during the insurrection gathered to grope for answers to the four questions above, the discussions turned very easily into disputes over what kinds of behavior by the contending parties of the insurrection were justifiable. Political scientists and students of political science did not distinguish themselves favorably in these discussions with mere laymen. For instance, at one point during the rebellion Vice-President Truman, one of the country's most eminent political scientists, offered the opinion that legality alone determines both morality and justice. That is, of course, an answer to the question of what acts are justifiable. But it isn't an answer which demonstrates that training in political science equips a man uniquely well to handle questions about the fundamental issues arising in politics.

However, he does have an excuse which other political scientists cannot lean on. His position in the administration obliged him to say something at the time to counter the rebels' claim of justification. But the mere fact that he had to respond teaches a lesson reflecting poorly on the customary omission of questions about justification from the concerns of political science.

He had to respond because this question had become not just an abstract discussion for the amusement of philosophers and theorists, but a highly political issue that would fundamentally influence the outcome of the insurrection. In relatively placid times for any particular society, justification is not an important political issue because the participants customarily and habitually accept the prevailing rules of political competition. At other times, however, when the rules themselves come under fire, then justification becomes a primary political issue.

Arguments which claim that action to alter the rules is justifiable are one of the few political resources available to elements challenging the rules. For sources of strength the challengers must rely heavily on their own numbers and on the acquiescence of the uncommitted. This means relying largely on arguments justifying the challenge, since the challengers must have vivid convictions to sustain them against the opposition they face and must strive to maintain the indecision of the uncommitted, at worst. The defenders, on the other hand, can rely on intransigence and coercion, although the results are often "counter-productive." Or they can try to undermine the challenge by striking at the rebels' own arguments of justification.

In these ways, justification becomes a highly political issue that must be dealt with very thoroughly by any analyst trying to understand the causes, course, and outcomes of the Columbia rebellion. For example, once the canard that the rebels can be dismissed as psychopaths has itself been dismissed, then answering the question of why so many students supported the rebellion requires an inquiry into how they justified to themselves their extraordinary behavior. But the inquiry cannot stop at merely making a catalogue of the justifications offered. It must move on to judging their validity.

When one faction of the rebels says that the insurrection occurred because Columbia is complicit in the repression of poor people in Vietnam and Harlem, another faction says the problem is the inept governance of the university, and a special fact-finding commission says bare light bulbs and bunk beds in the dorms are part of the problem, it is necessary to assess the validity of these justifications. Otherwise, the analyst is surrounded by a morass of issues and can come only to the useless conclusion that all the issues adduced by everybody must be counted as reasons for the insurrection.

Beyond this, the validity of justifications must be assessed before making any predictions about the future of the rebellion. Justifications that were a ruse or so utterly fanciful that they will wither rapidly when exposed to experience would not serve well in their essential role of mobilizing and maintaining support for the various parties. Any predictions that did not take account of this would also wither very rapidly.

Finally, only an analyst so thoroughly convinced of the worthlessness of his work that he knew no one would ever look at it could afford not to weigh carefully the validity of the justifications. The treatment he gives to the various justifications will influence his readers' opinions of them, and the readers' opinions will be reflected in their attitudes toward (and perhaps participation in) any continuation of the insurrection that he has analyzed or in future conflicts over similar issues.

Of course, saying that judgments are necessary on the validity of the various justifications offered does not clarify the standards to be used in determining their validity. The opposing standards used by different parties to the rebellion granted and denied justification to every brand of behavior. But the standards used by licensed political scientists caught up in the affair are the ones of particular interest here, for they indicate the present capacity of the discipline to deal with questions of justification. From the evidence available, it appears that political scientists employed three standards: disgracefully shallow, uselessly impartial, and grossly biased.

The first of these consisted of tactical and strategic advice parading as standards for judging whether the rebels' behavior in liberating buildings was justifiable. It almost always came from opponents who used it as a way of damning the rebellion without seeming to oppose the rebels' objectives. At its shallowest it asserted that the behavior was wrong simply because, "You're not strong enough. You can't win." More sophisticated versions went something like this: "You don't realize what you are doing. Action of this sort will bring on a fascist reaction that will make your original conduct seem like child's play." At best, this standard is a mere truism. Obviously, any action that severely challenges an established order will receive a strong reply, perhaps very much stronger than the original challenge. This will fail to happen only if the established order is so flaccid or decrepit that it is about to collapse anyway.

At worst, this standard is dangerously inverted. The rebels' general position on all the major issues argued implicitly (and occasionally this was made explicit) that the reaction preceded their action and that their acts were more defensive than offensive. An argument like this might be merely a self-justifying excuse for otherwise inexcusable behavior. But history knows occasions when the failure to resist repression quickly and firmly then invited further repression. Whether conditions like these existed at Columbia and in the university's off-campus activities is a crucial question, but the warning about provoking a fascist reaction doesn't even recognize that the question exists.

Finally, this standard based on fear of a fascist reaction contains only one small fragment of ethical content. The standard says, in effect, that it is better to endure whatever conditions exist than to risk provoking repression, since repression would be even worse. This brand of ethics reveals an almost total inability to cope with ethical questions. Whether repression would be worse and whether repression rather than the rebellion would win are both highly problematical issues. But the "fascist reaction" standard of judgment forces those who accept it to retreat meekly when confronted with risks. It always must warn against taking any risks because it provides no basis whatsoever for making an ethical comparison between what exists now and the kind of new order a successful rebellion might create.

The second general category of standards offered by political scientists was the uselessly impartial variety. These came mainly from members or camp followers of the Ad Hoc Faculty Group. When circumstances shoved upon them a need to choose, they refused to decide which side's behavior was justified and which wasn't. Instead they said, in effect, that neither's was by deciding to support whichever side would agree to cease doing what it was doing. This amounted to saying that the only behavior they could justify was behavior which restored the familiar peace and order to the campus. There is not much distance from this position to a position which holds that the only justifiable behavior is behavior that restores the political *status quo ante*.

The grossly biased standards make up the third category. They were based on four questions answered in ways that invariably justified the administration's acts while condemning the rebels.

First, what is an education? An education is what results when a number of people labeled students and a somewhat smaller number of people labeled teachers carry out a regular schedule of activities on the premises of an institution labeled a school, preferably "a great university." No defender of the administration ever answered the question with exactly these words, of course. But defenders did say many times that the rebellion must end so Columbia could return to its "primary educational function." In the context of events, this phrase and others similar to it meant merely that restoring order to the campus so the regular schedule of activities could resume was tantamount to resuming education on the campus. The rebels at least were asking whether education was indeed what resulted from the regular schedule of activities.

Second, what is Columbia? Some people said Columbia had become, in keeping with current trends, a diversified corporate conglomerate turning out graduates as only one of its many products and services. In general, these people were the ones who joined the rebellion or cheered it from the sidelines. Others, who said that Columbia was primarily a school educating under-graduates and graduate students, generally took some stand or posture justifying the administration's attempts to restore its authority. This view of Columbia could theoretically be accurate, but among the political scientists (both faculty and administrators) who took this position were several who had stated previously that Columbia existed not primarily to teach but to create new knowl-edge or who had helped turn Columbia into the diversified, multi-purpose enterprise that the rebels accused it of being.

Third, what is just authority? These men never denied publicly that legal authority equals just authority. But in trying to explain why it would be right and just for the administration to put down the rebellion, they usually argued that the rebellion was unreason-able, disruptive, coercive, physically dangerous, etc. They tended to avoid arguing that the administration's authority over the campus was right and just because it was based on a legal charter. However, in finally acceding to (if not endorsing) the two police busts, they necessarily fell back on the argument that the legal equals the just. Once the State was asked to send police onto the campus, it immediately became irrelevant whether the rebellion was unreasonable, disruptive, etc., since the State arrogates unto itself exclusively the presumption that its rules for conduct are, by definition, just and that the enforcement of these rules is therefore an exercise of just authority. To support the police action by arguing that the rebellion was unreasonable, disruptive, etc., would be to suggest that the acts of the State were not presumptively just, and these additional reasons for acting were necessary to confer justice upon the State's authority. A highly seditious suggestion, to say the least. The only way someone who supported the administration's call for cops can escape from these seditious implications is by believing that legality and justice are equivalent.

Fourth, what is legitimate force and violence? The answer that the political scientists justifying the administration gave to this question derives from the answer to the question discussed directly above. Therefore, it is unnecessary to discuss the three other ways that arose in various quarters to answer this question: (1) by distinguishing between violence against property and violence against persons; (2) by arguing over whether the rebels employed force first or whether the administration had struck first against oppressed people, if less overtly and largely off campus; and (3) by quarreling over the existence or not of other channels for expressing dissent. Even if the rebels could make conclusive arguments for their positions on all three of these issues, it would still be possible—and logically necessary—for supporters of the administration to deny that these arguments could constitute an answer to the question of what is legitimate force and violence. Most of the administration's supporters did, in fact, stand by such a denial. The reasons for adopting such a position are easy to see. Once it is accepted that the legal authority which the administration eventually relied upon was just, then it follows that the use of any force whatsoever to exercise that authority was legitimate, while the use of any force, no matter how little, to resist the administration was criminal. Thus, the question of the legitimacy of violence was also turned simply into a question of legality.

Such were the approaches advanced by political scientists for deciding what kinds of behavior were justified during the insurrection. The most that can be said for these approaches is that they were no more shallow and blindly biased than the discipline's approaches, discussed earlier, to answering some of the other main questions arising from the rebellion. The need for radically different approaches is obvious, if only to expose the obvious biases. A start can be made by deliberately viewing a few subsidiary issues of the rebellion in fashions that proper political science would consider quite bizarre, if not mad, and by showing these bizarre views to be quite plausible.

To Sanity Via Madness

Consider first the issue of why the cops were called in for the first bust when they were, rather than later or sooner. The most "sensible," "obvious," and generally accepted view is that the administration called down the bust when negotiations had reached an impasse. The attempts at mediation, particularly by faculty members, had failed to forge a settlement that both sides would accept. Therefore, this argument goes, the police were necessary, since the crisis had to be ended and there was no other way of ending it. This position came most clearly from the administration and its defenders. But it also appeared in the Ad Hoc Faculty Group's "bitter pill" resolution which, in effect, said among other things that if the rebels affirmed the impasse by turning down the terms of the settlement outlined in the resolution, then use of the police against them would be necessary and proper.

Instead of adopting the view that the police were called because negotiations had failed, an analyst could just as rightly (if not more rightly) conclude that the administration called the cops because negotiations were coming dangerously close to succeeding —for the rebels. The long liberation of the buildings brought the administration under increasing pressure, from the trustees especially, to restore normalcy to the campus. The trustees and others generating this pressure were outside agitators, people who do not live or work in the university community but leap into it at troubled moments to exploit these troubles for their own ends. Those ends required that the liberations cease very quickly.

Ending the liberations meant either that the administration

would have to accept most (perhaps all) of the rebels' demands or that the rebels would have to be hauled out by the cops. The outside agitators would not tolerate the former method of ending the liberations, but they would accept (perhaps relish) the latter. Columbia's administration had to use one of these two methods to end the liberations.

In the absence of calling the police, the rebels had the upper hand under these circumstances. If they held firm to their demands, the only way of ending the liberations by negotiations would have been for the administration to make major concessions to the rebels. Since the increasing pressure from the outside agitators was forcing the administration toward taking some decisive step to end the liberations, a negotiated settlement would necessarily have been a victory for the rebels. In other words, the negotiations had not failed but were moving perilously close to a settlement, on the rebels' terms Therefore, the final decision to call in the cops was made not because there was no alternative at that time but because the administration and the outside agitators needed an escape from a negotiated settlement.

The execution of this decision and of the subsequent one ordering the second bust raised the other two issues to be dealt with here. The first bust featured, among other things, a marked difference between the arrest of the blacks in Malcolm X University, (formerly Hamilton Hall), and the handling of white students inside the other liberated buildings on the campus. This contrast, whose existence no one has denied, raised the issue of reasons for the striking difference in treatment. The official explanation from university and civil authorities has been generally accepted. It asserts that there were two reasons for the contrast: first, that the police had also been ordered to handle the whites as gently as possible but that some of the men regrettably exceeded their order; second, that the university and civil authorities took special care to see that the police arrested and removed the blacks gingerly, since these authorities were properly, prudently mindful of the grave danger an angered Harlem would pose to Columbia.

In summary form, these reasons might seem to be a sensible, sufficient explanation, for the contrast in police conduct. Furthermore, they lend themselves readily to "deeper" analysis. A political scientist could seize on them, collect bushels of relevant data, and apply a wondrous panoply of decision-making, group-conflict, and communications-flow methods of analysis to show exactly how the contrast came into existence. But doing this would amount to nothing more than a torturous detour away from the more fundamental, and therefore more illuminating, reasons for the contrast. These reasons are, first, that the authorities are trying, where possible, to deal with blacks by buying them off, and, second, that these same authorities can deal with white rebels not by buying them off but only by beating them back. The care taken to handle the blacks gently and the broken orders in handling the white rebels are not explanations for the contrast in police behavior toward the two groups but rather the consequences of these paired policies.

The official explanation, of course, says that the desire to handle the blacks very carefully was a consequence of fears about Harlem. But, a longer look reveals instead that both the desire and the fears are mutual consequences of another circumstance, the conditions of life for Afro-Americans in general and for Harlemites in particular. Among the various ways that the authorities might choose for coping with the anger and unrest generated under such conditions of life, the authorities of Columbia, the city, and (to a lesser extent) the nation have chosen for the time being a course of pacification, or, in plainer terms, buying the blacks off. For Columbia, buying its own blacks off has meant giving them somewhat preferential access to places in entering classes and to financial aid, plus the appearance, at least, of trying to develop a sensitivity to the interests of blacks on and around the campus. During the rebellion, this policy particularly prescribed that the administration accommodate itself, if possible, to the black students' demand for ending the gym construction. When they showed themselves ready to take a strong stand against the gym, the administration had to back down on this issue or else allow the blacks to entertain grave doubts about the durability of the university's general policy of trying to buy them off. The administration's intense desire to smother such doubts explains why the gym demand was the only one of the rebels' six on which the administration was willing to make a major concession before the first bust.

If Columbia and the civil authorities had not decided to try buying the blacks off as the cheapest and easiest way of pacifying them for the time being, then Columbia would not have needed to be so frightened of Harlem, for two reasons. The administration would have known that insofar as any physical threat to the university actually existed, it would be dealt with swiftly, severely, and punitively. Second, were action of this sort ever taken, the administration would not have to worry about the inferences blacks would draw from it. When the authorities are trying to buy blacks off, they must take great care not to do anything that would suggest to the blacks that the buy-off is a ruse which gives way easily to repression. Such an inference would seriously wound the authorities' present efforts to buy the blacks off. But if buying-off were not the policy, then the authorities would not be engaged in strenuous efforts to win the blacks' good will. Repression then would be an efficient policy, since the repression couldn't compromise or destroy efforts that didn't exist. On campus, the administration would not have needed to deal preferentially with blacks, since many fewer would have been present in the first place and those present would have been more likely to accept much less than preferential treatment.

Understanding how the policy of buying off the blacks led the administration to speak and act as it did about the gym and the black arrests opens the way to seeing that the official and generally accepted explanation for the gingerly treatment of the blacks actually acts as a camouflage, intended or not, for four other matters that the administration would do well to conceal:

1. That the administration vastly overrated the so-called threat from Harlem. At no time since April 1968, have there been disruptions in Harlem aimed at Columbia, and even at the height of the rebellion black students on campus were never able to mobilize demonstrations of more than a few hundred people from Harlem. The administration has in fact felt so little intimidated by the "threat" from Harlem that now—more than two years after it officially stopped construction of the gym—it still has taken no steps to fill in the huge excavation scarring the park where the gym was to be built or to remove the fence surrounding the site, which cuts the park completely in two.

2. That the authorities' policy of buying off the blacks serves the

university and civil authorities' interests at least as much as the blacks' interests. The Columbia administration, by the logic of its policy of trying to buy off blacks, had good and sufficient reasons to reach a settlement with on-campus blacks even in the absence of any threat from Harlem. All the talk about threats from Harlem served to divert attention from this fact, while simultaneously giving supporters of the gym an easy way of transferring the blame for its death away from the administration and onto the residents of Harlem. In other words, the administration has subtly incited the gym's supporters to riot or at least to animus toward Harlem.

3. That blacks less noticed and less vocal than the ones who participated in the rebellion routinely receive much less than preferential treatment from the university.

4. That the treatment of the white rebels by the cops did not result simply from broken orders.

This last matter requires further inquiry, since it is the other half of the explanation for the contrast between the methods of arresting the blacks and the whites. Perhaps the cops did have orders to treat the whites as carefully as the blacks and then broke those orders. That fact, if it is one, would account by itself for the different treatment of the two groups—in the sense that the contrast could not have occurred if the orders had been obeyed. But the question that would still remain is why they broke the orders. The easiest explanation, one heard frequently from apologists for the administration, was that even a highly disciplined organization like a police force will have some deviants in its ranks who like to play rough and who break discipline. But this explanation explains nothing. It doesn't tell why the deviants deviated when dealing with the whites and not with the blacks. And it completely bypasses any inquiry into whether the violations of the orders had any sources except psychopathic ones.

An understanding, as opposed to a justification for, the police behavior must begin with the assumption that the deviations were not simply deviations. From that assumption an analyst can move on to consider the possibility that the orders were broken because circumstances virtually required that they be broken. Just as the conditions of existence for black people in America make a policy of buying them off plausible—if not inescapable—at the moment, so also the white rebels' mode of life dictated an opposite policy in dealing with them. White students and hangers-on at Columbia have, on the whole, been born into privilege and advantage.

When people born into such a status reject it by becoming rebels, they must be adopting a rather irreconcilable position toward the whole system that raised and nurtured them. If they are the natural heirs to that which the society has traditionally offered its most favored members, and they reject that inheritance, what could the authorities possibly offer if they decided they wanted to try buying these rebels off? These circumstances impel the authorities toward a policy—or practice, at least—of simply hitting the rebels on the head, figuratively and literally, since there is no other practical way of coping with them. Therefore, orders to handle the white rebels as daintily as the blacks, if indeed such orders were ever given, would have to be violated to carry out the authorities' only possible policy.

The circumstances which make it essential to the authorities' interests that such orders be violated also generate the means through which the violations occur. Because the white rebels have been born and raised in relative ease, they are relatively frail and soft, and, therefore, fairly easy prey for cops who might try to give them a thrashing. Because the cops have not been born and raised this way, they would easily resent these student rebels as young punks who ostentatiously cast aside advantages the cops privately yearn for. A vivid desire to give them a thrashing would not be a surprising result. Because the authorities were dwelling obsessively on the threats the rebellion posed to their policy of buying off the blacks, they concentrated on guarding that policy, as evidenced by the early concession on the gym and by the frequent processions of university and civil officials to Malcolm X University, particularly around the time of the arrests. By contrast, these officials and their sympathizers in the mass media directed much less concern toward, and many more polemics against, the white rebels. If the other reasons that the cops already harbored for meting out thrashings to the white rebels had not been sufficient, the echoes reaching the cops of these distinctions in official attitudes toward the black and the white rebels would have amounted, in effect, to orders for treating the white rebels precisely as the cops dutifully treated them.

Therefore, although the cops may, strictly speaking, have violated orders, they did so in obedience to an array of higher orders and necessities. The authorities, of course, expressed shock and dismay at what some of the cops had done in their name and muttered ominously about deviations from orders, departmental inquiries, and punishments. But these words served as camouflage, just as the words about the threat from Harlem did. When cops broke their orders so as to break students' heads, they were doing what they had been called to Morningside Heights to do.

The third issue to be considered reaches past the question of why there was such a contrast in the police treatment of the white and black rebels to ask what was the essence of the police action across the campus the nights of the first and second busts. Almost everyone would agree to the general statement that some time after the people in the buildings had been arrested and removed on those two nights, the police moved vigorously to clear the rest of the main campus. Beyond this, however, disagreements develop very rapidly over who ordered the cops to do what, whether the students provoked the cops or vice versa, whether excessive force was used, whether the clearing operations were necessary to prevent violence and destruction, etc. There is no need to enter here into the endless disputes that those questions generate.

For a political scientist, the important question should not be who deserves the blame for those police actions but what the political meaning of them was. President Kirk's decision to wage the second bust speaks eloquently to this point. His official explanation after the event said that it was regrettably necessary, since the university was in grave danger of destruction. Sometime before the bust, several windows had been broken, fires had been set in two buildings by unknown parties, and large crowds of students were roaming around the campus. But by the time the announcement of the impending bust was made—several minutes before the final order was given for the cops to move onto the campus—the breaking had stopped, the fires were out, and the crowds had begun to settle down quietly and aimlessly in an open area at the center of the campus. A few officers of the university, who presumably had access to the president's ear, were in the general vicinity and aware of these conditions. Yet the bust proceeded, although whatever danger to the university existed at the time was certainly less than

the danger of an hour or two earlier when the breaking and burn-
ing were in progress, with hundreds of police surrounding the
campus but having no orders to enter.

Under these circumstances, it is hard to believe that saving the
university from the torch was the actual motive for the bust, though
the president and others around him may have told themselves that
this is precisely what they were doing. Their fear of seeing the
university go up in flames was not well founded. However, if they
felt a vague, general fear and translated it into visions of leaping
flames, at least their vague feeling that something fearful roamed
the campus was well founded. The crowds had not only coursed
through the campus, but segments of them had also built barri-
cades at the two major gates and stood behind them defying the
police to enter. In other words, the students' crime was not that
they were trying to reduce the university to rubble. It was more
nearly the opposite: they had stopped damaging the university, had
seized control of it instead, and were successfully defying the
police, by whose grace alone Grayson Kirk could claim at that
time to be the president of Columbia University. That is why he
ordered the bust, though in those hectic hours he himself may not
have realized what his real reason was for doing so.

Understanding this helps, in turn, to understand the political
significance of the cops' actions once they came onto the campus
and got down to the business of clearing it. Most simply, of course,
during both busts they were restoring the administration's authority
by sweeping the campus clean of noise, disorder, disobedience, and
defiance. But they were doing it in a way characteristic of circumstances wherein despotic government has lost the last shreds of its
subjects' willful obedience. The masses, having long since lost
respect for their rulers, now have also begun to abandon the habit
of obedience. Therefore, the only method of controlling them is
to teach by terror the lesson that whenever some subjects step out
of line, then everyone is a potential victim of the random retribu-
tion rained down in response to the disobedience by those few.

This lesson, if well learned, produces two results essential for a
ruler in such desperate straits. First, since he has lost contact and
control so completely that he can no longer distinguish active
subversives from mere malcontents, he must force the subjects to
police themselves by showing them harshly what will happen if

they fail to keep the subversives in check. The second result is that if a revolt still manages to boil up somehow, then the subjects will know that for safety's sake, they must quickly remove themselves as far from the trouble as possible, pull their shades, and cower behind their locked doors. By doing so they inadvertently identify and isolate for the ruler his most ardent opponents, those subjects who fled less quickly than the others.

Some analysts might want to explore the arcana of whether this strategy used by the administration at Columbia should properly be called the "seize and hold" or the "search and destroy" brand of counterinsurgency and pacification program. That is was either one or the other should be clear to any fair-minded observer. Ex-President Johnson, certainly one of the world's most experienced men in the field, apparently was convinced that the Columbia operations fit into the general category. On June 20, 1968, as reported in the next day's *New York Times,* when the Columbia rebellion was still a very live topic, he told a group of prominent educators:

How times change. I suspect I ought to ask some of you for a battlefield report this evening. I'd be interested to know how the pacification program is doing, how much progress you are making in reform, how things are doing in the outlying buildings, and whether you still hold the central administration offices.[2]

The reporter swears that the president intended these words as a jest. He doesn't report the educators' response. The reader must assume that they seized the analogy instantly and shook it to death with laughter, lest anyone have time to believe that they didn't think it was a jest. But, on the other hand, no joke is funny and draws laughter unless it contains a core of truth.

Conclusion

Although many might disagree with the conclusions reached about the three issues discussed in the preceding section, agreement or disagreement is less important than demonstrating that those three issues could not have been dealt with at all except by first breaking loose from the shackles of political science. The discussion employed very little data, and that pittance consisted not of rare, previously unknown statistics but of generally known, generally noncontroversial information. The political system under analysis consisted not just of Columbia but included all levels of government and also reached out halfway around the globe. The justifications that certain parties to the insurrection offered for their behavior came under question, on grounds other than "practical" ones. And motives were attributed to certain parties who never acknowledged such motives and who, even in candid moments, might not recognize the motives as their own. This smashing of the shackles may have been haphazard and faulted in various ways, but it was not capricious. Rather it was essential if any true analysis of the three issues under consideration was to occur at all.

An analyst who tried to use the tools of the trade in dealing with the issue of why the administration called in the police for the first bust would necessarily reach a conclusion identical to the explanation that the administration and its supporters offered for the bust. All the available data show that negotiations had been at a standstill for the last few days preceding the bust. There aren't any data, nor are there likely ever to be any, revealing that the men who decided on the bust recognized among themselves that in the absence of such a police action, negotiations would have to resume and eventually end with a victory for the rebels. Furthermore, the good political scientist knows that since pluralist politics consists of the arguments and pressures at play among the contending parties, when one of the parties calls in the police, this is not a political move against its opponents but rather an attempt to restore the rules so politics may resume. Therefore, even if some data were available suggesting that the administration did, in fact, order the bust to prevent a negotiated settlement, the political scientist would tend to discount these data as dubious and irrelevant. The result, in sum, would be an analysis that did not analyze the issue at hand but merely confirmed in detail the administration's explanation of its decision to call the bust.

A similar result occurs when dealing as a political scientist with the issue of why the police treated the whites very differently from the blacks. Again, there are no data to support any view except the administration's. If an analyst is to investigate the event, he must step beyond the data about this particular event and then take three further steps. First, he must sketch out the administration's general policy for dealing with blacks. Then he must presume a connection between this policy and the administration's actions during the insurrection, even though the policy was not designed with such extraordinary circumstances in mind, and even though no connection has been admitted. Second, he must presume that Columbia, try as it might to create a citadel on Morningside Heights, still is not severed from its surroundings. There must be an intimate connection, explicit or not, between Columbia's policy toward blacks and the policies of local and national governments; otherwise Columbia's policy could not survive. Third, where neither practice nor words reveal the existence of any general policy, as in dealing with white rebels, the analyst must discover in existing circumstances the logic that explains the decisions which were made and the actions which were taken. None of these steps is possible without venturing far outside the bounds of political science with its insistence on data as a first priority in any analysis, on shunning presumptions that cannot be "proven" by amassing "evidence," on discouraging deductive reasoning, and on keeping the subject under analysis tightly constricted for the sake of precision.

Finally, an inquiry into the political character of the two busts cannot be carried out according to the canons of the discipline. Once again, the data show that the cops cleared the campus merely to restore order and remove any threat of physical damage to the university. Evidence of any designs beyond this on the administration's part is not available and probably never will be. No method of analysis current within the discipline allows a serious comparison between police action against lawbreakers on a university campus and military operations in a foreign war. And, any terrorizing effect that the police actions had on their victims or witnesses could not be confirmed empirically until subsequent police actions against the same people revealed that the first rounds of terror had indeed taught a pacifying lesson. Under these circumstances a professionally correct analysis would have to conclude that the busts were only what the administration and police officials claimed, with apologies for the occasional accidents and excesses.

The early pages of this paper showed only how political science dealt with the major issues of the rebellion in a highly arbitrary and biased manner that served status quo interests, without showing what could replace this way of analyzing the insurrection. Now that alternative approaches have been presented for the three subsidiary issues, the nature of the conceptions banished by the discipline starts coming into focus, and it thereby becomes possible to outline the preliminary steps necessary for creating alternative approaches to the major issues.

These steps number at least six. First, it is necessary to cultivate the will and then the skill to find in existing circumstances a logic that explains events when neither participants in those events nor any available data can produce a coherent and convincing explanation. Refusal to do this leaves the analyst at the mercy of those in a position to release or withhold data and of those in a position to formulate, publicize, and win acceptance for their own self-serving explanations. Second, the analyst must posit the existence of quiet, informal, submerged forces active in the governance of the country's complex of civil and private institutions. Then he must try to find, expose, and explain the operation of these forces. Unless the Columbia insurrection is a highly exceptional case, the analyst must do these things in dealing with any political event, for too many aspects of the insurrection cannot be explained except through such an analysis of it. Third, economics must be incorporated into the study of politics, and the study of politics must become the study of how men are governed rather than how laws, regulations, and administrative decisions are made. The rebellion revealed that the question of who stood to gain or lose control of dollars and property shaped the course of events as strongly as any other factor did. In other words, economics is a political issue just as much as the creation of rules and the administration of institutions are political issues, since economics shapes the circumstances in which men must live at least as much as rules and administration do. Fourth, the so-called First, Second, and Third Worlds must be recognized not as strictly geographical localities but as overlapping areas that girdle the entire globe. This step is necessary for several reasons, but there is only one reason that can stand alone as sufficient. If large numbers of people active in an event like the Columbia insurrection located nominally in the First World insist that they are part of the Third World, then this insistence and the conduct accompanying it bring the Third World into existence there. Fifth, and this follows very directly from the fourth point, the traditional distinction between domestic and international politics must be abandoned, or at least severely altered. It has traditionally been acceptable to argue that domestic disputes between political parties and their leaders can spill over into international politics by influencing the foreign policy decisions that their government makes. This perception remains as true as it ever was, but now something else must be added. When police actions at home and military actions abroad bear a startling resemblance to each other, then the question is not merely how domestic politics affects foreign policy but also what difference, if any, exists between domestic and international politics. Sixth, in times and places when the government—whether of public or private institutions—seems to regard the maintenance of law and order as almost its sole function, then the analyst must proceed with the assumption that other functions have a distant secondary status, regardless of periodic perfunctory denials by officials. For several years during the 1960's, John Doar headed the division of the Justice Department engaged in demonstrating that securing civil rights was a primary function of government, even at the occasional expense of law and order. In 1969, as head of the New York City school board, he declared flatly that "the first principle of government is to maintain order."[3] Transformations like this indicate that an analyst is being only sensible and scholarly if he assumes that he is in one of those times and places when government must be regarded as an instrument of law and order, and of little else.

These six steps hardly constitute what some practitioners of political science would call an integrated, well-articulated framework for analysis. They are, more accurately, logical deductions from a certain attitude toward politics and the study of it. It is true that the application of this attitude to the three issues analyzed in the preceding section might seem like a highly arbitrary and biased way of analyzing politics, but if the earlier pages showed anything, it is that these same charges must be leveled with equal force against political science as it is currently practiced. And if "predictive power" is a good way of measuring the soundness of any particular approach to the study of politics, as many political scientists assert, then the attitude displayed here stands up very well. That attitude grows from the same roots as the attitudes suggested by the following recollections:

In late 1960 and early 1961, the first reports of U.S.-financed training bases in Guatemala for anti-Castro Cubans began to reach the American citizenry. It soon became apparent that these men would try to invade Cuba, establish a guerrilla base, and do to Castro what he had done to Batista. Some people, with no particular expertise in Latin American affairs, political science, or military tactics, predicted flatly that the adventure would fail, because these anti-Castro men lacked even a shadow of the popular support essential for success and that they would be turned in rather than sheltered by the peasantry. Better-trained people, on the whole, either withheld judgement or predicted the opposite. They were wrong.

In late 1964 on the campus of a great university, the late Malcolm X and two eminent professors of political science participated in a panel debate. Malcolm said that civil-rights legislation was a hoax and a joke because it didn't get at the problem tormenting the ordinary black man, and life was getting no better for him, perhaps worse. The professors mobilized their knowledge and methodologies to show that things were quickly and steadily getting better. Now Malcolm is dead, the professors are professing and prospering, and events have proven him right, them wrong.

When the now-infamous Tonkin Gulf resolution was passed in 1964, some amateurs at political science gasped in shock at the realization that this gave President Johnson a blank check which he would draw on until he broke the bank, since the harder the United States fought there, the further it was doomed to sink into the bog. No respected professional in the discipline shared this assessment, or dared to say so anyway.

As long as six years ago, civil-rights workers in the South included as a common staple of their conversation the likelihood of mass black uprisings and urban guerrilla warfare as an ordinary feature of life in the near future. Only within very recent times, when these predictions had become common occurrences, did political science begin to take seriously the possibility that they could occur at all.

No matter how impressive this score on predictions may be, the general outlook on politics responsible for the score still remains just an attitude, and the six steps outlined above remain largely deductions from that attitude. Perhaps a coherent, consistent, and systematic scheme for the analysis of politics can be worked out from this beginning. But even assuming that it can be, political science could—and undoubtedly would—counterattack with a few objections substantial enough to be answered in advance.

The attitude offered here is obviously, frankly, value-laden. It sides much more with outraged and outrageous people and views well-established people and institutions with much more skepticism than is customary in political science. This seems to war wildly with the discipline's ideal of value-free political analysis. In fact it doesn't, for a value-free analysis has never been an end in itself but merely the supposed means of achieving the real goal, an objective analysis. But value-free does not necessarily equal objective, and value-laden does not necessarily equal nonobjective. To call an analysis of politics value-free has meant one of two things: first, that the methods or outlooks which the analysis draws on are themselves value-free—that is they accord no inaccurate influence or improper preference to certain actors, institutions, and conclusions over others. The failure to achieve this ideal in practice through using the standard methodologies of political science has been exposed for inspection several times since the first page of this paper. Or, second, once a method of analysis has been chosen, for whatever reasons, then the analysis may proceed objectively, within the rules and confines of the chosen method, and the analysis earns the label value-free if it succeeds at this. The type of analysis suggested by the attitude advocated in this paper is just as susceptible to value-free analysis, in the second sense, as is any standard method of the discipline.

Susceptibility, of course, is not synonymous with success, and the success anyone has in turning out an analysis that his readers will recognize as objective depends greatly upon the data he attaches to his arguments. Therefore, a natural second line of objections by the discipline would be that the attitude advanced here neglects data, even spurns it. But the objection would miss the point. This attitude does not neglect data but simply wants to keep them in their place. Very few questions worth answering can be answered by heaping up data. On the other hand, some questions that beg and scream for answers cannot be answered except by neglecting data, since relevant data are not available and never will be. Finally, the questions an analyst decides to answer and the methods he decides to use will shape his conclusions as much or more than the data he employs. Myopic concentration on collecting and manipulating data easily generates a mixture of intoxication and hypnosis that blots out a vigilant awareness of how these decisions overshadow data.

The next objection, then, would be that a method of analysis developed from the attitude advocated here would be one that presented a warped approach to politics which no amount of objectivity or data could rectify. In short, the objection would be that this approach does not analyze political reality as it really is. The standard approaches to domestic political analysis concentrate on the congress, executive agencies, presidency, and pressure groups. This supposedly allows an analysis of politics as it really is, since these institutions are presented as the decision-making centers of the political system. The influence of forces outside these institutions is not excluded summarily from the analysis. Any influence that these forces have will be reflected in the outcome of the decision-making process, be this outcome laws, regulations, administrative decisions or whatever. This influence can be traced back through the decision-making process to its point of entry. Therefore, the framework accounts fairly for everything, and the result is an analysis of politics as it really is.

This argument has two fractures in it. First, although a method of analysis that places pressure groups and the formal institutions of government at its center can be adapted to account for influences on politics from outside these institutions, the same could be said for a method of analysis that placed anything else there, too. An analysis based on the configurations of matter at the beginning of the universe could also be adapted to account for all the influences on politics, provided that the possibility of Providential Intervention at various times since the beginning of the universe is excluded. An analysis based on close textual study of laws and regulations could also be adapted to account for all the forces influencing politics. Saying that an analysis based at one point between these extremes has a greater grip on political reality than analyses based at other points is simply a statement of preference rather than a conclusive argument about the locus of political reality. The second fracture becomes apparent by looking into the reasons for and the consequences of choosing the particular point between the extremes that political science has chosen. The consequences are that the pressure groups and the formal institutions of government get cast in the role of a Mecca to which all other influences in the polity must make pilgrimages before they are recognized as political forces. This creates two misleading impressions: that decisions made in Mecca are political, while ones made on Wall Street and Madison Avenue and in Detroit are not, and that these places almost always make the pilgrimage to Mecca rather than the reverse. The reasons why political science advocates such a view are fairly simple. The discipline grew out of a philosophy of politics and a political system which believes that the locus of political reality is precisely where political science has dutifully discovered it to be.

But to argue that the reality political science analyzes can't claim to be the one and true reality is not to prove that the alternate view of reality advanced in this paper is the true version. The argument is designed merely to show that objections which assert that some newly proposed method of analysis does not deal with political reality mask the fact that this same objection can readily be turned back upon its authors.

The objection of last resort, if all others fail, is that the attitude advocated here looks with some favor upon an undemocratic, violence-proned movement. Granting, only for the sake of argument, that the movement is undemocratic and prone to violence, this objection, when launched from the preserve of political science, is delivered with very bad grace. The discipline has outdone itself in showing that American democracy is not strictly democratic, cannot be, and should not be but rather is a pluralistic competition among elites and pressure groups. Ordinary citizens, as many studies have striven to show, do not know or care enough about the affairs of state to have a responsible voice in them. Therefore, it is proper that these people should be effectively excluded, except for occasional ritualistic appearances at the polls. Yet the State so constituted can, with the blessings of political science, move beyond persuasion and use force to maintain itself against these same citizens, if they complain too vigorously about the share of values authoritatively allocated to them. The discipline has affirmed many times that the use of force by the State is legitimate, that indeed the State is defined in large part by its being the fount of legitimate force. In other words, political science customarily takes the position that the government of the country is undemocratic and also that the government can legitimately engage in violence against citizens. To deny the same privileges and immunities to a mere movement would be, putting it charitably, uncharitable.

Replying to objections in this manner does not really answer them, of course, but merely wards them off. The only way to answer them conclusively would be to show not only that the objections are faulty but also that the alternate attitude advanced here and the method of analysis which might be derived from it have a soundness based on something more than the infirmities of opposing attitudes and methods. This cannot be done simply by exercising great skill and inventiveness in constructing a new method of analysis. No matter how tightly it might be constructed, it could still be punctured in many places by arguments of the same sort used throughout this paper against the current attitudes and methods of the discipline. Manning the pumps and patching the leaks would become a livelihood for a whole new generation of political scientists. A sound ship could be built only on a keel of political theory. The theory would provide the rationale for all the methods, techniques, questions, data, and conclusions that an analyst of politics wanted to use and would force opponents to attack not only these tools of analysis but also the theory itself. Such a theory, like any other, would necessarily reek with unproven assumptions, ambiguous propositions, and value judgments. Yet it would still be an essential foundation for a sound method of analysis. The fact that this is true should teach a sobering lesson to any political scientist who claims his work neither contains nor is based on value judgments or any of their messy in-laws.

In addition to providing a rationale for the analysis of politics, theory also performs another function. It posits ideals and norms, and this function is not just a bonus feature. Theory does this necessarily because the positing of ideals and norms is integral to the very definition of political theory, and also because this function is an essential component in the construction and maintenance of physical conditions which will verify its soundness. To posit ideals and norms is to argue tacitly, at least, that political reality should be molded—or remolded—to conform to them. When it does not conform, then it must be made to conform, or the ideals and norms must be abandoned as irrelevant curios and pariahs. In other words, when any analyst adopts some method of analysis, he is also adopting the political theory that the method of analysis derives from, and by adopting this theory he is simultaneously taking a prescriptive stance toward politics.

A brief return to the Columbia insurrection reveals how the logic of this sequence is not a purely academic matter. Whether the insurrection was a revolutionary act, a reformist one, a regressive one, or merely a combination of psychodrama and mixed-media happening depends on what follows from it in the years ahead. What follows depends, in turn, partly on what political scientists say the rebellion was. Political theories and derivative methods of analysis that view it as less than a revolutionary act—or as a revolutionary but undesirable act—will implicitly, at the very least, prescribe subsequent behavior which would insure that history shall regard the rebellion as a nonrevolutionary one. Some readers may think that the attitude toward politics advocated in this paper and the method of analysis that might be derived from it would tend to have the opposite effect. If that is so, so be it.

NOTES

1. *New York Times,* May 23, 1968, p. 51.
2. *New York Times,* June 21, 1968, p. 6.
3. *New York Times,* March 10, 1969, p. 50.

10

THE PROFESSIONAL
MYSTIQUE • *Alan Wolfe*

The Caucus for a New Political Science has been interested not only in changing the nature of the reality which political scientists study, but also in changing the way in which they study it. This concluding essay is designed to represent that interest. It summarizes the criticisms made by a number of younger scholars of the profession itself, and then it suggests some difficulties and alternatives which grow out of those criticisms. What some of us have discovered is that if there is a bias in the methods and means by which reality is sought, it is hardly likely that the one found will be neutral. In this sense, a concern for a proper definition of professionalism is an integral part of the search for a new political reality. The intellectual and the organizational aspects of the caucus' activities are not distinct. Without some change in the rigidity with which academic professionals study politics, all other reforms will be meaningless. Any examination of this proposition must begin with the very word "professional" itself.

There is something powerful about professionalism. In an essay describing his experience teaching a seminar on the professions, Everett C. Hughes relates how, even though the course is one in sociology, people from fields as diverse as insurance, nursing, probation, and public health eagerly register. "As often as not, they want to write a paper to prove that some occupation—their own—has become or is on the verge of becoming a true profession."[1] The reasons are not hard to find. Hughes' comments on the insurance salesmen apply with few changes to any other similar group striving toward professionalism:

The insurance salesmen try to free themselves of the business label; they are not selling, they are giving people expert and objective diagnoses of their risks and advising them as to the best manner of protecting themselves. They are distressed that the heads of families do not confide in them more fully.[2]

Desires are often turned into realities. Title VIII, Articles 131–151 of the New York State Educational Law has given legal sanction as professions in recent years to such occupations as nursing, pharmacy, accounting, surveying, and shorthand reporting.[3] Two books dealing with institutions in urban areas have concluded that a drive toward professionalism on the part of school teachers and policemen is necessary for an understanding of their collective behavior in recent years.[4] In the face of this tendency to professionalize everyone, one can respond, as did Harold Wilensky, by being critical of the absurdity of the whole movement.[5] But I find it hard to criticize people for wishing to have more status attributed to the way they spend forty or more hours each week. The demand of groups such as these for professional status occurs at the same time as the economies of advanced, industrial societies offer fewer and fewer personal satisfactions on the job. As computers take the guess-work out of estimating, as programmed materials are presented to the teacher, as pharmacists have a ready-made pill for any prescription presented, one can summon up little indignation, but only pathos, at those who claim prestige for work which can be quite humiliating. Do we really care when the bail-bondsman tells his Long Island neighbors that he is "in insurance"?

Indignation may more justifiably be present when professionalism is claimed without the need for status being present, which is the case when we move beyond the occupations already mentioned to scholarship. In those "professional associations" like the Modern Language Association, the American Physical Society, and the American Psychological Association, a desire for status in the eyes of the rest of the population is rarely an important motive. Scholars and teachers know that they can achieve all the status they want by manipulating their classes into a submissive acceptance of their own authoritarian role. With a choice of being either "doctor" or "professor," with a captive audience that increases year by year, with the right to wear imposing and expensive academic paraphernalia at each graduation, with special parking lots, with the privilege of not paying library fines, with waitress service in the eating-place—college professors have much to buttress their claim to special status.[6] Any understanding of the professional activities they engage in must look elsewhere, then, to explain the attraction of professionalism.

Looking elsewhere, an alternative explanation for the importance of professionalism for academics might be found in the motives of groups traditionally labeled as professional. There is something positive about the word professional, especially when compared to one of its opposites, the word amateur. At one time, professionals were considered to be a group of people whose expertise, fairness, and devotion were so unquestioned that decisions about who was to be admitted to the group could be made by the group itself, privately, under special sanction from the state. So doctors, lawyers, and clergymen, to name the three most prominent traditional professions, developed apprentice systems and qualification tests for membership in the profession. The service to society performed by these groups was so demanding and important that only they should have the right to determine entry, they claimed. Much of the argument was valid. One has only to compare the strides made by modern medicine with the charlatanism of a not too distant past to realize the service which professionalism has performed in certain areas of life. The same comparison, however, also reveals the great danger always inherent in professionalism, that the chartering practice will lead to an exclusivist clique based, not on external expertise or fairness, but on internal conformity to certain values of the dominant professionals. Since most groups traditionally called professionals have both these external and internal functions associated with them, any evaluation of their performance should seek to find which was dominant in the minds of the ruling professionals at any one time.

From this point of view, there is much to be said that the purpose of academic professionalism, and of its organizational counterpart, academic professional associations, is more conformity within the profession than external service to society. This is especially true of many of the social sciences, including political science, for reasons of the ideology governing the field. If we are to listen to its practitioners, we would come away believing that political science is a neutral, "pure," science, not a body of expert and immediately applicable knowledge, like law or medicine. Therefore, service to any clientele, an important part of the traditional professions, is not a salient characteristic of the social sciences, except for certain fields like social work and educational psychology. Of course, we know that the ideology is false, that social science is very active in supporting a particular societal clientele.[7] But it is nonetheless interesting that the formal ideology of a field like political science, by implication, denies the external rationale for professionalism. If this interpretation is correct, here is a clue that those who maintain the value-free ideology *and at the same time* call for professionalism are doing so because the internal functions are uppermost in their minds. Why have professional political scientists? There would seem to be no reason as far as society is concerned. But there are many reasons as far as the professionals themselves are concerned. Having rejected the desire for status and external service as these reasons, let us now look at what are to me more convincing reasons, particularly those dealing with internal conformity.

A valid explanation of the contemporary attraction among academics for professionalism must take into account some of the changes taking place within academia at this time. For many years, it was just assumed that academics were professionals and were expected to act as such. After all, most universities had clauses somewhere in their by-laws or procedures to the effect that faculty members were not expected to engage in "unprofessional" conduct. Left intentionally vague, such clauses implied that there was such a thing as *professional* conduct which all college professors could fairly easily determine. Judging by the way such clauses were implemented, it would seem to be true that so long as a faculty member did not engage in illicit sexual relations with his students, his conduct was professional. Such clauses were not codes of ethics; they had nothing to say about a faculty member like J. Sterling Livingston, who turned a position at the Harvard Business School into a personal fortune; a university like the University of Pennsylvania which conducted secret research into biological and chemical warfare; or about the various institutes which helped fight wars overseas and have been recently recruited to help fight wars in American cities.[8]

In the last few years, academics have become more and more concerned that a proper definition of a professional role be developed. In part this is due to the various questionable activities which have taken place within universities, but even more it is due to the undertakings of the critics of these activities. For these critics have raised embarrassing questions about the proper role of the professoriate. Can one proclaim value-neutrality and still do counterinsurgency research? Can one remain silent in the face of an immoral war and counter that he is not being political? Does academic freedom give a faculty member the right to teach a course in riot-control? Is it the proper role of younger faculty to accept all the rules of careerism determined for them by tenured faculty? Is the demand for publication really a demand for political conformity? All of these are difficult questions. In many cases, young and radical faculty members and graduate students found that, when they raised them, no answers were forthcoming. Instead, the questioners themselves were attacked. A "responsible" and "professional" scholar does not take public positions on controversies where he does not have expertise. Nor does he appeal to the masses (i.e., students) in emotional terms when issues are dividing a campus, for such conduct is demagogic. Nor does the responsible academic question strenuously the rules of scholarly promotion, for then he will soon find himself no longer an academic. One convenient rubric which could be used for all of these charges was that the dissenter was acting "unprofessionally."

In this way, conservatives within universities made a distinction between acting politically and acting professionally. In the former capacity, the professor is equal to anyone else who acts similarly. So long as he publicly takes political positions outside his area of expertise, he has the same civil liberty as the barber or welder who does likewise. When the professor acts professionally, on the other hand, different criteria arise. It is then that he can use the umbrella of academic freedom, presumably because now he will never need it.[9] It is then that he is presumed to speak with authority. It is also then that his application for promotion will be considered more seriously. In other words, this attempt to define professional conduct is a political act, among other reasons because it is really an attempt to define political conduct. To those who make this distinction, what is political is unprofessional and vice versa. The concept of professionalism now beginning to emerge in many academic disciplines, then, stems from a motive which fears politics, challenge, and dissent. Advocating professionalism becomes a way by which academic conservatives can latch on to a respectable-sounding phrase to justify their adherence to the status quo. To paraphrase the famous character from Molière, they have only recently discovered that they have been acting professionally all their lives.

The attempt to operationalize this dichotomy between political and professional conduct can be seen throughout academia at this time. Take the changes going on within academic professional associations, for example. There, insurgent groups in a variety of fields have organized for different ends. Sometimes they have asked professional associations to go on record as condemning the war in Vietnam; this was countered, until it recently became more popular to take such positions, by the argument that to take political positions as an institution is an unprofessional way of acting. In addition, other groups, like the Caucus for a New Political Science, have decided to run candidates for office within the professional association as a way of demonstrating alternative approaches to the discipline. When the caucus announced that it was going to run a list of candidates for the elected positions within the American Political Science Association, marking the first contested election among political scientists in the twentieth century, the idea was expectedly denounced as unprofessional, even by groups running their own slate of candidates (presumably only as a last-gap measure to bring the profession back to its senses). One political scientist, Donald Herzberg, with the support of some of the most well-known scholars in the field, devoted nearly full-time to fulminating about the election. First, he formed a group called the Ad Hoc Committee for a Mail Ballot, designed (successfully) to insure that the election be taken out of the hands of any face-to-face group and be placed in the hands of an impersonal mail ballot. Herzberg had read the book by a former president of the association, David Truman, which showed how resorts to the mail are frequently used by the leaders of groups to keep themselves in power when dissenters begin to emerge.[10] Then, Herzberg formed another group called the Ad Hoc Committee for a Representative Slate. Under its name, he circulated a letter to all the members of the association (cost: $780) which made this statement:

This election will determine whether the Association is to be a *professional organization based on shared interests and expertise in scholarship, research, and teaching* or whether it is to be a *political action group.*

The Ad Hoc Committee for a Representative Slate wants to maintain the Association as a *professional organization* devoted to shared *professional purposes.*

For this reason we ask you to vote for the Ad Hoc Slate, all of whose members were chosen for *professional, rather than political reasons.* [Emphasis added]

The superficiality of this distinction is so apparent that the only thing more remarkable than the fact that an allegedly neutral and politically sensitive scholar made it is the fact that allegedly similar scholars will adhere to it.[11] A letter which claims to be nonpolitical but which urges people to vote for a particular slate is an interesting enough phenomenon. But this one goes beyond that. One of the two people supposedly picked for professional rather than political reasons is much more well known in his political capacity. He was one of the most outspoken critics of President Perkins at Cornell during the racial soul-searching there, and one of the first to announce his resignation. Since then, he has become a prominent speaker on the anarchy caused by white and black student unrest and the need for firm discipline to remedy it. But people are being asked to believe that his name is put forward at this time because of his (very good, as it happens) scholarship on the two-party system. At least Herzberg has made the paradoxes clear; we can see from this letter that, for many, acting professionally is a way of acting politically by denying the fact. Acting "professionally" does not allow one to escape from politics; it only appears to let him do so.

This same distinction between political conduct and professional conduct is used in academic departments with much more serious consequences. Because the removal of a member of a department for reasons of his politics is a direct violation of the conventional wisdom of academic freedom (and because it may also lead to censure from the AAUP), the rubric of unprofessional conduct has found a whole new outlet for its use. Surely a person who acts un-professionally has no recourse to academic freedom, for that is a protection for professionals only. Therefore, firing such an individual, while certainly distasteful, is still defensible. Consider the grounds for such action against a person dismissed from his position as a teacher of international relations. While teaching at San Francisco State College, John Gerassi helped students break into a building during a demonstration and, in a public speech, urged them to close down the college. Both a departmental committee and a faculty ad hoc committee agreed that Gerassi was guilty of "unprofessional conduct" (made punishable by the state's education code), and he was fired. Here politics is blatantly associated with professionalism. But in defending this action, one of the faculty members instrumental in firing him also said this:

. . . he declined to exercise the normal responsibility of academic authority. For example, he gave all his student's "A's." In style, dress, associations, and deportment, he made it clear that he·regarded the students, and not the faculty, as his peer group.[12]

The indictment, if it is meant to be one, is devastating. If you cannot get someone on his politics, get him on his deportment. If it is true that there is a direct correlation between informal dress and left-wing politics, one or the other would do. The possibilities are endless.

Another example is more interesting because it grows out of the "good side" in an academic freedom case. In 1969, Angela Davis was fired from the UCLA philosophy department by the California Regents because she was a member of the Communist party, although that action will most likely be reversed by the courts. Unlike the 1950's, when such an action would have been met with partial silence, the whole university has jumped to her defense. On the surface this would appear to be a positive development, for it indicates that people really believe in academic freedom. But a further look leads to a different conclusion, for defenders of Miss Davis may inadvertantly be laying the groundwork for more political repressions. In a statement issued on September 23, 1969, David Kaplan, Associate Professor of Philosophy and Vice-Chairman of the Philosophy Department at UCLA, took a strong stand in support of Miss Davis. After giving the conventional reasons for academic freedom, he goes on to note: "Academic freedom is not a license for irresponsible behavior. Indeed the academic profession has its own code of professional ethics, and one which many would find quite demanding." Kaplan the goes on to list these responsibilities, which include the intellectual honesty, avoidance of indoctrination, and respect for the opinion of others.[13] Angela Davis has all these qualities, so she should be defended. But the real question would concern those who allegedly did not meet these "responsibilities." I, for one, do not meet them, for there are others whose opinions I do not respect (at all) and whom I am quite intolerant of. Among them are outspoken racists, militarists, and neofascists. Does that mean that my conduct is irresponsible and hence not deserving of academic freedom? One could see how the case could be made. Were I to be fired, not, of course, for my politics but because of this "irresponsibility," where would those who defend Angela Davis on the quoted grounds stand? One would hope that they would have the sense to see how, even in defending someone, they are stating the opposite case from the one they intended. One would hope they would also have the sense to see how "responsible" and "professional" modes of behavior can be used as ways of insuring acceptable modes of political conduct.

At this point the argument I am making can be summarized. Recent talk of the importance of academic professionalism in many disciplines has not grown out of the external relationships between the discipline and society but out of internal pressures for political conformity. Hence the demand for professional conduct is a demand for a conservative politics. To evaluate such a thing as "the profession of political science," then, is to talk about politics. I have found that those who defend many of the present practices of political scientists do so under the name of professionalism. Among these practices are the following: accepting the emergence of an elite within the field which sets standards with little review or question; excluding points of view other than the prevailing ones; affiliating with client groups which are supportive of the status quo; and developing a model of proper scholarship which is exclusionary in effect. These practices are familiar enough to anyone who knows the discipline of political science, and repeating them here will add little information and much boredom.

But there are still some who are unfamiliar with them, and more importantly, the connection between these practices and how professionalism is used to rationalize their existence has yet to be made.

1. Professionalism is used to justify the formation of an unrepresentative elite which has determined the character of the discipline. In another paper I have shown how a small, unrepresentative sample of the membership of the American Political Science Association has dominated the important positions within that body.[14] No contested elections were ever held, until last year. No outlets were provided for the general membership to express its opinions. The affairs of the association, and to an extent the profession, were carried out by the APSA's Executive Director, Evron Kirkpatrick, a man trained in the arts of anticommunism to the extent of affiliating himself with more than one CIA front-group. No procedures were available for independently investigating his behavior. The constitution of the association mitigated against the emergence of democracy or representative government within it. Most of the membership felt unable to protest, but did denounce, in the only survey taken, the "establishment" which had developed. In short, political scientists—who always tell others how to govern themselves—did not do a very good job when it came to their own house.

The more interesting question is the relationship between the oligarchic character of the APSA and professionalism. Within the APSA, a kind of gentlemanly club atmosphere prevailed in which decisions were made by a small group of notables. In the strange logic which imbues these things, supporting this unrepresentative oligarchy and desiring little voice in the association which made decisions affecting your life was considered responsible and professional, while trying to change it through means considered highly proper in the larger political system (voting, persuasion, organization) was considered demagogic, unprofessional, and generally beneath contempt. This seems to be one of those cases, which political scientists should know about, where elites, in order to insure their position of power, define standards to which everyone in the political system is expected to adhere. Most people do, because they have not thought of other standards and because they aspire to or identify with those already existing elites. Whether the standards are good or bad is beside the point; it's who makes them up which matters. Professionalism, seen as such a standard, easily becomes translated into political quiescence, even by the quiescent.

2. Professionalism has been used to justify the exclusion of points of view from the discipline which run contrary to the established ones. The way this works has been summarized in the Gerassi and Davis cases discussed above. Few people dispute the idea that departments use the rhetoric of professionalism to gain total adherence within a department to one point of view.[15] In departments of political science, this refers not only to political viewpoints but methodological ones as well. There are departments which will not hire someone, no matter what his qualifications, if he is not trained in mathematics. There are others which will dismiss as unqualified anyone with extensive mathematical training. Both types of departments are suspicious of anyone who claims that the knowledge uncovered by a political science must be used by insurgent groups who are challenging those who now have power in America. People affiliated with the Caucus for a New Political Science, for example, have already found themselves blacklisted from many political science departments. One person, whose teaching and scholarly credentials were astounding in their excellence, was denied jobs at three different universities on the basis of his connections with the caucus. Many others have had similar experiences.

The secrecy and confidentiality which surrounds faculty-hiring procedures permits such informal blacklisting to take place. There are some senior professors who, when they hear of a caucus person being considered for a job in another department where they have a friend, dash off an immediate letter to him dropping the crucial code word, "unprofessional conduct." That is the end of the applicant's chances for a job, for what self-respecting department will hire an unprofessional when they can have a professional? The applicant does not know what happened because he can never see the letter which blackballed him, and in some cases, he may never know that a letter was written. The whole process of confidential letters, which is usually cited as the "professional" way of making new appointments, can easily be turned into a procedure which has no due process, no chance to reply to charges, and no redress.

In spite of the rubric of secrecy, there has been one study of the hiring process, and, even though it was done in an allied field, sociology, its findings are relevant to political science as well.[16] By studying 185 letters of recommendation written by 167 sociologists, Lionel Lewis strongly questioned the validity of this statement by Caplow and McGee: "The data leaves us with a strong impression . . . that although the scholar's judgment of his colleagues is often blind and biased, and occasionally crazy, it *is* professional."[17] On the contrary, says Lewis, interpersonal considerations dominate the letters written by sociologists. Portions of his analysis are indicative of his findings:

It is manifest, then, that departments are not interested in recruiting men who will disrupt social relationships and upset the *status quo* within a department. The distinguishing personality traits a prospective department member should have to ensure that he will not be an irritant are friendliness (amiable, warm, personable, pleasant) . . . gentleness (patient, modest, quiet, easy-going, relaxed), and soundness of mind (stable, well-adjusted, balanced, even-tempered). Possessing, or seeming to possess, such traits is deemed of greatest importance in defining a suitable colleague.[18]

Lewis feels that his analysis supports neither the traditionalists who argue that universities do operate rationally or critics who argue that it should. But it certainly is supportive of those who argue that it doesn't. What I find most interesting about it is that although professional conduct does not operate as a significant variable in letters of recommendation, unprofessional conduct does. An assertion of the candidate's friendliness, gentleness, and soundness of mind is an assertion that he can be trusted not to turn into a political radical, who would, of course, be bitter, distrustful, and intellectually insufficient.

3. Professionalism has been used to justify an affiliation with client-groups which are supportive of existing American policies, national and international. In spite of its ideology of neutrality, there is little doubt that most political scientists are working hard to support the contemporary American status quo. The ideology of pluralism is only the most blatant example. Many political scientists work directly for the State and Defense Departments at research institutes at universities like Columbia, Stanford, and Harvard. In addition, political scientists, despite an early promise

to the contrary,[19] find themselves collecting all sorts of information on nonelites, while totally ignoring research on elites, to the extent, according to Karl Deutsch, of spending about one hundred times the effort on the former compared to the latter.[20] Finally, as the introduction to this volume has pointed out, in their adherence to a value-free, limited-objective, "scientific" state of mind, political scientists have assured themselves that they would be incapable of dealing with the power of privileged groups in this country even if they accidentally stumbled across them.

The connections between this overwhelming proximity to power and the drive toward professionalism are intertwined with all of the things discussed so far. Power in America, insofar as it touches political scientists, does so through the foundations. Part of being a professional political scientist is doing research which has foundation support. Yet, it does not require much insight to conclude that foundations are going to be receptive to certain ideas—the ones defined by the discipline as compatible with professionalism—and hostile to others, those the profession has put outside the pale. Foundations, says Robert Dahl, "because of their enormous financial contributions to scholarly research, and the inevitable selection among competing proposals that these entail, exert a considerable effect on the scholarly community."[21] That effect, despite Dahl's denial of the point, is to reinforce notions acceptable to the foundations and to the national power-elite which funds them. Not only are left-wing scholars, particularly those who study the power-elite, cut off from foundation support, but even partially critical institutes, the moment they become critical of the direction of American policies, find themselves without funds.[22] Note the word "direction." To criticize the war in Vietnam is acceptable to the foundations; to even mention American imperialism is not. Once again, a situation exists in which support for existing power relationships is not considered "political" acitvity, while nonsupport for the same relationships is considered political. The urge to become professional, in other words, becomes so compelling that political scientists cannot even develop a sufficient definition of their own subject matter. But few seem to mind, for adherence to an incomplete definition of politics, which only views the action of insurgents as politics, is also a professional thing to do, while attempts to promote a more comprehensive definition of politics is not.

4. Professionalism has been used to justify a model of research which has been quite exclusionary in effect. Political scientists know that there are two kinds of journals, acceptable ones and nonacceptable ones. The former are those which, by some arbitrary criteria, are considered authentic publications in the constant search for new jobs. The latter group, demeaned as "popular" or "journalistic" are to be avoided and ignored, although they are (perhaps in secret) read more avidly than those in the first group. Acceptable journals are also considered professional journals; when one writes for them, one is writing for a group of similarly trained professionals. The others are considered "lay"; when one does write for them, he talks down to the audience, for they do not understand the details contained in the more sophisticated periodicals.

Since only "professional" journals count in one's career, most political scientists think only of publishing there. But what is acceptable for publication in such a journal must meet further standards justified under the name of professionalism. These standards cannot be dismissed as simply scientific criteria which apply equally to all. A study by Diana Crane of allied journals concluded that "the evaluation of scientific articles is affected to some degree by non-scientific factors."[23] That this proposition carries over to the *American Political Science Review* is scarcely debatable. Whether or not those nonscientific standards include political bias is the more interesting question. From everything I have been able to conclude, they do, but never explicitly so. Rather than reject articles for the critical stance of their politics and accept others because of their status quo politics, the Review determines the former to be unprofessional, while the latter, it is decided, meet the standards of the profession.

Since I have not been able to obtain (professional secrecy once again) any systematic information on which articles are accepted and rejected for the *American Political Science Review,* I can only use secondary evidence. David Kettler, who worked as an assistant to the editor of the *Review* for a few years, does not doubt that political factors play a role in the selection of articles.[24] His point is confirmed by an analysis of the actual articles published. In the last few years, articles in the *Review* can be broken down into the following categories: those with a political bias which is conservative; those with a political bias which is centrist; those with radical political biases; those which have no political bias because they are solely methodological or mathematical; those which had no political bias because of other reasons; those which formally had no political bias but which concluded by justifying the existence of current political institutions; and those which had no formal political bias but which concluded by justifying existing American policies. Since the categories are subjective ones, I did not rigidly break down all articles from one period to another into each category, but instead read through some recent issues to see, in my own mind, which categories predominated. I found that articles with explicit *left or right* biases were rare.[25] Nearly half the articles were scientific and "professional," while most of the remaining half, by implication, had implicit political biases which were supportive of existing institutions (nearly all the articles on the House of Representatives fit here) or policies (most articles on Latin America or foreign policy fit there). Thus, there is a bias against articles which are explicit in their politics but not those that are implicit. The norms of professionalism, then, discriminate against committed political scientists whose politics run in either direction. The only way to take a political position is to sneak it by the ever-watchful editors under the guise of "science" and "responsible scholarship." Since those who tend to have these implicit politics are supportive of the status quo, professionalism once again is used to justify the exclusion of divergent points of view.

To the extent that traditional professionalism supports and justifies these practices, critics of academia will find themselves becoming more and more distrustful of the use of the term "professionalism." Any merits which may have been present in the idea —insight, intelligence, critical stance—will become lost as the term more and more becomes synonymous with the politics of quiescence. Pseudoprofessionals will guarantee that no room is left for true professionalism. While this is happening, those dissatisfied with what professionalism has come to mean will attempt to develop for themselves some guidelines for their own action. In an important sense, the formation of groups like the Caucus for a New

Political Science is the first step in this process of redefinition. As one involved in redefining, I think it might be helpful to conclude this essay with some observations about what this process involved.

The profession of political science, as presently constituted, is not receptive to extended criticism. Certainly it should be, but merely to say so does not help very much. Everyone will agree *in abstracto* with the proposition that an academic discipline should welcome to it people of all points of view, in other words, that it should be guided by the principle of pluralistic liberalism. The trouble with such assertions, however, is that pluralism rarely works. It was under a permissive liberalism that the present situation came about. All were allowed to do their own thing, and all wound up doing the same thing. Is there a causal relationship between the two clauses of that sentence? I think there probably is. In the American political system, within the universities, and, as I have been trying to show in this essay within the academic professional associations, a rhetoric of liberalism has long been present. Yet the reality of the situation in all three cases has been to deny the development of any true pluralism, underrepresenting dissenting points of view in all three. In my view, this is not a coincidence. The ideology of liberalism becomes a two-edged sword. It guarantees diversity within the tenants of liberalism itself (where it is not needed), but it is incapable of extending those benefits outside of itself (where it is). To simply assert the need for many points of view, then, is not enough. Something must be developed which will actually bring that about. Whatever that something is, it will probably run counter to the central principles of liberalism.

Two activities have been the principal vocation of radicals within the academic disciplines until this point. Both are initially essential; both have now reached the point where at least in political science they are counterproductive. The first activity was to "muckrake" within one's profession. Proving the existence of political bias, showing how oligarchies control professional associations, confronting the limitations of the received wisdom of academic freedom—all of these activities, which I have been doing now for about two years, are fun. All of them, in addition, have become tiring. There is only so much rationality within the universities and the academic professions. Some will be convinced of the justice of your cause, but more will ingeniously develop rationalizations to avoid the points you are making. Thus, there reaches a point in the development of insurgent groups within academic disciplines where they have to stop being internally critical of the practices and content of their profession and turn their attention to more important things. I personally find, therefore, that this will be the last essay I write on the state of the political science profession, all my points having been made. And I similarly urge organizations like the caucus to turn their attention away from the discipline and its problems to more productive enterprises.

A second type of activity is organizing within the academic professions for radical ends. This grew out of a movement which was recently popular on the left called "radicals in the professions."[26] Recognizing that radicals would constitute a minority in whatever profession they happened to enter, this movement discussed organizing techniques for expanding the radical constituency. When it turned out that some professions, particularly secondary school teaching and welfare work, were attracting a high proportion of left-leaning college graduates, there was some possibility of creating relatively permanent organizations. Teachers for a Democratic Society, organized in New York City, is one such organization. Its success (measured by its continued existence, no small accomplishment these days) is proof of the basic lesson learned from all these activities: that radical organizing cannot take place in professions where there are few radicals.

I mention this experience because it is directly relevant to the problem of what radicals in the profession of political science can do. Political science is one of those professions in which radical organizing does not make sense. Something seems to happen to people when they become political scientists, or maybe people who become political scientists were strange to begin with. But whatever the causal relationship, this profession is one of the least movable there is. (Economics may be worse). Allied disciplines such as sociology and history have recognizable subgroups of scholars whose dissents from the prevailing orthodoxies were well-known to incipient radicals.[27] This means that these professions may be more likely to see radical organizing succeed. But in political science, the only criticisms of pluralism, the dominant ideology, came from people who were excellent scholars, but who could hardly be considered political radicals.[28] With a dearth of radical thought at the left end of the discipline, it is no wonder that political science is so conservative at the center and on the right. What other discipline has seen the development of a right-wing Conference—not Donald Herzberg's group but a group of actual *National Review*-type political scientists—to counter the "New Left" tendencies of the Caucus for a New Political Science? This is especially remarkable in the face of the caucus' own tendency to deny its radicalism by adopting a liberal rhetoric and welcoming to its ranks anyone interested in making political science "relevant."

Radicals, in a few words, do not really exist in the discipline of political science. At the September 1969 convention of the American Political Science Association, while the leaders of the association and *The New York Times* all waited for the young militants to disrupt the meetings, as was happening at the same time with sociologists in San Francisco and the psychologists in Washington, those of us who knew about these things were laughing. We knew that there might be somewhere between five and ten political scientists in the United States willing to challenge the basic notions of pluralistic liberalism, and only four or five of them were at the convention. This lack of radicalism within the profession does not contradict the point that radicals have been discriminated against in the profession. Rather, the two propositions feed each other. The rules of professional conduct discussed in this essay—the hostility of the professional journals, the difficulty of getting a job teaching, the lack of funds, the exclusion from the professional association—have left their toll. The reason radicals were not in New York at the APSA convention was that they were either in San Francisco with the sociologists or at home with themselves. The study of power and governance, it seems clear, has been left to those who deny the importance of power and governance.

With both internal criticism and radical organizing becoming less productive within the profession of political science, the question becomes one of defining certain positive steps which those branded as "unprofessional" can take. One of these would be to turn to places where there would be some support. The caucus is currently (and rightly, I feel) exploring the possibility of joining with insurgents in other disciplines around a journal and other activities for similar ends. The problem is that insurgents in other fields have more to do within their disciplines, but there is nothing in that problem to stop their also working with groups outside their own. This would make political science the weak sister in any such coalition, but it is better than being an only child.[29] In addition, dissenting political scientists can also obtain support by joining with people from other fields within their own university. This has the disadvantage of bringing together people who speak different languages, but at least it gives them a chance to speak. Both of these alternatives, however, are not the end of the problem; they are simply suggestions to avoid the problem of the radical political scientist going stir-crazy.

Ultimately, the "unprofessional" political scientist could, if he does somehow obtain job security somewhere, realize the virtues of a true academic professionalism, not because he hopes to convince anyone of his purity, but because it could be a very satisfying thing to do. In discussing the caucus and similar groups, David Kettler has noted that:

these groups will dissipate their energies and get caught in the senseless escalation of expectations to the point of cynical passivity if they do not recognize that their political activities within these associations and professions must first and foremost serve the theoretical goal of making the disciplines places where we can do our work, including, of course, work between teachers and students.[30]

This "work" is called by Kettler, in the title of his paper, "The Vocation of Radical Intellectuals." If we have been denied by others the title of professional, the answer is to claim for ourselves the title of vocational. In our process of redefinition, we could conclude that the true academic professional is one who never uses the word professional, because of its suggestion of internal conformity. Furthermore, true professionals would, in all likelihood, know that they were professionals and not have to repeat it every time they take an action which they feel might be unpopular. The true professional, on the contrary, has a vocation, and that vocation is the promotion of his own radical truth. It may be, because the university is what it is, that he will be unable to pursue that vocation within it. But that should not stop him, for neither Marx

ALAN WOLFE

nor Voltaire pursued his vocation within a university. So long as our true professional does not allow the pseudoprofessionalism of academia to convince him that he is crazy and they are sane, he, more than anyone else, can follow his questions where they lead him. So long as he maintains his real interest in questions of power and governance, it is he, and not those who currently misuse the title, who will be active in the profession of political science.

NOTES

1. Everett C. Hughes, "Professions," in Kenneth S. Lynn, ed., *The Professions in America* (Boston: Beacon Press, 1965), p. 4.
2. *Ibid.*, p. 5.
3. As cited by Arthur Niederhoffer, *Behind the Shield* (Garden City: Doubleday Anchor, 1969), p. 20.
4. *Ibid.;* and David Rodgers, *110 Livingston Street* (New York: Random House, 1968).
5. Harold L. Wilensky, "The Professionalization of Everyone?" *American Journal of Sociology,* 66 (January 1961): 325–334.
6. Jerry Farber has made all of these points in an essay entitled *Student as Nigger* (Ann Arbor: Radical Education Project, n. d.). Farber's experience had been at one school, California State College at Los Angeles, and since I teach at an experimental college which was highly informal and brand new, I tended to discount his essay as exaggerated. However, I recently taught a summer quarter at Cal State, L.A., and halfway through the summer I remembered that it was Farber's school. I then kept my eyes open to see whether he was overdoing it. He wasn't.
7. See the essay by Marvin Surkin in this volume for more on this proposition.
8. Livingston and Penn are discussed in James Ridgeway, *The Closed Corporation* (New York: Random House, 1968), pp. 70–74, 126. For a good overview of the research institutes, see David Horowitz, "Sinews of Empire," *Ramparts,* 8 (October 1969): 32.
9. This point is relevant to an understanding of the proposition that academic freedom has been achieved. Walter P. Metzger, in *Academic Freedom in the Age of the University* (New York: Columbia Paperback, 1955), seems to feel that academic freedom is much more of a reality now than it ever was. The only way he can maintain this position, it seems to me, in the face of the University's demands for near-total conformity, is to focus on the narrow issue of overt political conduct. From that point of view, there will never be an academic freedom case at any major university because all the scholars there have been turned into professionals. Once again, those who would need the protection of academic freedom are excluded from the university before they could ever use it, and those who

are in the university and able to use it will never allow themselves to do so.

10. "A device that must be classified with internal propaganda in most instances, although it superficially would not appear so, is the referendum. This is a widely employed instrument in chambers of commerce, trade associations, labor unions, and *professional associations.* By this device a question of public policy on which the association is to take a stand is sent to the members or constituent societies, frequently together with arguments on both sides of the issue. The recipients are to indicate their choice of policies on a ballot. The practice has been particularly used by the Chamber of Commerce of the United States. It is classed along with propaganda because judgments of it almost universally are that *it serves primarily to emphasize unity, to give sanction to previously determined decision, and, by the appearance of wide rank-and-file participation in policy making, to strengthen the group internally* and make it more effective externally." (Emphasis added.) David B. Truman, *The Governmental Process* (New York: Knopf, 1962), pp. 197–198.

11. Not all scholars. Herzberg's letter so incensed James Prothro of the University of North Carolina, one of the foremost scholars in the field of American Government, that he circulated to political science departments a defense of the men attacked in Herzberg's letter. This shows some humanity in the field, but does not deny the point. Prothro's approach was to show that the men under attack were indeed professionals, and not to question the whole notion of what professionalism is.

12. Marshall Windmiller, "Trouble at San Francisco State," *New York Review of Books,* 10 (April 11, 1968), pp. 41–42. That Windmiller is a member of the executive committee of the Caucus for a New Political Science only indicates to me how far the doctrine of professionalism has been allowed to go.

13. Press statement of David Kaplan, September 23, 1969.

14. Alan Wolfe, "Practising the Pluralism We Preach," *Antioch Review,* 29 (Fall 1969): 353–373.

15. When I wrote an essay devoted to making this point ("The Myth of The Free Scholar," *Center Magazine,* July 1969), few people disputed that it happened. Seymour Martin Lipset, certainly one prone to find nothing but goodness in existing institutions, argued that it would be "futile" to deny the point. He instead noted that ". . . as compared with other institutions and professions the university is the most critical one we have." (See *Center Magazine,* September 1969, pp. 93–94). Now I would agree that all institutions and professions have degrees of unfreedom. One of the activists in the Berkeley Free Speech Movement, for example, has been denied admission to the California Bar despite his excellent credentials. This exclusion was done, not for his left-wing views, but because of his having spent some time in jail (unprofessional) for offenses which grew out of his political views. Admittedly, the distinction is a difficult one for nonlawyers to grasp. Whether the university is less likely to engage in exclusionary tactics like this one is an interesting empirical proposition. It is not resolved by concluding, as Lipset did, that "scholars who are competent are as free as they choose to be." In face of all the unfreedom in the university, an unfreedom which Lipset has admitted is present, the only way for such a statement to make sense is through a narrow definition of competence. This would equate competence with "responsible" and "professional" behavior. Then

the statement would read that scholars who accepted the rules of professional conformity are as free as they choose to be. That is exactly the point.

16. Lionel S. Lewis, "The Puritan Ethic in Universities and Some Worldly Concerns of Sociologists," *American Sociologist,* 4 (August 1969): 235–241.

17. Theodore Caplow and Reece J. McGee, *The Academic Marketplace* (New York: Basic Books, 1958), p. 93.

18. Lewis, *op. cit.,* p. 238.

19. That promise can be seen in the early works by behavioral political scientists which did deal rather comprehensively with elites. See Harold Lasswell, *Politics: Who Gets What, Where, How* (New York: Meredian Books, 1958); and E. E. Schattschneider, *Politics, Pressures and the Tariff* (New York: Prentice Hall, 1935) as representative examples.

20. As quoted in David Horowitz, "Billion Dollar Brains," *Ramparts,* 7 (May 1969): 42.

21. *Ibid.*

22. The story of how the Ford Foundation, Standard Oil, and powerful individuals in Washington and California brought about the end of the Institute of Hispanic American and Luso-Brazilian Studies at Stanford University, which had been critical of American policy, and replaced it with a heavily financed and more controllable institute is fully told in Horowitz, "Sinews of Empire," pp. 39–40. Few can read that story and come away with idealistic thoughts about contemporary American universities.

23. Diana Crane, "The Gatekeepers of Science: Some Factors Affecting the Selection of Articles for Scientific Journals," *American Sociologist,* 2 (November 1967): 200.

24. In a letter to *P.S.,* newsletter of the APSA.

25. I considered an article by Wilmore Kendall and George Carey to have an explicit right bias, one by Lewis Lipsitz or Peter Bachrach to have a left political bias, one by Nelson Polsby to have implicit support of existing institutions, and any article on a socialist country to be implicitly supportive of American policies.

26. See the *Radicals in the Professions Newsletter* for insights into this movement's philosophy and tactics.

27. Historians with dissenting views were attracted to the University of Wisconsin, particularly by William Appleman Williams and Harvey Goldberg, but also for William R. Taylor and George Mosse. After obtaining their degrees, they went to other institutions where they carried on the tradition. Sociologists were attracted by the works of Robert Lynd and C. Wright Mills, although they could attend Columbia only with difficulty because of Paul Lazarsfeld and Robert Merton. What they tended to do was to go someplace else, but to read the dissenting books on the side. The result is that there are some radical sociologists in little groups throughout the country and in Canada.

28. Particularly Henry Kariel and Theodore Lowi. See the essay by Michael Parenti in this volume for references.

29. There are two already existing umbrella groups of radicals within universities, the New University Conference and the Socialist Scholars Conference. Neither has very many political scientists associated with it.

30. David Kettler, "The Vocation of Radical Intellectuals," in Godfried van den Bergh and David Kettler, eds., *Reason Against Power* (Amsterdam: Vangenner, forthcoming).

Report on the
American Political Science Association Convention

Washington, D.C.
September, 1968

A phoenix
With greater predictive power
Than those of yore
Rising presciently
Not out of but
Before the ashes.

Atop a commanding promontory
Its immense skeletal wings
Of steel and pale cement
Arch out
Across the face
Of the Vesuvian evening sun
And cast a cold shadow
For miles
Over the grid of hovels below.

The Washington Hilton,
A citadel of progress,
Where teams of waiters
Ply the reclining patrons
Around the pool
With juleps and delicate pastries,
While leashed German shepherds
Pad across the terrace,
Their fangs decorously sheathed
Behind sleek jowls.

Steel beetles bearing the embodied law,
Its majesty insured by the officers' arms,
Circle the citadel
And patrol the surrounding streets—
Endlessly.

At the doors
Uniformed mercenaries stand watchful guard
Admitting only the anointed,

Who enter the veneered interior
For their ritual, fraternal business
And for their solemn resolutions
Not to sully themselves
By convening next year in Chicago.

Moving with the measured grace
But ponderous incapacity
Of men in a movie
Shot
On the floor of the sea,
They open their mouths
And utter
Glistening clouds of bubbles.

Outside,
Deep in the shadow,
Patient lynx eyes
Watch unblinking
And wait,
Stalking
Goldfish in a bowl.

—Eyewitness

INDEX

JK
271
.E65   An End to political
         science: the Caucus
         papers

DATE			
FEB 2 6 1980